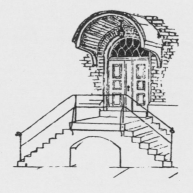

FEARS AND FASCINATIONS

FEARS AND FASCINATIONS

Representing Catholicism in the American South

Thomas F. Haddox

Fordham University Press

New York 2005

Library of Congress Cataloging-in-Publication Data

Haddox, Thomas F. (Thomas Fredrick)
   Fears and fascinations : representing Catholicism in the American South / Thomas F. Haddox.—1st ed.
      p.   cm.
   Includes bibliographical references and index.
   ISBN 0-8232-2521-6 (hardcover)
      1. American literature—Southern States—History and criticism.   2. American literature—Catholic authors—History and criticism.   3. Catholic Church—Southern States—Historiography.   4. Catholics—Southern States—Intellectual life.   5. Christianity and literature—Southern States.   6. Southern States—Religion—Historiography.   7. Catholic Church—In literature.   8. Catholics in literature.   I. Title.
PS261.H23   2005
810.9′92128275—dc22   2005016713

Printed in the United States of America
07   06   05   5   4   3   2   1
First edition

Contents

Acknowledgments

This book has been seven years in the making and has gone through several incarnations. The English department of Vanderbilt University generously funded a year of relief from teaching, and the English department of the University of Tennessee provided me with a summer grant that enabled me to travel to libraries. Both institutions also provided supportive environments in which to complete the work.

Several of my teachers, mentors, and former colleagues at Vanderbilt University read, commented upon, and gave other forms of guidance on this project at various stages: Thadious Davis, Teresa Goddu, Kurt Koenigsberger, Deandra Little, J. David Macey, Kevin Matthews, Eliza McGraw, Gary Richards, Sheila Smith-McKoy, and Eugene TeSelle. I owe a particular debt to Michael Kreyling, whose careful reading and direction of this project when it was still a dissertation were invaluable, and to the late Nancy Walker, whose intellectual generosity was always inspiring. I am equally grateful to my friends and colleagues at the University of Tennessee who provided close reading of chapters and savvy advice at a later stage of the project—above all, Amy Elias, Allison Ensor, Heather Hirschfeld, Chuck Maland, and Dorothy Scura. Conversations with fellow southern literary and cultural scholars elsewhere—including Deborah Cohn, Anne Goodwyn Jones, and Farrell O'Gorman—have also been valuable.

The staffs of the special collections departments at the following libraries have been particularly helpful to me during the course of my research: the Jean and Alexander Heard Library at Vanderbilt University; the Wilson Library at the University of North Carolina at Chapel Hill; the Firestone Library at Princeton University; the Southern Baptist Historical Library and Archives in Nashville, Tennessee; the Howard-Tilton Memorial Library at Tulane University; and the Local History and Genealogy Library in Mobile, Alabama. Bill Sumners at the Southern Baptist Historical Library and Archives generously granted me permission to quote from *The New Challenge of Home Missions* by Eugene P. Alldredge.

I want to extend special thanks as well to Helen Tate, for permission to quote from Allen Tate's unpublished letters; to Nancy Wood, for permission to quote from Caroline Gordon's unpublished letters; and to Régine Latortue, for permission to quote from her translations of the poems of *Les Cenelles*.

Two portions of this book have been previously published. A portion of Chapter 4 appeared in a slightly different form as "Contextualizing Flannery O'Connor: Allen Tate, Caroline Gordon, and the Catholic Turn in Southern Literature" in *Southern Quarterly* 38 (Fall 1999): 173–90. A portion of Chapter 1 appeared in a slightly different form as "The 'Nous' of Southern Catholic Quadroons: Racial, Ethnic, and Religious Identity in *Les Cenelles*" in *American Literature* 73 (December 2001): 757–78. I am grateful to both journals for permission to reprint these articles.

I would also like to thank those at and associated with Fordham University Press who helped see this book into print, especially my readers, whose suggestions for revision were enormously helpful; Mindy Wilson, who provided thorough and meticulous copyediting; Chris Mohney, managing editor; and Helen Tartar, editorial director.

Finally I wish to thank my family: my parents, James and Margaret Haddox, and my sister, Katherine Jollit, for their love and moral support through the years. And the lion's share of gratitude goes to my wife, Honor McKitrick Wallace, who has seen me through every crisis and without whose love, constructive criticism, and faith in me this book would never have been completed.

Abbreviations

AA	*Absalom, Absalom!*, William Faulkner
ACD	*A Confederacy of Dunces*, John Kennedy Toole
CA	*Cannibals All! or, Slaves without Masters*, George Fitzhugh
CD	*Critical Dialogue Between Aboo and Caboo; or, A Grandissime Ascension*, Adrien-Emmanuel Rouquette
CY	*A Connecticut Yankee in King Arthur's Court*, Mark Twain
DC	*Decadence and Catholicism*, Ellis Hanson
DP	"The Displaced Person," Flannery O'Connor
DS	*Divine Secrets of the Ya-Ya Sisterhood*, Rebecca Wells
FAS	*The Feast of All Saints*, Anne Rice
GWTW	*Gone with the Wind*, Margaret Mitchell
IA	*The Innocents Abroad*, Mark Twain
JA	*Personal Recollections of Joan of Arc*, Mark Twain
L	*Lancelot*, Walker Percy
LAE	*Little Altars Everywhere*, Rebecca Wells
LC	*Les Cenelles*, trans. Régine Latortue and Gleason R. W. Adams
LCG	"The Little Convent Girl," Grace King
LLB	*Letters of the Late Bishop England to the Honorable John Forsyth, on the Subject of Domestic Slavery*, John England
LR	*Love in the Ruins*, Walker Percy
MD	*Madame Delphine*, George Washington Cable
MW	*The Member of the Wedding*, Carson McCullers
RSR	"Remarks on the Southern Religion," Allen Tate
SJ	"Sister Josepha," Alice Dunbar-Nelson
SP	*Selected Poems of Father Ryan*, Abram J. Ryan
TF	*The Fathers*, Allen Tate
TLG	*The Last Gentleman*, Walker Percy
TM	*The Malefactors*, Caroline Gordon
TMG	*The Moviegoer*, Walker Percy
TSC	*The Strange Children*, Caroline Gordon
VV	*A Vocation and a Voice*, Kate Chopin

Introduction

"He is the one who is curious to me."[1] Jason Compson Sr.'s offhand remark about Charles Bon identifies a persistent source of fascination in William Faulkner's *Absalom, Absalom!* "Curious" Bon certainly is: as Thomas Sutpen's unacknowledged son and wrecker of his dynastic "design," a man of French ethnicity and uncertain race, a languorous and fatalistic decadent, and "a Catholic of sorts" (*AA* 94), he astonishes Yoknapatawpha County and provokes widely divergent responses from the novel's characters. On the one hand, Bon suggests to some the horror of miscegenation—"the nigger that's going to sleep with your sister" (*AA* 358), as Quentin and Shreve imagine him telling Henry Sutpen—and embodies what the white South both disavows and fears that it might become. Yet "Charles the Good" is also an object of desire and envy, representing European standards of refinement and exposing the pretensions of the South's uncouth would-be aristocrats, who build elegant plantation homes and fashion themselves as lords of the manor to hide the fact that they have broken with a genuinely feudal culture. As Jason Sr. suggests, Bon fascinates and frightens those "who have not quite yet emerged from barbarism, who two thousand years hence will still be throwing triumphantly off the yoke of Latin culture and intelligence of which they were never in any great permanent danger to begin with" (*AA* 94). By bringing into sharp relief several of the white South's obsessions—racial mixing, decadence, nostalgia for lost cultural glories, and fear of cultural inferiority—Bon crystallizes, in a powerful but contradictory way, the anxieties and investments that surround any narrative of identity.

What accounts for these contradictory responses to Bon? Certainly the fact that the novel's narrators reconstruct Bon's story from incomplete (and sometimes dubious) information and often revise their judgments contributes to the sense of contradiction. More fundamentally, however, of all the markers of Bon's difference, only his Catholicism binds together the rest and offers an adequate explanation for the full range of his significations. Though Bon's faith in Catholicism has lapsed, Catholic practices and associ-

ations surround him, from the *voudun* ceremony that he allegedly participates in with his octoroon mistress to his dandyish style of dress. *Voudun*, a
syncretic mixture of Catholicism and west African religions practiced in
New Orleans and the West Indies, highlights the openness of Catholicism
to different religious and cultural traditions, while its use in the novel to
consecrate a relationship between a putatively white man and a woman of
mixed race suggests that Catholicism tacitly or actively supports miscegenation. At the same time, Bon's sartorial splendor, perennial ennui, and penchant for making rural adolescents of both sexes fall in love with him
connect him to styles of decadent and homoerotic sexuality that have often
been associated with Catholicism, as Ellis Hanson and Eve Kosofsky Sedgwick have shown.[2] Against an assumed background of what Jason Sr. calls
"[that] puritan heritage—that heritage peculiarly Anglo-Saxon—of fierce
proud mysticism and that ability to be ashamed of ignorance and inexperi-
ence" (*AA* 108), Bon's Catholicism signifies as a dimly understood threat
that is deeply involved with and even responsible for his racial and sexual
mystery, his cultural capital, and his undeniable appeal.

Bon is not an isolated figure. The heady mixture of fear and desire that
his Catholicism awakens can be found, in different guises, across a wide
swath of American literature, and it first emerges as a major phenomenon
in the antebellum years. As Jenny Franchot has argued in her magisterial
Roads to Rome: The Antebellum Protestant Encounter with Catholicism, "anti-
Catholicism operated as an imaginative category of discourse through which
antebellum American writers of popular and elite fictional and historical
texts indirectly voiced the tensions and limitations of mainstream Protestant
culture." This antebellum anti-Catholic discourse, originally intended both
to strengthen the concept of a national Protestant culture and to emphasize
the primacy of New England within this culture, frequently proved a double-
edged sword. According to Franchot, antebellum anti-Catholicism shows
how easily "a rhetoric of theological attack can twist from enemy back to
self and how a religious zone like popery that is made to contain the con-
taminated, the exotic, and the fearful comes to be entered by the Catholic
convert."[3] It should not surprise us, Franchot suggests, that the same decades
that saw shocking acts of violence against Catholics and the rise of the
Know-Nothing Party (1830–60) also saw a large number of conversions to
Catholicism, including those of such luminaries of the American intelligen-
tsia as Orestes Brownson and Isaac Hecker.[4]

A complete picture of Catholicism's function as a set of tropes within
American literature and culture, however, must include the primary re-

gional antagonism of the nineteenth century between North and South. This book argues that beginning in the 1840s, Catholicism repeatedly figures, in the work of both Catholic and non-Catholic southern writers, as a linchpin that connects anxieties about and emotional investments in southern identity. The fears and fascinations that Franchot traces in nineteenth-century antebellum culture function quite differently in a southern context. Not only do they first emerge at a slightly later historical moment, establish themselves more gradually in the culture, and persist well into the twentieth century (as Charles Bon's iconic example reveals), they also tend to cluster around a distinctly southern set of preoccupations. Indeed much of the force of southern representations of Catholicism derives from the tension between the changelessness and universalism often invoked by the church—evident in the very word *catholic*—and the culturally specific, historically variable objects of desire and terrors that southerners found in or projected onto the church. For many southern writers, the church is a malevolent force connected with miscegenation and sexual perversity, determined to extend its dominion through force or guile and to stamp out cherished (and racist) values and folkways. For others the church figures as a source of aesthetic wonder, a locus of blissfully erotic sensations and a potential rallying point for differently raced and sexed identities. For still others, attracted to the church's associations with a vanished feudal world, Catholicism becomes an eminently southern institution, whose commitments to order, hierarchy, and tradition are compatible with and even indistinguishable from those of the white South as a whole. In short, Catholicism becomes evocative and powerful precisely because it eludes fixed definition and encompasses opposites: universal equality and local, coercive hierarchy; decadent eroticism and transcendent spirituality; the promise of racial justice and the guarantee of white supremacy.

Regardless of whether Catholicism figures as an evil, a splendid fetish, or a focus of white southern cultural nostalgia, it becomes, from about 1840 on, a presence that cannot be ignored in southern self-definition. It also becomes invariably disruptive—either because it is perceived as a challenge to that self-definition or because the arguments used to affirm the church's southernness prove counterintuitive and require a complex elaboration. The diversity of these representations of Catholicism in southern literature—and of the ideological uses to which they have been put—is the focus of my investigation. By tracing how these diverse representations compel a continual rethinking of southern and Catholic identities alike, this book sheds new light on the history of Catholic and anti-Catholic discourses in

American culture and on the tangled series of attempts to define southern identity in contradistinction to a normative "Americanness." It also shows that such celebrated southern and Catholic writers as Flannery O'Connor and Walker Percy are not anomalous figures but simply the most distinguished participants in a long-standing conversation about the relationship between the church and southern identity that includes Catholic and non-Catholic writers, political theorists, and religious leaders.

To argue that Catholicism compels a rethinking of southern identity is to challenge the still powerful notion that the most authentically southern literature and cultural practices embody conservative values and reflect a constant, implicitly white identity. The list of now clichéd preoccupations that earlier southernist critics often traced back to the Agrarians' *I'll Take My Stand* and then retroactively applied to southern literature as a whole— sense of place, community, consciousness of defeat, a tragic view of history, reverence for nature, and so on—has been recognized as insufficient to describe the full range of conflicts and identifications in southern literature, and much important scholarship in the last decade has begun to uncover the challenges posed to a traditional definition of southern literature by the claims of race, gender, sexuality, subregion, and global economic context.[5]

Impressive as this scholarship is, however, it has tended to neglect the claims of religion as a constituent of identity—an omission all the more significant not just because of the centrality of religion to such writers as O'Connor and Percy, but also because traditional southernist criticism relies on the notion that southern literature has an ultimately religious grounding. To be sure, this grounding is often vaguely stated, as in O'Connor's famous assertion that the South, while "hardly Christ-centered . . . is most certainly Christ-haunted" or, more abstractly still, in John Crowe Ransom's definition of religion as "our submission to the general intention of a nature that is fairly inscrutable."[6] Taken at face value, such axioms could mean anything from unease with secularism to nostalgia for an established church to pantheism inflected by Christianity—and indeed, as Michael Kreyling has noted, southernist critics often carefully chose the term *religiousness* so as to refer to "an attitude or temperament rather than to a body of doctrine, to the idea of religion rather than to the social history of a particular sect."[7] What these definitions share are their alleged opposition to the liberal individualism of the United States (and its economic wellspring, industrial capitalism) and a willingness to appropriate available forms of religious discourse as weapons against that individualism. Yet just as traditional accounts of southern literature often fail to register the challenges to their coherence posed by the claims of race, gender, class, or sexuality, their inclusion of a wide range of specific religious beliefs and groups—from Appalachian snake-handlers to High Church Episcopalians to practitioners of *voudun*—under the rubric of a Christ-haunted and inscrutable sense of "submission" overlooks the diversity and conflicts of southern religious practice and the crises of southern identity that these conflicts have fueled. Similarly, criticism that focuses on the specific religious difference of Catholicism, such as theologically informed readings of individual Catholic writers or examinations of American Catholic literature more generally, also typically overlooks the specific cultural and political differences of Catholicism in the South.[8]

Accordingly I consider Catholicism not as a new grounding for a definition of southern literature, but in order to emphasize the contested nature of southern and Catholic identities, the interrelations among them (including their vexed connections to notions of an American identity), and the cultural changes that these interrelations have wrought. Even as I recognize the historical dominance of conservative Protestantism in the South and the long hegemony of white supremacist ideology, I show how these forces were often challenged and failed to remain coherent in the face of these challenges. At the same time, however, I do not argue that either the mere recognition of multiplicity in the South or the existence of particular subject positions within this multiplicity is inherently progressive. Instead I examine how these multiple identities function in varied historical circumstances. The literary and cultural history presented in this book moves within a dialectic of hope and suspicion: Catholicism in the South functions simultaneously as a site of tremendous liberatory potential and as territory peculiarly vulnerable to co-optation.

～

Though Catholicism has been a minority religion in the South for as long as notions of a collective southern identity have existed, Catholics have been a distinct presence in the region since the first days of European colonization. Indeed the first Catholics to settle in what would become the South were the Spanish, who landed at St. Augustine, Florida, in 1565—a presence largely ignored by southern historians and literary scholars. Among English settlers and their descendants, Catholicism did not become a focus of distinctly southern anxieties until the middle of the nineteenth century. The second of the southern English colonies to be established, Maryland, was originally intended by Lord Baltimore as a haven for Catholic gentry,

although this intention could not be openly avowed because of the prohibition against Catholics in England. The travel narratives and promotional
tracts of Maryland colonist Andrew White, S. J., arguably the first southern
and Catholic writer, do not differ significantly from those of the Protestant
Virginians. "A Briefe Relation of the Voyage unto Maryland" and "A Relation of Maryland," for instance, recall the writings of John Smith in their
praise of the landscape and the opportunities available in the new colony;
despite their frequent, formulaic allusions to God and his protection, neither
work has much to say about the theological or social difference of Catholicism, and both acknowledge the legitimate authority of Charles I. Though
in fact Protestants outnumbered Catholics in the colony from the beginning
(and attempted, during the English Civil War and the period following it,
to restrict the rights of Catholics), there is little evidence that these anti-
Catholic sentiments were related to distinctly southern questions or that
they continued into the early national period. Indeed the colony and future
state would long retain its historical and symbolic importance as the center
of American Catholicism and pride itself on its early religious toleration.[9]

The greatest concentration of Catholics in the South, however, would
arise in Louisiana, where French settlement predated the arrival of Protestant *Américains* by nearly a century and where a thriving Catholic Creole
establishment maintained its sense of elite exclusivity (if not its political supremacy) and cultural influence well into the nineteenth century. Nor was
anti-Catholicism much in evidence in regions of the South where Catholics
were scarcer. Indeed Eugene D. Genovese argues that the antebellum South
was "the least anti-Semitic and anti-Catholic region of the United States, as
a long list of Jews and Catholics certified. . . . Convent-burning disgraced
the cities of the Northeast, not those of the South."[10] As a result, the common stereotype of Catholics that evolved in the eighteenth- and nineteenth-century United States—in Paul Giles's words, "poor, lazy, ignorant,
undemocratic, devious, psychologically intemperate, sexually perverse, and
often drunk"—appeared remarkably late in the South and even then dif-
fered in significant ways from its northern counterpart.[11]

Catholicism first begins to figure as a significant marker of difference in
the South in the 1840s, and this emergence goes hand in hand with the
increasingly strident attempt to define a white southern identity in consciously reactionary terms. The notion of the South as a political bloc was,
of course, already in place by 1840, thanks in part to the Missouri Compro-
mise and other political measures that had established the idea of parity in
the Senate between free and slave states. A string of significant events in the

previous decade, however, played a crucial role in transforming this political stance into an emotionally resonant identity: the Nat Turner slave uprising of 1831, which coincided with the rise of militant abolitionism in the North (William Lloyd Garrison's *The Liberator* began publishing in the same year); the 1832 nullification crisis in South Carolina, which led to the canonization of John C. Calhoun as the leading proponent of a southern political philosophy; and the first stirrings of Manifest Destiny, with its attendant visions in the South of a "cotton kingdom" stretching to the Pacific. This consolidation of a white southern identity would continue to gather momentum, culminating in the establishment of the Confederacy in 1861—and the revelation that even thousands of men who did not belong to the planter elite were willing to die for its ideals. It would also produce, in such writers as William Gilmore Simms and Henry Timrod, the first consciousness of southern literature as a body of work that dissents from an American mainstream.

Within this historical moment, the identification of Catholicism as a marker of identity distinct from southernness springs primarily from three historical developments. The first was the large influx of immigrants from Ireland and Germany during the 1840s to the United States, which provoked an unprecedented outbreak of xenophobia and anti-Catholicism. Relatively few of these immigrants settled in the South, and expressions of anti-Catholicism directed against southern Catholics were infrequent. Even so, the concentration of immigrant Catholics in northern cities did lead to new suspicions; in James J. Thompson's words, "Its strength in the North lent to Catholicism an identity with a region and culture to which Southerners displayed mounting aversion. The North, they lamented, vomited up every variety of weirdness: Transcendentalists, Unitarians, utopian socialists, abolitionists, health reformers, free-love advocates, feminists—and Roman Catholics."[12] Some of these perceptions merged with anti-Catholic rhetoric that had circulated during the Mexican War, a rhetoric that identified Catholic countries with despotism, technological backwardness, and evil, mind-controlling Jesuits. These perceptions of Catholicism would continue to spread in the late nineteenth and early twentieth centuries, finding expression in the more virulent anti-Catholicism of Populist demagogues such as Tom Watson, the resurgence of the "nativist" Ku Klux Klan in the 1920s, and the southern reaction to Al Smith's presidential candidacy in 1928.[13] Perhaps their first significant literary expression in the South was Augusta Jane Evans's novel of 1855, *Inez: A Tale of the Alamo*, in which virtuous southern ladies transplanted to San Antonio (as well as the beautiful, free-spirited Mexican woman of the title) must free themselves from the clutches of the evil Padre Mazzoni, who seeks absolute control over his congregation and the expulsion of freedom-loving Americans from Texas.[14]

The second development fueling perceptions of Catholic difference was the need to justify the institution of slavery. Recognizing that their system was growing less compatible with the liberalism and industrial capitalism developing in the North, southern apologists sought models of society that made virtues of inequality and hierarchy. The Roman Catholic church, with its sharply defined hierarchy, its ruling patriarch with political as well as spiritual power, its assertions of universality and divine protection, and its apparent hostility during the nineteenth and early twentieth centuries to modernizing impulses in politics, fit the bill well. Whereas before, Catholicism had been invisible to many southerners, now some southerners noticed it precisely to press it into the service of a reactionary southern identity. Indeed, since the 1850s, one intermittent narrative in southern discourse has cast the Catholic Middle Ages as a kind of Eden and the threefold phenomenon of Reformation, Enlightenment, and capitalism as the Fall.

Finally, the fear that Catholicism might prove an ally to the aspirations of African-Americans and even an abettor of miscegenation begins to appear among white southerners in the 1840s—a fear derived both from the outspoken abolitionist sentiments of some prominent Catholics, such as Daniel O'Connell, and from the way that many free people of color in the South (especially in Louisiana) clung to their Catholicism as a badge of identity and a source of dignity. This particular source of anxiety becomes more prominent after the Civil War, converging with the nativist strand of anti-Catholicism that had long flourished in the North, so that by the 1920s, arguments that attack the church as "foreign" and as friendly to black political aspirations become inseparable.

Whether Catholicism figured in the South as threat or savior, its presence often required explanation after the 1840s; the possibility that it could be a private belief system unconnected with regional identity became increasingly remote. Yet even if many specific accounts of southern Catholicism functioned, broadly speaking, as defenses or critiques of white southern ideologies (in which Catholicism's relation to these ideologies would come in for approbation or for attack), the sheer diversity of these accounts also reflected the church's great capacity for mediation and for the negotiating of difference. Despite the universalizing claims and reverence for authority promoted by the church, the structure of Catholicism allowed for mediated relations that would by their very nature complicate binary structures and require negotiation with them. For instance, the presence of priests and nuns as mediators between the people and God raised the possibility of positions misrecognized, debated, or even subject to local variation. Similarly, Catholic iconography and devotions often expressed local influences and proved amenable to syncretism rather than outright schism, perhaps most strikingly in the case of *voudun*. In an American context, the usual alignment of Catholicism with a variety of non-Anglo ethnicities also highlighted difference, as even a cursory comparison of, for instance, the cultural styles of Irish-American Catholicism and Creole-American Catholicism shows. Against the self-conscious "purity" and simplicity of many southern Protestant denominations, which made their negotiation with a white southern identity that saw itself as monolithic a comparatively simple matter, Catholicism's variety and potential for mediation displayed no obvious affinity with that identity and would require a more careful thinking through. To what extent would French Creole Catholics disrupt the unity of a South defined as Anglo-Saxon and Protestant? What effect would the aesthetic excess of Catholic churches and liturgies have on southerners' moral constitutions or on white southerners' ability to control African-Americans? How might wily Catholic clergy undermine the southern racial order by encouraging miscegenation and advocating racial equality? These questions, raised at different times by different southern partisans, all derive their force from the church's capacity for mediation, its ability to align itself with and be appropriated by a variety of racial, sexual, and political positions.

This book's chapters, then, attempt to do justice to this variety—to catalog and investigate the full range of quadroons, decadents, priests, and others that emerge as figures of Catholic southernness. Chapter 1 ("Catholic Miscgenations: The Cultural Legacy of *Les Cenelles*") examines the most persistent source of anxiety surrounding Catholicism in the South—the association of the church with miscegenation that began to emerge in southern texts in the 1840s. This association begins with the poems of *Les Cenelles*, an anthology published by a group of free people of color, ethnically and culturally French, in New Orleans in 1845. In these poems, Catholicism plays a key role in the construction of both racial and ethnic identity: even as Anglo-Protestant Louisianians deny the *gens de couleur libres* their distinct racial identity and their privileges, grouping them together with all African-Americans, the *Les Cenelles* poets appeal to Catholicism as a space within which they can preserve their identity. Yet even as they affirm their faith, the *Les Cenelles* poets criticize the church for turning a blind eye to the institution of *plaçage*, the system of concubinage that simultaneously preserved some free black Creoles' material well-being and ensured white sexual exploitation. The poems of *Les Cenelles* thus contribute to a perception that the church encouraged miscegenation, integration, and a general laxity in the maintenance of racial distinctions. Later southern writers, such as George Washington Cable, Grace King, and Alice Dunbar-Nelson, continue to explore the associations between Catholicism and miscegenation, providing unwitting justification for the anti-Catholic propaganda of politicians such as Tom Watson and religious leaders such as Eugene P. Alldredge. The association of the church with miscegenation finally reaches its imaginative zenith in the figure of Charles Bon, the most famous and most resonant Catholic of uncertain race in southern literature.

Even as the church began to figure in many white southerners' minds as a frightening force that enables miscegenation, some white southern intellectuals contested this picture, valorizing Catholicism as the ideal southern religion, uniquely suited to the quasi-feudal and racialist order of a plantation economy. Chapter 2 ("Medieval Yearnings: A Catholicism for Whites in Nineteenth-Century Southern Literature") focuses on this effort, beginning with the attempt of John England, the Catholic bishop of Charleston, to declare southern slavery compatible with Christianity despite the presence of abolitionist Catholic voices. George Fitzhugh and George Frederick Holmes, two of the white antebellum South's leading political theorists, would build upon England's position, erecting the first theoretically developed characterization of the South as a feudal, anti-Enlightenment, highly cultivated, and unconsciously Catholic society. The figure of Abram Ryan, the "Poet-Priest of the Confederacy" who became popular in the decades following the Civil War, would combine this discourse of a feudal Catholicism with a celebration of chivalric southern heroism on the battlefield. Like Robert E. Lee, Ryan would function symbolically as an embodiment of southern bravery and eloquence, memorializing the Lost Cause and implicitly contrasting its glories with the bankrupt capitalist values of the North. Such medievalist ideology, however, did not go unchallenged by southern writers: most famously, Mark Twain responded to these developments with a scathing critique of a feudal Catholicism in *The Innocents Abroad* and *A Connecticut Yankee in King Arthur's Court*. Twain's depiction of Catholicism would prove both inconsistent and oddly productive. On the one hand, he would repeat in his hagiographic *Personal Recollections of Joan of Arc* some of the same lineaments of the feudal heroic myth that he rejected in the earlier works. On the other hand, he would, by connecting Catholicism with decay and necrophilia, anticipate later formulations of southern Catholicism as decadent.

Chapter 3 ("The Pleasures of Decadence: Catholicism in Kate Chopin, Carson McCullers, and Anne Rice") traces the emergence of this decadent Catholicism around the turn of the century, with its homoerotic undercurrents, its preoccupation with languor and terror, and its affinities with today's queer theory. This Catholicism figures most prominently in the work of Kate Chopin, who participates in the fin de siècle tradition of Catholic decadence most commonly associated with such European writers as Oscar Wilde and Joris-Karl Huysmans. Just as associations between the church and miscegenation were taken up by southern writers across the political spectrum, the image of a decadent and homoerotic Catholicism would recur for decades, celebrated by some writers and reviled by others. The same tropes of a decadent and "queer" Catholicism on display in the stories of Chopin's *A Vocation and a Voice* reappear in texts as different as Carson McCullers's *The Member of the Wedding* and Anne Rice's *The Feast of All Saints*—the latter a historical novel about the New Orleans *gens de couleur libres* whose continued popularity suggests that associations among miscegenation, homoeroticism, aristocratic privilege, and Catholicism persist today.

Chapter 4 ("Agrarian Catholics: The Twentieth-Century Catholic Turn in Southern Literature") turns first toward Flannery O'Connor, the most canonical of southern Catholic writers, and, through a reading of her short story "The Displaced Person" (one of the few works in her oeuvre to present Catholic characters), argues that she takes part in a continuing effort to connect Catholicism to a conservative and medievalist southern politics. The key figure behind this effort is Allen Tate, whose tortured efforts to align Catholicism with the Agrarian movement in the 1930s would eventually culminate in his own religious conversion. In his essay "Remarks on the Southern Religion," his novel *The Fathers*, and his essays of the 1950s, Tate mounted the most comprehensive attempt to equate the tenets of the white southern order with the unchanging dogmas of Catholicism—an attempt that comes in for implicit critique in that most popular of southern novels, Margaret Mitchell's *Gone with the Wind*. Although Tate's theories about Catholicism in the South remained contradictory, both O'Connor and Caroline Gordon attempted to put them into practice, asserting in such novels as *The Strange Children* and *The Malefactors* and in the essays of *Mystery and Manners* a virtual equivalence between southernness and Catholicism. Here, however, we see also the collision of competing discourses of Catholic southernness: Gordon's *The Malefactors* simultaneously embraces Catholicism as a mark of a conservative southern identity and revels in its affinity with the decadent and the flamboyantly queer. The effort to characterize southern culture as essentially Catholic, always historically dubious, lost much of its force in 1965, the year that saw the end of the Second Vatican Council and demonstrated that the Catholic church was no more immune to historical change than the South.

Indeed the rapid changes produced in the church by Vatican II, combined with the changes produced in the South by the civil rights movement, were instrumental in bringing about a new set of southern Catholic tropes that began to appear in the early 1960s: a "deconstructive" brand of Catholicism that rejects the metaphysical grounding of its earlier incarnations and comes increasingly to function as a marker of what we would today call "lifestyle." Chapter 5 ("Toward Catholicism as Lifestyle: Walker Percy, John Kennedy Toole, and Rebecca Wells") charts this new development, beginning with Percy's complex, "postsouthern" portrayal of Catholicism as an attempt to reject the stoic and quasi-feudal traditions of white upper-class southernness while acknowledging the lingering presence of those traditions' tropes. Though Percy sought to make Catholicism a substitute for southern identity, one that would be comparable in its metaphysical gravitas, he portrays Catholicism in such novels as *The Moviegoer, The Last Gentleman,* and *Love in the Ruins* as a relentlessly ordinary and domestic set of practices that rejects both southern medievalism and decadence. Such portrayals suggest a postmodern "micronarrative," a way of life that works best when it does not seek to establish a new and totalizing framework of identity— despite Percy's intense, even apocalyptic desire that Catholicism do just that. At the same time, whatever politically progressive potential Percy's depiction of southern Catholicism may have quickly finds itself co-opted by the blandishments of consumerism, which transforms Catholicism into a practice that can be either working-class and cheerfully tacky—as in John Kennedy Toole's *A Confederacy of Dunces*—or middle-class, feminist, and multicultural—as in Rebecca Wells's *Little Altars Everywhere* and *Divine Secrets of the Ya-Ya Sisterhood*—but which in both cases signifies as a solipsistic, consumer-driven practice that contributes to little more than the accumulation of goods on the one hand and smug, therapeutic self-satisfaction on the other.

Throughout this book, I foreground the contested nature of both southernness and Catholicism in the literature I examine. Certain styles and characterizations of both may come into being, flourish for a time, disappear, and reappear, but their variety precludes any stable definition of either term in the larger American cultural arena. Each new text does not simply take its place in an unbroken and self-evident tradition, but plunges into a welter of ongoing debates. The aesthetic, historical, and political significance of each new text is neither known in advance nor determined for all time, and I hope to show that the work of cultural analysis must involve grappling with each instance of southern, Catholic, and American representation in its own context, fashioning a literary and cultural history that at any given moment might offer grounds both for pessimism and hope.

I   *Catholic Miscegenations: The Cultural Legacy of* Les Cenelles

In 1845 a group of seventeen free Creoles of color in New Orleans published *Les Cenelles* (*The Holly Berries*), a volume of lyric poems in French. The fruit of an endeavor that had begun two years before with the establishment of *L'album littéraire*, the first "little magazine" in Louisiana, *Les Cenelles* emphasizes its communal production and adheres closely to a shared romantic aesthetic. Many poems in the collection imitate the French Romantic poets, taking up their characteristic meters and familiar themes: unrequited love, death and suicide, dreams and visions, the vagaries of longing and melancholy. Others are witty exercises: acrostics, displays of elegant repartee, assertions of poetic one-upmanship. The editor, Armand Lanusse, proclaims in the introduction that *Les Cenelles* was compiled to promote the cultivation of art and the cause of general education. Affirming that "a good education is a shield against the spiteful and calumnious arrows shot at us," Lanusse expresses his deepest sympathy with aspiring poets, who suffer not just from active malice, but also from the indifference of those who fail to see how poetry "peut avancer le progrès des lumières chez nous" ("may advance the progress of the gifted among us").[1] This invocation of a "nous" raises the question: what are the identity, the audience, and the politics that *Les Cenelles* constructs and defends?

For a number of critics, this "nous" should be understood as the African-American community. Henry Louis Gates Jr., for instance, calls the collection "[t]he first attempt to define a black canon" and considers Lanusse's introduction "a defense of poetry as an enterprise for black people, in their larger efforts to defend the race" and to validate "the collective black intellect." According to this reading, the absence of overt racial, political, or social themes in the poems and their frequent, reverent allusions to Hugo, Lamartine, and Dumas constitute a deliberate strategy. Racism is untenable, the logic goes, because black poetry can aspire to the same aesthetic standards of the masters. Just as Phyllis Wheatley voiced the aspirations of African-Americans through a politically subversive use of eighteenth-century

English poetic forms, *Les Cenelles* illustrates, in Gates's words, "An apolitical art being put to uses most political."[2]

Gates's contention, however, relies on an implicit definition of nineteenth-century African-American literature that regards the experience of slavery—and the necessity of combating the "peculiar institution"—as central. William L. Andrews, for instance, in his introduction to one section of *The Norton Anthology of African American Literature,* maintains, "The engendering impulse of African American literature is resistance to human tyranny. The sustaining spirit of African American literature is dedication to human dignity."[3] Such a definition privileges certain genres (the slave narrative, the spiritual, the folktale, the abolitionist lyric poem) and certain recurring figures (the heroic slave, the tragic mulatta, the orator, the trickster) while identifying the tradition's authors and reading public with slaves, former slaves, and whites with unambiguous abolitionist sentiments. *Les Cenelles,* however, corresponds to none of these categories. The poems' imitation of French Romantic models conflicts with the emphasis on the vernacular that is the corollary of this definition (so that the poets' preference for standard French over Creole French or African-American English presents a potential problem), while their subject matter often seems indifferent or hostile to political activism. Perhaps not surprisingly, *Les Cenelles* has often been excluded from major anthologies of African-American literature: both *The Norton Anthology of African American Literature* and *Call and Response,* probably the most well known of such anthologies today, contain no selections from *Les Cenelles.*[4]

More significantly Gates's positioning of *Les Cenelles* ignores the cultural conditions that separated the *gens de couleur libres* from the vast majority of the African diaspora. Although their "blackness" would become increasingly enforced by an interlocking network of legal and cultural discourses as the nineteenth century progressed, there is little evidence to suggest that the *Les Cenelles* poets identified themselves as simply "black" in 1845. As Régine Latortue and Gleason R. W. Adams observe, free Creoles of color in New Orleans carefully distinguished themselves from both whites and blacks:

> They were neither Negro nor white; certainly not slaves but free only in a circumscribed way; culturally French but citizens of an American state. They were looked upon with envy by slaves and free Negroes, and with suspicion by the predominant whites. They jealously guarded the prerogatives which their color, their culture, their social standing, and their money afforded them, for they were a people proud of their heritage.[5]

This "heritage" is defined by race but just as passionately by class, by Latin ethnicity, and by Roman Catholicism: the adjective "créole," repeated at several points in *Les Cenelles*, signifies the French or (in the case of one poet, Manuel Sylva) Spanish antecedents of the poets, proclaimed in proud contradistinction to the Anglo-Protestant, "American" ethos that gained ground in New Orleans throughout the nineteenth century.[6] The *gens de couleur libres* distinguished themselves not just from slaves but from other free blacks who were not Creole. Furthermore, many of this class, having been left considerable property by white forebears, were wealthy enough to be educated in France, and some settled there permanently. Still others were slaveholders themselves.[7] These poets, in other words, belonged to a class whose record of solidarity with African-Americans and resistance to slavery was less than exemplary during the antebellum period.

Armand Lanusse's life points up the difficulty of positioning the poets of *Les Cenelles* and their work squarely within the African-American tradition. A well-respected civic leader in antebellum and Reconstruction New Orleans, Lanusse was known for his efforts to improve the lives of free blacks. He helped to establish the Catholic School for Indigent Orphans of Color in 1848 and served as its principal from 1852 until 1866. Yet he was also conscripted into the Confederate army during the Civil War and refused to fly the Union flag over his school after New Orleans had been occupied by General Butler—an act which provoked severe criticism. Before the war, he refrained from attacking slavery and accepted financial support for his school from slaveholding members of the free black community. Indeed the black Creole historian Rodolphe Lucien Desdunes suggests that Lanusse identified politically with both his ethnicity and his race: "[He] never boasted of being an American. His pride in being Creole was more dear to him than his being a Louisianian or anything else pertaining to his origin."[8] Given such a background for its editor, it is not surprising that *Les Cenelles* reads less as an intervention in an African-American tradition defined by a common cultural and political framework than as a work that disrupts that tradition's homogeneity: French ethnicity, Catholicism, and relative material privilege all undermine the applicability of the term *African-American* to *Les Cenelles*.

Of course, the very existence of the *gens de couleur libres* was a consequence of miscegenation—a practice forbidden by the Louisiana Code Noir. Because of this prohibition, free Creoles of color had to emphasize both their visibility and their invisibility when defending their privileges. Because these privileges ultimately depended upon an admixture of white ancestry, to deny the white racial component would be to abolish the crucial distinction between free Creoles of color and other people of African descent, slave or free. Yet because their very persons drew attention to the forbidden mixing, the *gens de couleur libres* also undermined the notion of two monolithic races, suggesting that multiple and even unforeseen racial designations could flourish—a notion that became more significant as the American order in Louisiana began to replace the multiple racial categories associated with the West Indies (including mulatto, quadroon, and griffe) with an enforcement of the "one drop" rule.⁹ This deconstruction, then, also entailed a considerable risk: how could privileges based on race and pride in one's identity be preserved if race and identity were themselves exposed as mutable?

Catholicism offers a kind of solution to this problem. For the *Les Cenelles* poets, the church allows a space within which free Creoles of color can preserve their highly differentiated yet tenuous identity—and thus guarantee their continued elite status. On the one hand, the church's universalizing rhetoric—evident in the word *catholic* and in the insistence that all souls are equal before God—offers a justification for the aspirations of *gens de couleur libres* that claims to transcend politics. At the same time, however, Catholicism's association with French ethnicity suggests resistance to the comelately Protestant Americans. In other words, Catholicism allows the *gens de couleur libres* to construct their identity in terms of both equality and difference: assertions of Catholic brotherhood emphasize commonality with the white Creole population and seek to dilute the social significance of race, even as the same assertions oppose, in the name of cultural and religious difference, the Anglo-Protestant order that sought to enforce a rigid division between black and white and to strip the *gens de couleur libres* of their rights and privileges. Catholic identification, then, proves inseparable from affirmation of race and ethnicity.

This identification, however, does not imply an unthinking endorsement of Catholic practice as a whole, for even as these poets affirm their faith, they register ambivalence toward the church's tolerance of miscegenation. Although they praise the church's kindness toward the children of such unions, the poets also criticize Catholic acquiescence in *plaçage*, the system of concubinage that simultaneously contributed to the *gens de couleur libres'* material well-being and ensured continued white sexual exploitation. As a result, the identity, politics, and religious stance constructed in *Les Cenelles* prove curiously contorted: the already paradoxical use of a universalist creed to buttress a sharply demarcated racial, ethnic, and socioeconomic identity becomes still more troubled when identification with that creed cannot consist of simple affirmation. The associations first developed between Catholicism and miscegenation in *Les Cenelles,* however, would go on to become staples of Louisiana local color fiction in the decades after the Civil War, particularly evident in the work of George Washington Cable, Grace King, and Alice Dunbar-Nelson. What was for the poets of *Les Cenelles* a strategy to assert their dignity as free people of color would become, by the turn of the century, a trope that reinforced both racism and anti-Catholicism in white southern imaginations.

꙳

Catholic imagery and belief pervade the eighty-five poems of *Les Cenelles.* References to God, heaven, and the Catholic clergy recur in a decorous, self-consciously pious language equally removed from the highly emotional rhetoric of much southern Protestantism and from the syncretic ambience of *voudun.*[10] As Alfred J. Guillaume Jr. observes, "Nothing seems to diminish [the poets'] faith, neither rejection in love nor the loss of a loved one. To the contrary, tragedy increases their fervor."[11] Yet though such staunch traditionalism might seem at odds with any expression of social protest, the most overtly religious of these poems reveal a faith informed by their racial and ethnic identity and capable of stances no less political for their quietness.

"An Impression," a poem by Mirtil-Ferdinand Liotau, provides the most striking example of the poets' faith and its oblique but crucial connection to race and ethnicity. One of only two poems in *Les Cenelles* that refer to actual locations in New Orleans, "An Impression" describes an empty St. Louis Cathedral and bemoans the decline of the faith affirmed there:

> Eglise Saint-Louis, vieux temple, reliquaire,
> Te voilà maintenant désert et solitaire!
> Ceux qui furent commis ici bas à tes soins,
> Du tabernacle saint méprisant les besoins,
> Ailleurs ont entraîné la phalange chrétienne.

> (Church of Saint-Louis, old temple, shrine,
> You are today empty and deserted!
> Those who were entrusted in this world to your care,
> Scorning the needs of the sacred tabernacle,
> Have led the Christian army elsewhere.) (*LC* 88, 89)

Liotau's plaintive lines, however, do not specify why the cathedral has been abandoned. What has led "the Christian army elsewhere"? Clearly the poem does not refer to a specific ecclesiastical event: St. Louis Cathedral continued to occupy the seat of Catholic power in New Orleans throughout the nineteenth century (as it still does today), and there is no evidence of mass desertions from Catholicism in the city during the 1840s. Despite the more general adjective "Christian," the emphasis on the neglected sacred tabernacle—the home of the consecrated host that Catholics believe to be the literal body of Christ—draws attention to a distinctly Catholic anxiety, as do the next lines of the poem, which worry that the cathedral's "ancient images" and "sacred relics" are threatened with "profound oblivion" (*LC* 89). Since the cathedral went on celebrating its liturgies with its usual trappings, one must look elsewhere for the source of this anxiety.

In the second half of the poem, Liotau explains how the cathedral may be restored to its former glory:

> Puisque jamais en vain nous prions le Seigneur,
> Chrétiens, unissons-nous; quand ce Dieu tutélaire
> A versé tout son sang pour nous sur le Calvaire,
> Espérons qu'en ce jour lui seul puissant et fort,
> En le priant du cœur changera notre sort;
> Prions si nous voulons que sa miséricorde
> Détruise parmi nous la haine et la discorde.

> (Since we never pray to the Almighty in vain,
> Christians, let us unite; when this tutelary God
> Had shed all His blood for us on Calvary,
> Let us hope that today, all mighty and strong,
> Granting our prayers, He will change our destiny;
> Let us pray if, through His mercy we wish Him
> To destroy among us hatred and discord.) (*LC* 88, 89)

The danger that the cathedral faces, then, springs from division in the Christian community: only Christian unity can bring back "the true happiness [that] was shining in all eyes" (*LC* 89). In this context, the implied division seems to result from the influx of Anglo-Protestants into New Orleans after 1803, an influx that destroyed the "unity" of Christians in New Orleans. While Catholicism did not suffer an absolute decline in membership—indeed, with the arrival of large numbers of Irish and German immigrants to New Orleans after 1830, there were more Catholics in the city than ever—its strength relative to Protestantism waned, and the potent symbols of Catholic worship no longer commanded universal reverence.

Yet even this explanation seems inadequate to account for the poem's exaggerated lament. Why should the arrival of Protestants in New Orleans prove so catastrophic? Here it is worth remembering that the Catholic / Protestant divide in New Orleans was as much ethnic and cultural as religious, and these cultural differences contributed to different models of race relations. Although neither the French and Spanish colonial governments nor the American regime in New Orleans condemned the institution of slavery, evidence suggests that racial policies were much more tolerant and that the segregation of races was much less rigorously enforced under the French and Spanish. Particularly during Spanish rule (from 1763 to 1800), churches were integrated, clergy members spoke out against the cruel treatment of slaves, and such rights as self-manumission were widely allowed, if not universally guaranteed. Perhaps most significant from the point of view of the *Les Cenelles* poets, French and Spanish authorities recognized free Creoles of color as a distinct class and upheld the three-tiered racial order that ensured this class its privileges. Even after New Orleans became an American city in 1803, Catholic influence on the treatment and status of blacks and mixed-race individuals persisted: Catholic worship, for example, remained racially integrated, in sharp contrast to nearly everywhere else in the South. In the words of Caryn Cossé Bell, "Until the 1830s, the city's liberal religious culture helped to delay the imposition of a sharply defined, two-tiered racial hierarchy . . . [and] forestalled the emergence of a conservative proslavery orthodoxy."[12]

Liotau's poem thus appears at a moment when the previous racial and ethnic order was disintegrating, as American and Protestant attitudes grew in power and as newly arrived Irish and German immigrants eroded the hegemony of French Creoles within the church.[13] In this context, it seems best understood as a protest against the Americanization and Protestantization of New Orleans—a process that would entail ominous implications for people of Liotau's own race, culture, and religion. Whereas once, one could have used the terms *Catholic*, *Christian*, and even *Creole* synonymously in the city, the influx of Americans, Protestants, and even non-Creole Catholics was in danger of dividing the local church, infecting it with a more virulent strain of racism, and eventually denying slaves and free persons of color equal access to the church, the sacraments, and the splendors of the liturgy. Liotau's profession of faith and concern for its survival, then, are inseparable from his concern about the survival of his race and culture.

At the same time, the poem's location of a better world in the past rather than the future reveals the limits of Liotau's progressive stance. The poem is conservative in the strict sense of the word: despite its recommendation of a specific course of action, it seeks to preserve rather than alter a status quo. If the Christians of New Orleans follow the poem's injunction to unite and forget past hatreds, then the result will be a return to a lost universal brotherhood: "Have we not seen the crowd of New Orleans, / When came the Noble Feast, at ease in the old temple?" (*LC* 89). The heterogeneity of people and experience implied by the word "crowd" here is balanced against the unanimity of sentiment that its "ease" would suggest. Diversity becomes praiseworthy only because it does not finally matter much, because Catholicism erases the social stigma that attaches itself to racial and ethnic difference. Like most invocations of past harmony, this idealization of a "noble feast" indicative of Catholic unity has little basis in Louisiana history: integrated Masses and Catholic advocacy on behalf of the *gens de couleur libres* may have mitigated but did little to challenge the fundamental inequalities of Louisiana society. Even the poem's optimistic conclusion, which states baldly that only "another effort will tip the scale / Undoubtedly toward peace, we can be sure of that" (*LC* 89, 91), appears as wishful thinking. Not only is there no specification of what this "effort" might be, but the ease and certainty with which it can be achieved ring false: if a single "effort" can magically restore the past, then the danger cannot help but appear less dangerous. Because it holds up Catholicism as a uniformly positive expression of Creole identity, denying the complicity of both the church and the *gens de couleur libres* themselves in an unequal class structure, Liotau's poem must simultaneously register a sense of threat and suggest that a mere change of heart can overcome the threat.

Other contributions to *Les Cenelles*, however, record a more complicated relationship with the church. While faith and devotion remain keynotes, expressions of this faith and devotion betray hints that the price paid for the church's protection includes a troubled acquiescence in the racial injustices surrounding miscegenation. To be sure, church law prohibited interracial marriage and concubinage under both the colonial and the American regimes, but in practice church leaders tolerated such liaisons and generally did not condemn either those who engaged in them or their children.[14] While this unofficial tolerance helped free Creoles of color to preserve their privileges, it also helped to perpetuate the sexual exploitation of free women of color—and ensured that free men of color, insofar as they cast themselves as the guardians of these women, continued to be humiliated.

"The Orphan of the Tombs," a long poem by the poet Bowers, whose first name is unknown, comments in a particularly camouflaged form on both the church's cherished protection of free Creoles of color and its complicity with the racial power structure. The speaker of the poem, lingering in a New Orleans cemetery, overhears the lament of an orphan who lives among the tombs, having been left destitute after the death of a kind protector. The child relates how his protector encountered him one day in the cemetery and offered to take him in:

> " 'Je serai désormais ton parent adoptif;
> J'adoucirai ton sort; hélas! il est à plaindre!
> Enfant, dans mon séjour tu n'auras rien à craindre;
> Des orages du temps j'abriterai tes jours;
> Car tu seras mon fils, et le seras toujours.
> J'endormirai tes maux. Dans ma demeure antique,
> Oh! viens te reposer, enfant mélancholique.' "

> (" 'Henceforth will I be your adopted father;
> I will cushion your fate; alas, it is to be pitied!
> My child, in my home you will have nothing to fear;
> I will shield your days from the ravages of time;
> For you will be my son, and will be so forever.
> I will make you forget your pains. In my ancient lodging,
> Oh! come here and rest, melancholy child.' ") (*LC* 22, 23)

The kind "father's" address contains several scriptural echoes: the "For you will be my son" recalls both God's covenant with Abraham ("I will be your God, and you will be my people") and Paul's declaration that Christians become "sons of God" and brothers of Christ. Moreover, this father's pity at the fact that "the world hates you" suggests Christ's words of comfort to his disciples ("If the world hates you, know that it has hated me before you"). Indeed the kindness extended to the orphan transcends both the material comforts of a home and the filial bonds of affection: the adoption will last "always," will protect the child even from "the ravages of time" (a hint of immortality), and will afford shelter in an "ancient lodging." In short, the "father" in the poem figures as God himself, whose habitation is the church and who loves even the outcast and downtrodden. At the same time, the orphan—rejected or left behind by his true father—functions as an extraordinarily apt symbol for the child of miscegenation, whose existence is officially denied, whose father has no legal obligation to him, and upon whom the powerful in society pour contempt.

The church, then, welcomes the orphan, who for a time experiences a happiness tempered only by "[t]he sad memory of a touching voice," which sometimes surfaces "[a]nd suddenly force[s] me to burst into tears" (*LC* 23). This unspecified voice, however, introduces a link to the orphan's origins—a link that must be suppressed if the adoption is to be sustained. The protection of Christ's church, even as it guarantees the orphan a place in the world, carries with it the price of forgetting. As Joseph Roach points out, the civil code of law "never explain[s] the presence of the mixed-blood subjects whose existence it both forb[ids] and recognize[s]"; neither can the church afford to recognize too openly this class of human beings whose existence attests to violations of church law.[15] Thus the only means of acceptance for mixed-race individuals is to deny or erase their origins, particularly in an Americanizing society (and church) busily abolishing the rights and privileges of such individuals. Read in a positive light, this acceptance might suggest that all, regardless of race, find equality within the church, as Liotau's poem fervently hoped. Yet the pain that the orphan feels points to a more vexed interpretation: while racial identity may be mutable, it possesses a tenacious memory not easily dissolved in religious faith.

In fact the problematic nature of the church's demands becomes evident when the orphan returns from a visit to his sister's tomb to discover that his adopted father is dying. Just as he has paid his respects to his past, his protector in the present deserts him. Perhaps Liotau's fears that the church was becoming more racist and Americanized may be apropos here. This reading would imply that while the church would never *really* desert the orphan (that is, his eternal life in heaven remains secure), life on earth would become much harder. The protector's dying address, however, suggests a bleaker prospect:

> " 'C'en est fait, ô mon fils, je te quitte à jamais;
> Sur mon tombeau désert tu prîras désormais.—
> Chaque jour tu viendras au lever de l'aurore,
> Enfant—pour y gémir t'agenouiller encore—
> Que je serre ta main! C'en est fait—je me meurs' "—

> (" 'It is finished, O my son, I leave you forever;
> On my solitary tomb henceforth will you pray.—
> Each day will you come at the break of day
> My child—kneel there and moan—
> Let me hold your hand! It is done.—I die.—!' ") (*LC* 24, 25)

Here the echo of Christ's last words on the cross resonates with irony. The "father" leaves his son miserable, even as he requires him to keep up the

forms of belief, to pray every day. Yet this prayer seems patently ineffica-
cious, because the father claims to leave "forever," thus contradicting his
earlier promise of eternal adoption—and departing from the example of
Christ, who rose from the dead and promised his followers that he would
return after his ascension. The orphan, enjoined to live out his days in the
cemetery, despairs of ever attaining the love of Anastasie, a woman described as "an angel of fifteen, crowned with jasmines" and "that timid virgin" (*LC* 25). His only consolation is the fantasy that after his death,
Anastasie may remember him with love when she reads the inscription on
his tombstone: "He lived and died amidst the tombs" (*LC* 25). When the
orphan does die at the end of the poem, his facial expression suggests to the
speaker no eternal bliss but rather "that sleep whose lugubrious aspect /
Prints in our hearts an eternal regret!" (*LC* 27). If, then, the protector allegorically represents Christ and the church, the prospect that "The Orphan
of the Tombs" outlines for the *gens de couleur libres* is hopeless indeed: whatever the church's promises of protection and solace may be, in the end, they
will be abandoned. The suppression of racial difference, however well in-
tentioned, carries with it a heavy price.

The brief mention of unrequited love in the poem (Anastasie does not
appear until the end and then vanishes quickly) raises the interconnectedness
of race and sex among the *gens de couleur libres*—a nexus that provokes specific anxieties for the *Les Cenelles* poets. The orphan's generic description of
Anastasie includes nothing that would identify her race, but the French
name and the implicitly mixed-race background of the orphan himself argue
that she is probably a free Creole of color. *Les Cenelles* is dedicated by Lanusse "To The Fair Sex of Louisiana" (*LC* xxxiv), and although his dedica-
tory quatrain contains no racial allusions, the coquettish women who
populate the poems are often given racial and ethnic markers, unlike the
lyric speakers themselves: "blue-eyed creole," "blonde creole" (*LC* 35, 37).
Sometimes these markers combine with allusions to an unknown ancestry
and with the suggestion that these women must be exiles from heaven, because no earthly women could be so beautiful. Joanni Questy's poem "A
Vision," for instance, addresses to a "[v]irgin expelled from heaven" the
pointed question, "Tell me, who was your father, / Airy child?" (*LC* 61).
Just as the familiar children's story about the stork who delivers babies conceals the truth of sexual reproduction, these hints of divine origin conceal
the truth of miscegenation that accounts for these women's actual origin. In
the context of the collection as a whole, Anastasie appears as one of these

cruel, unattainable women who fail to recognize the worth of their virtuous lovers.

In a groundbreaking reading of *Les Cenelles*, Floyd D. Cheung proposes that the poems be read "in imaginary conversation with the performative text of quadroon balls, [so that] the dark undertones of the balls come into relief."[16] Quadroon balls, a New Orleans institution begun in the colonial period and continued with the sanction of the American government, were occasions at which wealthy white men gathered to choose concubines from a selection of beautiful and accomplished free women of color. Latortue and Adams note that "Among those *gens de couleur libres* who had not yet reached the highest stratum of their society, interracial liaisons were often a means to achieving that end. Mothers, especially among quadroon and octoroon women, would seek to 'establish' their daughters with white male 'protectors.' This would assure the daughter's financial support, and frequently, her social rank."[17] Such financial support typically included a gift of money or a house, so that the women would retain some property if they were later deserted or if their protector died.[18] *Plaçage*, or "establishment," was the name given to the process of making such arrangements.

With clarity and brio, Cheung argues that in the larger cultural narrative of antebellum New Orleans, "free women of color [are] the symbolic prize in [the] competition for cultural superiority" between white men and free men of color. Accordingly the *Les Cenelles* poets position themselves as "jealous lovers and protective brothers," who seek to steer free women of color away from the degradation of *plaçage* and toward unions with men of their own race and caste. In this way, the poems constitute a kind of "hidden transcript" with a definite but disguised political message: "Winning a coy glance from an octoroon . . . represents a triumph in the war for rights and respect that deteriorated a great deal for free black Creoles with the introduction and increasing dominance of American rule in Louisiana."[19]

There is much to recommend Cheung's thesis. He shows that such poems as Valcour B.'s "To Miss C" and Lanusse's "The Young Lady at the Ball," which, respectively, criticize women for listening to the lies of other suitors and for caring more about riches and hedonism than true love, do indeed resonate as protests against quadroon balls and the frankly material aspirations that young quadroons and their mothers entertained. Perhaps Questy's "Chat," which Cheung does not cite, supports his argument more openly: it presents a brother who threatens his sister for flirting with a man, saying, "do you know, my cruel one, / What is going on inside me, in my heart, in my blood, / When I happen to catch one of them with my eyes?"

(*LC* 69). If Cheung's argument is extended to the productions of *L'album littéraire*, even clearer denunciations of *plaçage* appear. "A New Impression," a poem by Liotau that appeared in the issue of 15 July 1843, admonishes a mother who pressures her daughter into an arrangement with a white man; "A Marriage of Conscience," a short story by Lanusse in the issue of 15 August 1843, exposes the way a young girl is tricked into a "marriage" that, although sanctioned by a priest, is neither legally nor religiously binding.[20] In both works, the poets' abhorrence of the practice is straightforward and unambiguous.

Cheung overstates his case, however, when he proposes that "[m]ost commonly, the poems overturn white hierarchies by valorizing in their place those of the Catholic church," because this formulation suggests an opposition between "whiteness" and "Catholicism" that simply did not exist.[21] While the poets do appeal to moral laws and the need to remain close to God in their efforts to persuade free women of color (and sometimes to praise, using strongly religious language, those few women who cling to their virtue, as in Liotau's "To Ida"), they cannot rely too much on the church's injunctions against miscegenation, since such unions often received the church's tacit approval. The priest in "A Marriage of Conscience" who officially sanctions the false marriage has nothing to say when the man abandons his partner for a white wife; he thus shares the responsibility for the young woman's descent into madness and suicide. By appealing to Catholic morality, then, the poets place themselves in the awkward position of affirming their faith while sometimes condemning its clergy and practices. Nor is it simply a matter of a few corrupt priests contradicting the true and accepted practice of Catholics, for Protestants in New Orleans had no monopoly on *plaçage*: it was a familiar custom well before the establishment of American sovereignty.

The poets' attitude toward *plaçage* is further complicated by the material benefits that they acquired as a result of the practice. Blyden Jackson reports that at least two of the *Les Cenelles* poets—Pierre Dalcour and Camille Thierry—"were conspicuously the children of *placées*."[22] A third, Victor Séjour, may also have been. All three were educated in France, eventually settled there, and died there (in Séjour's case, after a long and acclaimed career as a playwright). The material well-being that such educations required was almost certainly gained from the inheritance of white forebears. While little biographical data on the other poets' parentage remains extant, their comfortable positions in society sprang, if not always directly from instances of *plaçage*, from acts of miscegenation and probable attendant financial gains in the recent or distant past. In fact there is even evidence that Séjour's father may have taken part in the promotion of quadroon balls at the Washington Ballroom in the Vieux Carré—a suggestion that free Creole men of color, as well as free Creole women of color, sometimes had a vested interest in the continuation of *plaçage*.[23] The ringing denunciations of the practice in Liotau and Lanusse's work, although undeniably sincere, come from those for whom miscegenation has brought social prestige and financial security.

In what may be the most remarkable poem in *Les Cenelles*, Lanusse confronts the problem of *plaçage* squarely. "Epigram," the only poem in the collection to allude openly to racial matters, presents an exchange in the confessional between priest and penitent:

> "Vous ne voulez donc pas renoncer à Satan,"
> Disait un bon pasteur à certaine bigote
> Qui d'assez gros péchés, à chaque nouvel an,
> Venait lui présenter l'interminable note.
> "Je veux y renoncer," dit-elle, "pour jamais;
> Mais avant que la grâce en mon âme scintille,
> Pour m'ôter tout motif de pécher désormais,
> Que ne puis-je, pasteur—Quoi donc?—*placer* ma fille?"

> ("You really do not want to renounce Satan,"
> A good preacher was saying to a certain zealot
> Who, every year, came to present him
> Her interminable list of rather mortal sins.
> "I do want to renounce him," says she, "for ever,
> But before grace sparkles in my soul,
> To remove henceforth all incentive to sin,
> Why can't I, father—what?—*establish* my daughter?") (*LC* 94, 95)

Readings of this poem have assumed that the priest's moral authority is clear. For Cheung the poem's message is simple: "*plaçage* is sinful . . . [and] such behavior will only lower [the mother] in the cosmic scale." Michel Fabre states his judgment even more strongly: the poem presents "a scathing critique of (unofficially) institutionalized white (sexual) supremacy."[24] Such readings rest on the correct assumption that *plaçage* and miscegenation in general were condemned by both church and state, in conformity with Catholic teachings against extramarital sex and legal prohibitions against interracial marriage. Yet both the text of the poem itself and its situation in dialogue with other works by Lanusse suggest a more conflicted stance toward the woman and her plan.

As "A Marriage of Conscience" shows, Lanusse does not always represent the clergy as paragons of virtue. The priest who arranges the marriage of conscience violates the church's law and earns condemnation. Another poem, however, expresses sympathy for a priest wrestling with his desire for a young penitent—and goes so far as to hint that moral dogma may not always be absolute. The lyric speaker of "The Priest and the Young Girl," reduced to desperation by the violence of his lust, exclaims, "this law is far too cruel! / Do these vows correspond with [*sic*] our nature?" A few lines later, he protests "the decrees of an inhuman council" that enjoin him to celibacy and thinks of telling his love that "No one is capable of feeling only pure sentiments." At the end, he gives up any pretense of being able to control his feelings and cries out, "My God! protect her, please!" (*LC* 117). While the poem reveals the race of neither the priest nor his penitent, in the context of the collection as a whole, the possibility of a forbidden interracial desire in this poem cannot be discounted. If Lanusse is ready to excoriate priests who depart from the teachings of the church, he also betrays sympathy with their failings—and again reveals the implausibility of the view that the church is always intrinsically moral.

The priest in "Epigram" does appear in a better light than his counterparts in "A Marriage of Conscience" and "The Priest and the Young Girl." He certainly does his job correctly, as Cheung and Fabre maintain, by reminding the woman that her machinations are sinful. The encounter in the confessional, however, is no isolated event: both her yearly presentation of "the interminable list" and the phrasing of the priest's words suggest that the two are enacting a familiar, often repeated ritual. The priest does not expect her to "renounce Satan," but he also shows no sign that he will send her away or refuse to give absolution. Indeed his manner can be read just as convincingly as cynical jocularity or turpitude rather than moral earnestness: he warns the woman but does so formulaically and may even consent to her plans, just as the woman's hesitation before pronouncing the euphemism "establish" shows a desire to observe proper forms without adhering to their spirit. The woman's response reveals her awareness of the moral problem involved. As a "zealot," she probably desires the grace that she speaks of, yet her allusion to the material benefits of *plaçage* displays an honest shrewdness. Grace may be well and good, she implies, but it is partially enabled by financial security. "Establishing" her daughter—one final sin—thus becomes a positive good because it will foreclose any number of future temptations. The devoutly Catholic Lanusse may well intend to decry her theologically unsound logic and to pronounce her words hollow. Yet by giving her the last word, and allowing his priest no opportunity to refute her claim, he foregrounds the competition between economic and moral claims without providing any resolution. Moreover, the universalizing thrust of church teaching—concubinage, after all, would be presented as always wrong, regardless of who engages in it—pales before the woman's sound grasp of very specific economic realities that cannot be divorced from her racial and ethnic difference. Universal, "catholic" standards of virtue, the poem implies, prove more difficult for those marked by difference.

The construction of Catholicism in *Les Cenelles*, with its mixture of sincere devotion and pointed criticism, springs from a unique confluence of circumstances that existed between 1803 and 1845: the presence of a free, racially mixed, and ethnically French population forced into a defensive posture by the pressures of an Americanizing government committed to a biracial order. Such an account necessarily emphasizes the apartness of the free Creoles of color, the difficulty of describing their identity as unproblematically African-American, and the reality of their class separation from others with African ancestry. These conditions, however, were in rapid flux even as *Les Cenelles* was being published. Cheung reports that "[d]uring the period from 1850 to 1865, free persons of color as a class virtually disappeared, since those who could left for other cities to pass as white, and since the legal category itself was subsumed into 'Negro' after the Civil War."[25] Traces of this disappearance can be discerned even in the literary production of Creole blacks in New Orleans in the years during and after the Civil War. Whereas *Les Cenelles* is the product of a moment at which free Creoles of color still sought to preserve their identity and to chart a destiny separate from those of all African-Americans, journals such as *L'Union* and *La Tribune de la Nouvelle Orléans* (launched respectively in 1862 and 1864), although published by the free black Creole elite, announce themselves self-consciously as vehicles for the voice of all African-Americans. Protected by the Federal forces then occupying the city, these publications take a pro-Union stance and call for the abolition of slavery.[26] Even Lanusse, whose reputation was tarnished by his service in the Confederate army, came to believe before his death in 1867 in, as Edward Maceo Coleman puts it, "the hopelessness of any attempt on the part of the Creoles to build for themselves a future apart from other persons of color."[27] The disappearance of free Creoles of color as a category of race and class is consistent with the larger trajectory of "mulatto" identity that Joel Williamson has sketched:

> Essentially, what happened in the changeover [between 1850 and 1915] was that the dominant white society moved from semiacceptance of free

mulattoes, especially in the lower South, to outright rejection. As mulatto communities in the 1850s confronted an increasingly hostile white world implementing increasingly stringent rules against them in the form either of laws or of social pressures, they themselves moved from a position of basic sympathy with the white world to one of guarded antagonism. In the movement the mulatto elite gave up white alliances and picked up black alliances. The change accelerated in the Civil War, took its set during the critical year 1865, and continued through Reconstruction, post-Reconstruction, and into the twentieth century. . . . In white eyes, all Negroes came to look alike.[28]

Williamson's rather schematic account does not quite convey the racial flux of the Reconstruction years: the movement of the *gens de couleur libres* into the designation *Negro* was an uneven process, and the consciousness of a distinct and proud *gens de couleur libres* identity would persist into the twentieth century, long after the legal designation had ceased to exist. Nevertheless the basic outline remains accurate: free Creoles of color, even as they clung to their unique history, would take part in this "changeover" and come to identify with the aims of African-Americans as a whole. As a result, the emphasis on Catholicism as a badge of identity among free Creoles of color would never again resonate as strongly as in *Les Cenelles*. Yet the associations between the church and miscegenation evident in that collection continue to circulate in the postwar period—and indeed take on a more sinister tone from the perspective of a white world increasingly committed to the "one drop" rule and to the denial and prohibition of miscegenation.

❧

From the point of view of white New Orleans Creoles, the Protestant *Américains* were cultural invaders, determined to stamp out the leisurely pace and charm of Latin culture and to impose their own joyless way of life on the city. Protestantism, signifying within this context delayed gratification, moralism, and a spiritually bankrupt economic calculation, was seen as a threat to the spirit of *laissez les bon temps rouler,* that elusive and embattled ethos that would eventually overcome its defensive posture through mythologizing and the savvy marketing of New Orleans as a tourist destination. New Orleans in the 1840s was, however, a small cultural enclave not just within the nation as a whole but also within the more circumscribed boundaries of the South, and the cultural narrative of invasion and dispossession that white Creole Catholics of the period took up was echoed in regional and national contexts. The waves of Catholic immigrants from Ireland and Germany that began to arrive in the United States in the 1840s quickly produced political reactions that included physical attacks on Catholics, burnings of convents, and the brief rise in the 1850s of the American or Know-Nothing Party, which sought to strip Catholics and "foreigners" of their voting rights.

Since few of these immigrants settled in the lower South (New Orleans was, in fact, one of the few lower southern cities to absorb them in significant numbers), the primary loci of anti-Catholic feeling during the antebellum period were northern cities. Anti-Catholic violence and Know-Nothing political gains were, accordingly, rare in the South and occurred there most conspicuously in the border states. In Maryland, for instance, the Know-Nothing Party elected the mayor of Baltimore in 1854 and captured the state legislature the following year. (Only in Louisville, Kentucky, did significant violence take place: on "Bloody Monday" in 1855, mobs provoked by the Know-Nothings moved through Catholic neighborhoods, killing nearly one hundred people.)[29] Nevertheless the concentration of Catholics in the North did contribute to suspicions that the church might find itself opposed to certain key aspects of the southern way of life—particularly in the years just before the Civil War, when the attempt to defend a white southern cultural and political identity distinct from that of the nation became acute. By the turn of the century such suspicions had, in James J. Thompson's words, "metamorphosed into . . . the most poisonous strain of anti-Catholicism the United States has ever seen."[30]

Of the various anti-southern forces perceived to be aligned with Catholicism, none proved more terrifying to white southern imaginations than antiracist movements. For much of the century following Reconstruction, racist arguments in favor of segregation and the restriction of suffrage from African-Americans claimed that the end result of social equality would be universal miscegenation—a prospect too horrible to contemplate. The fact that New Orleans, the southern city with the highest concentration of Catholics, also possessed an unusually large number of mixed-race residents contributed to fears that the church tacitly supported miscegenation—fears that were sometimes justified. New Orleans and southern Louisiana also possessed the largest number of free men of color in the antebellum South, and many of this class assumed roles of political leadership during the early Reconstruction period.[31] For both these reasons, New Orleans itself would come to figure in some southerners' minds as an anomalous place, a place that, while in the South, was not of it.

Initially postwar perceptions that New Orleans' race relations and Catholic ethos were at odds with southern Protestant culture (and the larger national culture) expressed themselves in a fascination with the city's exoticism, an atmosphere used to great effect in the enormously popular and often nostalgic local color writing that flourished in the last decades of the nineteenth century. Many of the local color writers who took Louisiana as their subject were Protestant, but they tended to represent Catholicism more as part of a richly textured local fabric than as a menace. Nevertheless their association of the church with miscegenation—often in ways that uncannily resemble the same association in *Les Cenelles*—provided disquieting food for thought to forthrightly anti-Catholic southerners of the early twentieth century. In particular Cable, King, and Dunbar-Nelson, three southern local colorists divided by race, gender, and political ideology, provide related accounts of the connections among Catholicism, miscegenation, and racial identity to a much larger reading public than the intended audience of *Les Cenelles*. Although their subject matter remains much the same, these writers' attitudes toward the church and miscegenation are more varied and reflect the changing attitudes in the South toward the church.

Of these writers, Cable was the most typically "Protestant" in his beliefs and ideology. A devout Calvinist whose piety could provoke exasperation in the famously skeptical Mark Twain, Cable was a native of New Orleans but a product of Virginian and New England ancestry whose fiction registers both fascination with the white Creole population and stern disapproval of its perceived laziness and moral laxity.[32] Many of Cable's most famous works center on the confrontation between white Creole and *Américain*, exposing the Creole as a shallow, hedonistic hypocrite and the American as a kind of latter-day Yankee Jonathan, essentially decent and moral but not immune from temptation.[33] "Posson Jone," a short story of 1875, presents this contrast at its most exaggerated in its portrayal of Jules St.-Ange, a pleasure-loving, frivolous Creole Catholic, and Parson Jones, a straitlaced and kindhearted soul from West Florida. St.-Ange is wily enough to persuade Parson Jones to get drunk, but in the end the good parson's moral influence proves stronger: St.-Ange resolves to pay his debts and sends Parson Jones away, admonishing him never to return to such a wicked place as New Orleans.[34] Although Cable was capable of creating sympathetic Creole characters—indeed, even St-Ange possesses a certain amoral charm—in most of his works their Catholicism functions less as a system of belief than as a mere trapping of Creole identity.

Cable's most accomplished novel, *The Grandissimes,* set during New Orleans's transition from French to American rule in 1803, softens the contrast between Creole and Yankee, but the broad outline remains. On the one hand, the novel revels in sensual local color tropes: charming women (some of whom may have African blood) and hot-blooded Creole partisans who twitter in broken English or in patois; lush descriptions of swamps, the French Quarter, and *bals masqués*; the tragic story of a heroic slave, Bras-Coupé. Yet the novel's moral center is Joseph Frowenfeld, a painfully earnest, even priggish American who arrives in the city in the second chapter, establishes himself as a druggist, and spends the rest of the novel lecturing on the inferiority of Creole culture, the idleness of the Creole population, the inevitability of American rule, and the racial prejudices and injustices perpetuated by the Creole social structure. From a post-Reconstruction vantage point, Frowenfeld's belief that the cession of Louisiana to the United States augurs a brighter day for enslaved African-Americans appears naive: American rule not only failed to abolish slavery but in some respects worsened living conditions for slaves and free blacks alike. This naiveté, however, becomes less problematic if the novel is read as an intervention in the politics of post-Reconstruction New Orleans, so that the Creoles in the novel forced by the Louisiana Purchase to submit to an American regime against their will become, allegorically speaking, those New Orleanians resisting the hated policies of the occupying Yankees after the Civil War. Louis D. Rubin Jr. observes that just as the Creoles of 1803 found themselves incorporated against their will into a new government, "the New Orleans of the years following the Civil War had a government imposed upon it by force, and pledged, in theory at least, to political and social principles very much at odds with those of the society thus subjected."[35] Despite occasional ironic pricks at his protagonist's innocence, Cable's position on this "subjection" is much the same as Frowenfeld's: the newly reunited American dispensation should be welcomed, because it represents freedom and progress, while the defeated southern order offers nothing but continued prejudice and oppression. Frowenfeld's task, to persuade the dashing Honoré Grandissime to acknowledge his brother, welcome the American regime, and heal the feud that has long festered between his family and the de Grapions, is much the same as Parson Jones's, and, though Honoré wins both the glory and his beloved when he finally yields, Frowenfeld has been the agent of his moral transformation.

The contrast between Yankee and Creole here turns on ethnicity, but race and religion are both implicated in the contrast—race because of the mixed bloodlines of the Grandissimes (they even, somewhat contradictorily, boast of their Native American ancestry), and religion in the universal adherence of the Creole population to Catholicism. When Cable represents Catholicism in *The Grandissimes,* he notes its essential hypocrisy, its distortion of Christian charity and love, and its acquiescence in racial injustices. He rarely voices his criticism as directly: for example when he mentions the priest who marries two slaves, Bras-Coupé and Palmyre Philosophe, against the will of Palmyre, he presents this clerical atrocity without comment. Indeed the novel's most biting indictment of the church comes in a brief flashback to the days of Louis XV, when the "Grand Marquis" De Vaudreuil governed in New Orleans. When Clotilde, the orphan daughter of a murdered Huguenot, arrives in Louisiana as a *fille à la cassette,* she proves difficult because she refuses both to marry and to pray to the Virgin Mary. De Vaudreuil attempts to overcome her religious scruples by convincing her that Catholic belief is "actually a joke, every whit; except to be sure, this heresy phase; that is a joke they cannot take."[36] The governor's suggestion that even bishops and cardinals do not believe in Catholicism, except as a necessary pillar of the social order, far exceeds in cynicism the use that the *Les Cenelles* poets made of Catholicism to buttress their own identity and privileges. Against such brutal nihilism, the association of Protestant heritage with individual freedom is clear.

The Grandissimes provoked a storm of criticism from white New Orleans Creoles, who maintained that their culture, customs, and religious beliefs had been maligned. The most flamboyant attack on the novel came from a priest, Adrien-Emmanuel Rouquette, who anonymously published his pamphlet *Critical Dialogue Between Aboo and Caboo; or, a Grandissime Ascension* later the same year. This remarkable work presents Agricola Fusilier, Cable's representative of Creole racism in *The Grandissimes,* risen from the dead, renamed Aboo, and returned to Louisiana after the Civil War. While weeping bitterly over the ruined plantations he sees, he is accosted by his kinsman, Caboo, and the two immediately focus their dialogue not on the destruction of the war but on the insults to their family bandied about in *The Grandissimes.* That book's author, Aboo maintains, "is, we have been told, a native of Louisiana," but he reveals himself as a cultural scalawag, pandering to northern prejudices and grossly misrepresenting the glories of Creole culture.[37] Though Aboo and Caboo dwell at considerable length on the barbarity of Cable's language, the disordered, phantasmagoric pictures that he paints, and the disregard he shows for fact, they return obsessively to the likelihood of "Negro" influence on the book: Aboo, for instance, sneers that "he got his *historical* information from some old negresses, reeling on the brink of Eternity" (*CD* 11).

Most damning, however, are the insinuations that Cable himself supports and practices miscegenation. "This impec-*cable* Exquisite," says Aboo, "has decked his head with a *jet-black* plume, fallen from the *tail* of a crow,—which remar*kable* circumstance warns us to distrust this Grandissime TELL-TALE" (*CD* 10). Caboo agrees, warning his cousin to be careful in his attacks on Cable: "Beware! He is a High-Priest of Negro-Voudouism, and you known what Negro-Voudousim means" (*CD* 20). Their worst fears are quickly confirmed: a chorus of bullfrogs appears on the scene to sing Cable's praises, and a "Weird Solo By a Zombi-Frog," sung in Afro-Creole French, claims that Cable has married "mamezelle Zizi," the most beautiful of black women, under the auspices of *voudun* priestess Marie Laveau and fathered numerous mixed-race children. It is no wonder, then, that he maliciously calls New Orleans a "HYBRID CITY" (*CD* 17); he advocates a "beautiful palengensia, heretofore undreamed of,—which will consummate all *fusion* and *confusion,*—making all diverse colors intermarry and blend into one sole and mongrel color,—symbolical of highest perfection,—highest, in sooth, if *highest* means *lowest*" (*CD* 19, emphasis in text). In fact the cacophony of Cable's language, which swings from broken English to Afro-Creole, merely illustrates the ideal to which he aspires. The fear of "fusion and confusion" that haunts white southern imaginations and leads to an inability to tell white from black, *Américain* from Creole, could not be more baldly stated.

At first glance, Rouquette seems an unlikely candidate to have published this attack. Locally famous for his missionary work among the Choctaws and for his conventionally romantic French nature poetry, Rouquette was a thoroughgoing Unionist who had opposed secession and cooperated with Federal forces occupying New Orleans during the Civil War. More surprisingly he had incurred the displeasure of his superiors during the 1850s by supporting the anti-Catholic Know-Nothing Party—an astonishing position for a priest to take and comprehensible only if, as his biographer has suggested, the patriotic association of the party's name blinded him to its unpalatable politics.[38] Why, then, would Rouquette later malign a man who, despite his earlier service in the Confederate army, had come to believe in many of the aims of Reconstruction?

The most likely explanation centers on Cable's linkage of Catholicism, miscegenation, and Creole culture, for Rouquette's pamphlet also associates Cable's moralizing, straitlaced Presbyterianism with his general audacity.

The fictional "editor" who presents the *Critical Dialogue* to readers describes Cable's "spiteful mood and style," which has "the pedantic phraseology of a sunday [sic] school-master, who pedagogues before a ravished audience of gaping boys and girls" (*CD* 4). Later Caboo refers to the "finical refinement of disguised puritanism [sic] that informs *The Grandissimes*"—undoubtedly a response to Cable's unflattering portraits of Creole laziness and moral turpitude, which a slack and worldly Catholicism allows to flourish. In this way, Rouquette seeks to turn the tables: Cable may consider miscegenation a product of Creole and Catholic apathy and cruelty, but given his own erotic pursuits, the "puritans" of Cable's stripe are the ones who really contribute to moral outrage. Cable's alleged involvement with "Negro-Voudousim" thus serves both to paint Cable in the most diabolical light and to distract from the reality that *voudun*, as practiced in New Orleans, proved quite compatible with Catholic belief, iconography, and liturgy.

Perhaps as an attempt to placate his critics, Cable included in his next major work, the novella *Madame Delphine*, the most sympathetic of all his Catholic characters, the good Père Jerome, who combines Frowenfeld's moral idealism with a stereotypically Creole love of worldly pleasures. Not surprisingly Cable achieves this effect only by making this priest as Protestant as possible. Père Jerome's rotundity, love of good food, and mirth are excusable, the narrator implies, because he knows where Christianity's true authority lies: "Among the clergy there were two or three who shook their heads and raised their eyebrows, and said he would be at least as orthodox if he did not make quite so much of the Bible and quite so little of the dogmas."[39] This priest also declaims from the pulpit that the racial caste system is sinful and admonishes his congregation that they share guilt for consenting to it—a view, one would think, that would hardly endear him to his white parishioners. Nevertheless, the narrator insists, "he was much beloved" (*MD* 17). By the end of the novella, Père Jerome has become an accomplice to a union that involves racial mixing and passing, making him overtly subversive as well as implausibly liberal.

The novella centers around the efforts of Madame Delphine, a quadroon, to find a white husband for Olive, her octoroon daughter, and thus to ensure her social rank and her escape from poverty. Père Jerome, who helps to engineer a match between the daughter and a reformed pirate, is, to be sure, somewhat disturbed by the fact of the miscegenation that he accomplishes, and his contradictory attitude toward this subject seems to mirror Cable's own.[40] In *The Grandissimes*, the quadroon character Palmyre had been held up as a living emblem of sin, a "poisonous blossom of crime growing out of crime" whom "one would want to find chained."[41] Madame Delphine, who resembles the timid but resourceful Nancanou ladies more than she resembles Palmyre, escapes such loathsome description, but Père Jerome's kindness to her springs entirely from his judgment that white men are responsible for the quadroons' "sin"—a judgment repeated several times in his quotation: "Lord, lay not this sin to *their* charge!" (*MD* 19).

Père Jerome's efforts to help Olive take several forms. His first "happy thought" upon learning of her predicament is to recommend the cloister, but then he reflects that Madame Delphine must have "intentionally" overlooked that choice (*MD* 28). Here he echoes the view first suggested in "The Orphan of the Tombs" that the church itself is the best refuge for the outcast children of miscegenation. Later he arranges to send Olive and her fugitive husband-to-be to France, where the two can marry without breaking the law (*MD* 65). Madame Delphine, however, finally removes all obstacles to the marriage by declaring publicly (and falsely) that Olive is in fact white—that she is not her daughter. Immediately afterward she dies in the confessional. Thus the story ends balanced between tragedy and happiness, with the priest uttering as his last words, "Lord, lay not this sin to her charge!" (*MD* 81). Yet while Père Jerome does all he can to help Madame Delphine, forgives her "sins," and seems sincere in his belief in the immorality of segregation and "caste," he never speaks against slavery itself, the institution originally responsible for such "sins." His two closest friends, Jean Thompson and Evariste Varrillat, are slaveholders, and he never condemns them either for owning slaves or for trying to prevent Olive's marriage. Moreover, by considering only the cloister and marriage in France as possible alternatives to a straightforward marriage, he leaves the law intact and unchallenged, while the story itself suggests that death may be an appropriate punishment for the mother who dared to transgress the color line so boldly. For all of his indisputable good will, Père Jerome lacks the courage or the moral clarity to proclaim what he has done and thus to challenge the racial order openly. The poets of *Les Cenelles* would no doubt have recognized, understood, and been pained by his dilemma.

✤

Père Jerome's initial belief that the daughter of mixed-race parents might be happiest in a convent recurs in a number of short stories published near the end of the nineteenth century. Before the Civil War, convents had often been portrayed in American literature as places in which virtuous women forcibly separated from their families endured tomblike imprisonment and sexual torture. As Jenny Franchot has shown, the most popular anticonvent texts, such as Maria Monk's *Awful Disclosures of the Hotel Dieu Nunnery* (1833), emphasized the contrast between the secrecy of the convent and the open, healthy freedom of American Protestant (and middle-class) life.[42] Anticonvent literature, however, had achieved its greatest popularity in the North, and the difference between texts such as Monk's and the southern convent stories of the 1880s and 1890s confirms not just Eugene Genovese's observation that the antebellum North was far more anti-Catholic than the antebellum South, but also that the first significant expressions of anti-Catholicism in the South emerge largely out of the association of the church with miscegenation. When in 1880 the Orleans Ballroom, one of the main sites at which quadroon balls were held, was taken over by the Sisters of the Holy Family and became St. Mary's Academy, a boarding school for young black women, the symbolism was perhaps too apt. The same church that had turned a blind eye to the sexual exploitation of *plaçage* now found new ways to "establish" its mixed-race children.[43]

The best known of these southern convent stories, Grace King's "The Little Convent Girl," appeared in 1893, just twelve years after *Madame Delphine* and during a decade that saw the rapid erection of Jim Crow laws across the South (after *Plessy v. Ferguson* in 1896, with the Supreme Court's blessing). King's story begins with an eighteen-year-old, who has grown up in a convent in Cincinnati, returning home to her mother in New Orleans after the death of her father. The journey down the Ohio and Mississippi rivers lasts for a month, and during the course of the journey the girl, who at first "could not do anything of [*sic*] herself" and spends most of her time praying or worrying about her sins, discovers the pleasures of freedom and movement.[44] She soon delights in the spectacle of the boat's loading and unloading, watches the stars, and listens eagerly to the pilot's fabulous stories about a subterranean river flowing beneath the Mississippi. Only when she arrives in New Orleans does she discover that her mother, whom she has never met, is "colored" (*LCG* 158). A month later, when the boat returns to New Orleans, the girl's mother brings her back for a visit with the captain, thinking that it might lift her spirits. While no one is looking, she jumps or falls into the river, and her body is never discovered.

Thematically "The Little Convent Girl" resembles both such narratives of mistaken identity as Mark Twain's *Puddn'head Wilson* and the narratives of "passing" that would become popular in later decades. Like them, it depends, as Thadious M. Davis has noted, upon an implicit "acceptance of diversity and complexity as the textures of African-American female life . . .

even though it explores the cultural conditions and proscriptions that shape, but do not determine, the life of a female of color."[45] King's acknowledgment that such "passing" can take place even without the passer's knowledge is potentially shocking, for it not only points to (as Davis suggests) a degree of diversity within African-American life that whites would have wished to suppress but also to the terrifying possibility of what could happen to the entire white race. Despite occasional hints in the story as to the girl's race—for example, the reference to her hair, which had "a strong inclination to curl, but that had been taken out of it as austerely as the noise out of her footfalls" (*LCG* 144)—the girl is as surprised as anyone at the discovery of her mother's identity, although she conceals her agitation as she walks away from the boat, not looking back (*LCG* 158). Only the environment of the convent, set for good measure in a northern city, has prevented her from this deadly knowledge.

In addition to shielding her from the horrors of racism more broadly, the nuns protect her from the sexual predations of white men. Her slow, awkward movement in climbing the stairs, accompanied by "such blushing when suspicion would cross the unprepared face that a rim of white stocking might be visible" (*LCG* 153), indicate how thoroughly she has internalized the nuns' rigid requirements for dress and comportment. Post-Freudian readers may view such indoctrination as unhealthy sexual repression, and we do indeed learn that she lives in terror of "her sins! her sins!" (*LCG* 149), but as a disincentive to lustful male gazes and the consequences that might follow from them, the nuns' program succeeds. The captain and pilot of the ship never think of her in sexual terms and even modify their own rough behavior and idiom so that their language "flowed in its natural curve" (*LCG* 153) only in her absence.

Like Kate Chopin's *The Awakening*, "The Little Convent Girl" invites feminist readings that stress the girl's discovery of personal freedom and discern in her apparent suicide an attempt to preserve that freedom in the face of a society that finds it intolerable. Anne Goodwyn Jones, for instance, describes it as the story of "[the] girl's aborted journey to her self"—a hidden, genuine, and healthy self represented both by the confident black mother and by the hidden river into which the girl finally disappears. Even if King, who was "thoroughly . . . a part of the traditional white South," cannot tolerate the fact of miscegenation and must therefore kill off the girl rather than allow her to grow up with her mother, Jones ascribes a proto-feminist logic to the story: "In drowning herself, the girl may have saved herself. . . . Unable to accept consciously the fact that her mother—hence her self—is black, she affirms that awareness by the manner of her dying."[46] Persuasive though Jones's reading is, it suggests that the girl possesses an essential self that is merely waiting to emerge. But just as the nuns at the convent fashion one "self" for the girl, the captain and pilot who widen her horizons contribute to the construction of a new self. The reading here will focus less on the story as a narrative of awakening than on the social implications of the girl's identity as it is presented, an identity defined by race and religion as much as by gender. Readings that focus only on the repressive atmosphere and fear that characterize the girl's sheltered life, then, fail to take into account the real benefits afforded by the church's protection—and may even unwittingly reproduce the bigotry of antebellum convent exposés in their suggestion that the girl's fear indicates a clerical reign of terror.[47]

The question of whether the story advocates the girl's awakening thus remains open. The girl's death at the end of the story need not be attributed solely to King's traditional racial attitude, as Jones suggests; rather it indicates that in the array of options then open to a young woman in her position, none are particularly attractive. Jones is right to dwell so appreciatively on the girl's awakening: such a multitude of new sights and sounds, of "so much unpunished noise and movement in the world" (*LCG*152), do indeed show her what she has missed in the convent, and readers may conclude that giving it up is too high a price for her protection. This conclusion, however, should be balanced against the realization that once in New Orleans, her zest for life disappears: as her mother reports, she "don't go nowhere, she don't do nothing but make her crochet and her prayers" (*LCG* 160)—and this new confinement is arguably worse than her previous life in the convent, since she now possesses awareness of the world's delights. Like Nella Larsen's *Passing*, which closes with a death that might be accident, suicide, or homicide, "The Little Convent Girl" closes with similar ambiguity. Her disappearance into the fabled subterranean river beneath the Mississippi may signify, as Jones suggests, as a journey to a freer (if not necessarily a more genuine) self—but the ambivalence in such an outcome, and the inability to imagine a more satisfactory outcome, nevertheless remains the final note.

No less than "The Orphan of the Tombs" or *Madame Delphine*, then, "The Little Convent Girl" suggests that Catholicism may be the best friend to individuals of mixed-race ancestry, offering women in particular the opportunity, through a kind of passing, to live a life free of racial oppression and sexual exploitation. At the same time, however, the story registers an awareness that entry into the convent forecloses a wide range of freedoms and provides its own set of terrors. Interestingly enough, King's attitude toward Catholicism and the Creole culture of New Orleans could not have been more opposed to Cable's. Although a Protestant herself, King aligned herself with patrician Creole traditions. Like Rouquette, she reacted with outrage to Cable's depiction of Creoles in *The Grandissimes*; indeed she cast her first efforts at writing as a deliberate rebuttal to his work.[48] The fact that writers as politically different as she and Cable could depict the Catholic church—and more specifically the convent—as a benefactor to racial outcasts suggests that suspicions of a relationship between Catholicism and miscegenation, a connection with both positive and negative implications, continued to gain in cultural currency.

By the end of the nineteenth century, the association of Catholicism and miscegenation explored in *Les Cenelles* had crossed racial and religious boundaries enough to figure in the imaginative work of white southern Protestants. Alice Dunbar-Nelson's writing, however, shows that it also persisted in the work of African-Americans. Usually grouped together with the early writers of the Harlem Renaissance because of her long residence in Brooklyn, Washington, D.C., and Wilmington, Delaware, Dunbar-Nelson spent her first twenty-one years in New Orleans and used the city frequently as a setting in her early fiction. Although a non-Creole Protestant whose forebears were slaves from the small Louisiana town of Opelousas, Dunbar-Nelson was familiar with the literary and cultural traditions of the New Orleans free Creoles of color and identified with them—an identification perhaps facilitated by her own light skin and ability to pass for white on occasion.[49] Although her voluminous journalism and political activism indicate that she cannot be accused of trying to maintain racial distance from African-Americans as a whole, she does share with the *Les Cenelles* poets a consciousness of her mixed-race ancestry, of the special prominence that free people of color had achieved in New Orleans, and of the possibilities that their heritage offered for a fiction writer. She likely knew of the lives and work of Lanusse and other free Creole poets of color and had absorbed their direct influence. In "The Stones of the Village," a short story typescript that was never published during her lifetime, she presents a young Creole, neither black nor white, a French speaker in a rapidly Anglicizing rural area, whose earliest memories include being pelted with stones by all the boys, "white and black and yellow," who "hooted at him and called him 'White nigger'" not just because of his skin color, but because his attempts to speak English produced only "a confused jumble."[50] The unique position and tribulations of free Creoles of color could not be more sympathetically sketched.

Catholicism enters Dunbar-Nelson's depiction of free Creoles of color in a short story of 1899, "Sister Josepha." This story, which combines elements of both "The Orphan of the Tombs" and "The Little Convent Girl," emphasizes yet again the stark contrast between the church as protector of the outcast and as the repressive, life-denying jail. Its central figure, Camille, is a young orphan who appears "without an identity," speaking "monosyllabic French," one day at the Sacré Cœur convent.[51] For the first few years of her life, she is racially unmarked, characterized only as part of the orphanage's cultural mélange: "She grew up with the rest of the waifs; scraps of French and American civilization thrown together to develop a seemingly inconsistent miniature world" (*SJ* 157–58). Even the convent, however, cannot wholly separate her from a culture that regards Creole women of color as sexual commodities, and the onset of puberty reveals both her racial makeup and her probable destiny in the world:

> One day an awakening came. When she was fifteen, and almost fully ripened into a glorious tropical beauty of the type that matures early, some visitors to the convent were fascinated by her and asked the Mother Superior to give the girl into their keeping. . . .
>
> Camille stole a glance at her would-be guardians, and decided instantly, impulsively, finally. The woman suited her; but the man! It was doubtless intuition of the quick, vivacious sort which belonged to her blood that served her. Untutored in worldly knowledge, she could not divine the meaning of the pronounced leers and admiration of her physical charms which gleamed in the man's face, but she knew it made her feel creepy, and stoutly refused to go. (*SJ* 158–59)

Thus, without giving Camille a definite history, Dunbar-Nelson establishes her mixed-race origin through both the allusions to her "tropical beauty" and "quick, vivacious" blood and through the obvious suggestion that the white would-be guardian wishes to adopt her for his own sexual satisfaction.

Until this point, the church has served Camille well, not only providing her with food and shelter but even allowing her a kind of coquettish power: "Mademoiselle Camille was a queen among [the orphans], a pretty little tyrant who ruled the children and dominated the more timid sisters in charge" (*SJ* 158). Her refusal to go home with the couple, however, angers the Mother Superior—perhaps an indication that even long after the official demise of *plaçage* and quadroon balls, religious leaders continued to ignore and collaborate in the sexual exploitation of women of color. The Mother Superior does not, to be sure, compel Camille to leave, but her anger, coupled with Camille's horror at the prospect of adoption, drives Camille to a solution that will ensure both her protection and the Mother Superior's favor: she begs to become a nun.

Whereas *Madame Delphine* had treated the convent as an unambiguous haven for the child of miscegenation, "Sister Josepha" recalls "The Little Convent Girl" in its portrayal of the convent as both a place of both security and confinement. Dunbar-Nelson's story, however, presents a young woman whose desire is awakened even before she has the chance to contemplate what she has been missing. As Sister Josepha, Camille quickly comes to regret her decision: she loathes the stupidity of many of her fellow nuns, the pettiness of her daily chores, and above all, the repetition of her religious routine, suggested by the rosary devotions that leave her fingers numb (*SJ* 155). When she catches a glimpse of a young man in church and falls in love, she makes plans to desert, intending to "rely on the mercies of the world to help her escape from this torturing life of inertia" (*SJ* 169).

The story, however, does not end happily. Even in the midst of Sister Josepha's happy reveries about what the future holds, the narrator intrudes with disapproving, moralistic commentary: "Sister Josepha did not know that the rainbow is elusive, and its colours but the illumination of tears; she had never been told that earthly ethereality is necessarily ephemeral, nor that bonbons and glacés, whether of the palate or of the soul, nauseate and pall upon the taste" (*SJ* 164). When she overhears the conversation of the detested Sister Francesca, however, she experiences a painful epiphany: "In a flash she realised the deception of the life she would lead, and the cruel self-torture of wonder at her own identity. Already, as if in anticipation of the world's questionings, she was asking herself, 'Who am I? What am I?'" (*SJ* 171). Again there is no direct allusion to race in her train of thought, but her realization that one's identity must be known and established intimates the cruelty that awaits those who cannot define themselves. Chastened by her new knowledge, Sister Josepha confesses her sins at once. In the story's final sentence, she hurries back into the convent "with a gulping sob" (*SJ* 172) after gazing out at Chartres Street, presumably never to consider leaving again.

The young nun's unmitigated misery—only partially offset by the narrator's conventional moralizing—is far from the more mediated treatment of the same conflict in "The Little Convent Girl." While King's narrative provides only the merest hints as to the young girl's consciousness and suggests that knowledge necessarily leads to misery, Dunbar-Nelson's records Sister Josepha's thoughts in exhaustive detail and no less forcefully affirms the misery of ignorance inside the convent. This difference in emphasis and tone may be enough to cause one to question whether Dunbar-Nelson subscribes fully to the notion that whatever the church's involvements with racism and injustice, it serves as a true protector to mixed-race individuals.[52] If *Les Cenelles* marks one endpoint of the identification of mixed-race individuals with the church, "Sister Josepha" might be one of the last attempts to sustain this identification while critiquing it and might even be—depending on how closely we wish to identify Dunbar-Nelson with the *Les Cenelles* poets—the end of a discrete tradition.

❧

The demise of a distinctly Catholic *gens de couleur libres* tradition, however, did not mean that the associations generated by this identification ceased to exist. In the context of a culture governed by the "one drop" rule in all racial matters, miscegenation becomes an even graver danger in southern white imaginations because it implies the colonization and slow extermination of the white race by the black.[53] It follows, then, that the church's reputation as protector of the outcast mulatto would easily slide into a perception that the church backed African-American aspirations toward social and legal equality. Cultural manifestations of such a perception begin to appear in the South in the 1910s and 1920s—the period that saw the rise of nativism nationwide, and, as was not the case during the Know-Nothing furor seventy years before, of a widespread, venomous anti-Catholicism in the South.

Walter Benn Michaels has argued that cultural pluralism, or the belief in the value of identity as difference, is itself a product of the 1920s, a discourse of "nativist modernism" that adapted a fundamentally racial definition of identity to a newer, cultural definition.[54] "Race" came to signify not only the difference between black and white but also any difference from a putatively authentic "American" identity defined by whiteness, Anglo-Saxon ethnicity, and Protestantism. Perhaps the most disturbing manifestation of this change was the resurgence of the Ku Klux Klan, whose former preoccupation with African-Americans was now also extended to "foreigners," Jews, and Catholics as well. Particularly in the South, the new forms of racist discourse emerged alongside anti-Catholic rhetoric and were often explicitly linked. In Georgia, Tom Watson, who had achieved considerable power as a Populist politician in the 1890s, reinvigorated his political career in the 1910s by publishing in his *Jeffersonian Weekly* a series of vehemently anti-

Catholic pieces, accusing the church of wishing to undermine American sovereignty, violating women in confessionals and in convents, and promoting racial equality ("The Sinister Portent of Negro Priests" was the title of one article).[55]

The specter of "Negro priests" that Watson pointed to was more thoroughly spelled out in *The New Challenge of Home Missions*, a 1927 report by Eugene P. Alldredge, a member of the Southern Baptist Sunday School Board. The product of five years of fact-finding among Southern Baptist churches, Alldredge's book presents a progress report on the task of saving souls. Two chief obstacles lie with "the Negroes" and "the cities"—and Roman Catholicism is deeply implicated in both of them.

Alldredge's argument proceeds at first along familiar nativist lines, focusing on the essential unsuitability of foreigners for American democracy and the moral evils spawned by the urban areas in which these foreigners concentrate. Correctly observing that most Catholics in the South live in urban areas, Alldredge discerns in the tendency of Catholics to vote in ethnic or religious political blocs the designs of a pope bent on world domination. Yet Alldredge, like Watson, perceives a special danger in the appeal of Catholicism to blacks, who, as the census figures show, had been moving from rural to urban areas in great numbers:

> The great congested masses of Negroes in our big Southern cities are thrown . . . with the great congested masses of foreigners who know nothing about the Negro and many of whom know far less about American ideals and American life. . . . Roman Catholics have long since discovered this great opportunity and are doing their utmost to reach and convert the Negroes.

This appeal, Alldredge argues, comes in three forms. First, Catholics have built "schools and still more schools" for African-Americans, which can have no effect but to stir discontent. Next, Catholics often allow integrated worship in their churches, which suggests to blacks that Catholics will support full social equality. Finally, the church has made special efforts to recruit a black priesthood, opening Negro seminaries, which will draw on "the almost limitless religious (and perhaps political) possibilities which are locked up within the American Negro," appealing to their superstitious nature and seducing them with displays of pomp and power.[56] Although he does not say so directly, Alldredge's invocation of black priests, like Watson's, poses the intolerable possibility of blacks in positions of spiritual leadership over whites. It is, of course, extremely unlikely that Watson and Alldredge were familiar with the literary tropes associating Catholicism with the threat of miscegenation and even less likely that they would have known of *Les Cenelles*. Alldredge's invocation of integrated worship and the political menace of religious education, however, draws upon two elements of concern that extend as far back as the poems of Lanusse and Liotau—indeed, Lanusse's situation as the principal of a school is worth remembering.

The identification of the church with people of mixed race that finds expression in *Les Cenelles* would come to pervade southern culture so thoroughly that it would long survive the demise of mixed-race individuals as a legally distinct caste. The same qualities that Lanusse and Liotau celebrate in the church would be excoriated, eighty years later, by politicians, religious leaders, and others who saw only "black" and for whom blackness was an omnipresent threat. When William Faulkner portrayed Charles Bon in *Absalom, Absalom!,* a man of indeterminate race, a participant in *plaçage,* and a lapsed Catholic, he highlighted anew the complex set of associations that had developed between Catholicism and racial mixing in the South. Bon's transformation from Henry's devoted friend into a threat who must be destroyed—"the nigger that's going to sleep with your sister" (*AA* 358)—appears as the necessary consequence of a cultural logic that would link Catholics and African-Americans together as Others by the 1920s.

Medieval Yearnings: A Catholicism for Whites in
     Nineteenth-Century Southern Literature

Of the many attempts to explain the causes of the American Civil War, Mark Twain's assigning of the blame to Sir Walter Scott is among the wryest—second, perhaps, only to Abraham Lincoln's judgment that Harriet Beecher Stowe was responsible. According to Twain's attack on Scott in *Life on the Mississippi,* at the beginning of the nineteenth century both North and South were committed to the Enlightenment ideals of liberty, equality, and progress consecrated by the American Revolution. Scott's novels, however, would soon effect a cultural catastrophe below the Potomac and the Ohio:

> Then comes Sir Walter Scott with his enchantments, and by his single might checks this wave of progress, and even turns it back; sets the world in love with dreams and phantoms; with decayed and swinish forms of religion; with the sillinesses and emptinesses, sham grandeurs, sham gauds, and sham chivalries of a brainless and worthless long-vanished society. He did measureless harm; more real and lasting harm, perhaps, than any other individual that ever wrote. . . . But for the Sir Walter disease, the character of the Southerner . . . would be wholly modern, in place of modern and mediaeval mixed, and the South would be fully a generation further advanced than it is. It was Sir Walter that made every gentleman in the South a Major or a Colonel, or a General or a Judge, before the war; and it was he, also, that made these gentlemen value these bogus decorations. For it was he that created rank and caste down there, and also reverence for rank and caste, and pride and pleasure in them.[1]

This portrayal of Scott as a romantic reactionary has, of course, been challenged—most famously by Georg Lukács—and even critics who acknowledge Scott's influence on southern culture have often concluded that it was Scott's progressivism, not his medieval nostalgia, that appealed most to nineteenth-century southerners.[2] And yet Twain's assessment of Scott's influence is difficult to dismiss, for upper-class southern whites did indeed often legitimate their peculiar institutions by appealing to the glories of a bygone feudal age opposed to the liberal capitalism of the nineteenth-century North. While such southerners may have misread Scott and misunderstood their own relationship to capitalism (the South's plantation economy was, after all, firmly embedded within global networks of capital and trade, southern pretensions to feudalism notwithstanding), Scott's novels of medieval life, with their celebration of the local and their sympathetic por- trayal of chivalry, proved undoubtedly useful to "gentlemen" eager to jus- tify their "bogus decorations." As late as 1941, William Alexander Percy could employ a familiar cultural shorthand that associated Scott with the figure of the benevolent planter. Writing in *Lanterns on the Levee* of his father, LeRoy, the prototype of the brave but modest southern gentleman, Percy notes, "He read *Ivanhoe* once a year all his life long, and *The Talisman* almost as frequently."[3] If LeRoy's accomplishments as defender of the weak and downtrodden (for instance, his battles against the vulgar, antipaternalist, and violent Ku Klux Klan of the 1920s) are not enough to convince readers of his nobility, his favorite author should remove all doubt.

The planter as kindly lord of the manor is a familiar trope in nineteenth- century southern literature—*pastoral* and *paternalist* are the standard adjec- tives used to describe this characterization—and its relation to a proslavery ideology that would equate the plantation system with feudalism has been widely recognized.[4] Southern partisans, both in literature and politics, tended to view both slavery and the tightly controlled republican govern- ment that protected it as extensions of the patriarchal family—an institution that, having existed since the beginning of human society, appeared self- evidently preferable to newfangled arrangements based on social contract theory or notions of universal equality. As possibly the last surviving incar- nation of feudalism in the world, such thinking held, the South was also the last place where a happy and stable order prevailed.

What has been less recognized is that for many southern apologists, this "medievalist" ideology ultimately required a religious grounding.[5] The ir- ruption of "history" into medieval Christendom under the rubrics of En- lightenment, Reformation, secularization, and emerging capitalism could only be combated by the recovery or preservation of medieval principles— one of which was the totalizing and hierarchical ordering epitomized in the Great Chain of Being and underwritten by Roman Catholicism, the alleg- edly "decayed and swinish" religion of which Twain speaks. Accordingly, even as one construction of Catholicism in the South, associated primarily with New Orleans and its distinct racial and ethnic milieu, became linked to fear of miscegenation and the collapse of social order, a competing construction began to reconfigure the church as a quintessentially southern institution. In this view, not only does the church underwrite a feudal economy and therefore justify slavery, its structure, with the pope as supreme patriarch and individual priests as local shepherds, provides a useful social model for antidemocratic thinkers.

The emergence of this medievalist model of Catholicism in the South must be viewed in connection with the great migrations from Ireland and Germany to the United States in the 1840s and 1850s. As Chapter One argues, the South was largely free of the xenophobia, anti-Catholicism, and violence that often greeted immigrants to the North during this period. Even so, this large population constituted an unforeseen variable in national politics, and given the increasingly precarious nature of political compromises between North and South, the immigrants' growing political clout became a source of concern for white southerners as well. What would the immigrants' stance toward slavery be? Would their religion lead them to oppose slavery and to join the often religiously inspired abolitionist movement? In the decades before the Civil War, white southern ideologues gradually excluded any middle ground: one had to be for or against the slaveholding order. The historically dubious notion that Catholicism may be the most authentic southern religion originates in the efforts of white southern Catholics confronted with such anxieties to reassure their fellow southerners of their regional loyalties. It would, however, develop into a comprehensive conservative ideology that would be taken up with equal enthusiasm by non-Catholic southerners eager to justify inequality through a more formidable authority—and would not reach its zenith until the mid-twentieth century.

As this particular construction of a medieval and southern Catholicism took shape, it also became intertwined with representations of the southern hero. Unlike the typical Romantic hero, with his alienation from society and his all-encompassing egoism, the antebellum southern hero emerges from, embodies, and legitimates a medievalist social order, acting always with bravery, kindness, and understatement. Like the prosaic heroes of Scott, who (pace Lukács) compel admiration through their ordinariness and even their lovable eccentricity, southern heroes derive their authority not from the depths of their personality but from what Michael Kreyling calls "an inherent and instantaneously acknowledged capacity to render the provisional nature of any situation or condition into part of a consecrated pattern"—the ability to bestow a transcendent meaning upon the contingencies of history and thus consecrate an enduring, ahistorical southern identity.[6] The purported transcendence that heroic figures guarantee validates the hierarchical, antidemocratic social structure defended by the Old Southern planter elite and their like-minded descendants. Implicitly or explicitly, southern heroes demonstrate that even when this structure is threatened by the forces of bourgeois liberalism—what Twain would simply call "progress"—it proves itself morally superior, if not always triumphant. In Kreyling's words, "Inherent in heroic narrative is the conflict between [heroic and democratic] paradigms—either the heroic prevails (the outcome of most antebellum narratives) or it falls before a modern order universally acknowledged to be powerful but morally and culturally bankrupt (the frequent pattern after Reconstruction)."[7] Appropriately enough, many heroic figures prove their heroism in political or military combat, for conduct on a battlefield, in both victory and defeat, provides the most effective means to distinguish true heroes from impostors and the transcendent order from the fallen. Robert E. Lee, whose representation among postbellum southerners combined dashing military genius, kind and benevolent master, and world-weary but dignified relic of a purer, bygone order, is perhaps the most obvious example. And yet even Lee, whose status in the postbellum South approached that of a saint, lacked the Catholicism that would have made him even more coherent and representative as a champion of a putatively feudal order.

This medievalist ideology begins to appear in the 1840s, in part as a reaction to the xenophobic suspicions aroused by Daniel O'Connell's antislavery and pro-Irish politics, but it only becomes a fully formed ideology in the work of such southern intellectuals as George Fitzhugh and George Frederick Holmes. It would achieve literary expression and become linked to the figure of the hero in the postbellum work of the enormously popular Abram Ryan, the "poet-priest of the Confederacy." Indeed, well into the twentieth century, associations between Catholicism and a medievalist, Old Southern order would persist, despite the sustained but often inconsistent critique of this ideology in the work of Mark Twain. In *The Innocents Abroad, A Connecticut Yankee in King Arthur's Court,* and *Personal Recollections of Joan of Arc,* Twain scrutinizes this nexus of medievalism, heroism, and Catholicism, suggesting that one of its logical consequences is a preoccupation with death and decadence. Yet at the same time—particularly in *Joan of Arc*—he displays his own attraction to a southern and Catholic heroism and perhaps unwittingly participates in the continuation of this ideology into the twentieth century.

In the early 1840s Daniel O'Connell, the leading spokesman for Irish independence, created controversy within his organization, the Repeal Association, by denouncing slavery. Though the association accepted financial support from American sympathizers and operated branches in many American cities, O'Connell condemned those donors who were slaveholders or publicly friendly to slavery, blasted the hypocrisy of American racial attitudes, and urged support for the abolitionist movement. When justifying his views, O'Connell rested his case not just upon the Enlightenment notions of universal equality but also on appeals to Catholic teaching. In a letter of 14 October 1843 to the Cincinnati chapter of the Repeal Association, O'Connell asserted that "every Catholic knows how distinctly slave holding, and especially slave trading, is condemned by the Church."[8] This characterization of the church's position on slavery at the time, although not entirely accurate, was plausible enough—if one read the right documents and put the most liberal construction on them—to frighten southern slaveholders. The obvious identification of some persons of color with the church was already beginning to raise suspicions that Catholicism might promote miscegenation. When Catholicism was further linked with foreign immigration from Europe and the unambiguous abolitionism of O'Connell, the sense of threat became more palpable.

O'Connell's injunctions fell largely on deaf ears in the United States. Irish-Americans, hated and feared by many Anglo-Protestants, faced with an abolitionist movement that was often vehemently anti-Catholic, and disturbed by the prospect of competing with free blacks in the labor market, tended, as Noel Ignatiev has shown, to prove their national loyalty by opposing African-American aspirations (indeed, some American chapters of the Repeal Association disbanded rather than endorse O'Connell's position).[9] The need to reject an abolitionist politics would have been most acute for Irish and Catholics in the South, particularly because evidence that Catholicism was beginning to figure as a southern political issue appears in the wake of O'Connell's public statements. In an address at Fredericksburg, Virginia, on 29 August 1840, John Forsyth, who served as governor of Georgia and as U.S. secretary of state under Jackson and Van Buren, condemns the "World's [Anti-Slavery] convention" that had recently met in London for its attacks on American slavery. Decrying the convention's "compound of ignorance, folly, and insolence" in which "[t]he brutal O'Connell was quite at home," Forsyth went on to suggest that the British government was acting as "selected agent of the Pope" by distributing an apostolic letter against slavery to a number of Latin American nations.[10] The utter implausibility of Forsyth's charge both reflects and contributes to the siege mentality that white southern political leaders increasingly invoked: the hint that Britain might be acting as an abolitionist Vatican puppet not only sounds uncannily like the contemporary conspiracy theories associated with far-right groups in the United States but also demonstrates the increasing unwillingness of white southern leaders to tolerate dissent from proslavery positions.

While it is unclear how widely disseminated Forsyth's address was, its potential for furthering anti-Catholic sentiment was undeniable, and John England, the Catholic bishop of Charleston, South Carolina, responded to Forsyth's allegations in a series of letters that were published in 1844 along with the full text and translation of the apostolic letter to which Forsyth had alluded, Pope Gregory XVI's "De Nigritarum Commercio Non Exercendo" (literally, "Concerning the Not Carrying on the Trade in Negroes"), which was issued in 1839. Faced with charges that their allegiance to the pope made them potential traitors, southern Catholic leaders hastened to reaffirm their regional loyalties. England, who had already aroused the ire of white Charlestonians by briefly operating a school for free blacks—and who, moreover, was a friend of O'Connell's—would thus need to proclaim his fidelity particularly loudly.[11]

England begins by suggesting that Gregory XVI's letter has been willfully misinterpreted. According to the letter, the papacy has spoken out against the African slave trade ever since Europeans began to engage in it. The first traders who "reduced to slavery Indians, Negroes, or other miserable persons" (*LLB* x) were rebuked by the Vatican in a number of official documents, but these warnings were not heeded. Positioning itself as a definitive statement, the letter condemns the slave trade as un-Christian and forbids "that any ecclesiastic or lay person shall presume to defend that very trade in negroes [sic] as lawful under any pretext or studied excuse" (*LLB* xi). As England points out, contrary to what Forsyth suggested, the letter prohibits only the "reducing" of free people into slavery and the importation of slaves from Africa—acts already prohibited by the U.S. Constitution since 1808— and has nothing to say about domestic slavery or the sale and transport of slaves within the United States. Thus the claim that American slavery in toto contradicts church teaching cannot be substantiated, and England states that he has personally "reproved Mr. O'Connell's assaults upon our planters, more than eleven years ago: and [his] judgment and feeling are now what they were then" (*LLB* 14).

Having established this principle, England undertakes a meticulous (not to say mind-numbingly repetitive) examination of the history of church teaching on slavery, citing scripture, Aquinas, and the whole succession of papal statements on the subject from Clement I forward. No matter what the context of the quotations he chooses, England interprets them all as evidence that slavery is not intrinsically incompatible with Christian practice. Yet despite his mighty efforts to reassure, England's citations cannot put the fears that Forsyth had invoked completely to rest. Forsyth refused to admit the humanity of slaves at all, referring only to the outrageous claims of those who would presume to restrict what one could do with one's personal "property" (*LLB*13). This dehumanizing rhetoric, with its clear implication that masters have absolute power over slaves, conflicts with the assertions sprinkled throughout England's examples that slaves possess human dignity, the capability for spiritual, moral, and intellectual advancement, and certain rights that masters cannot abrogate. Indeed Gregory XVI's letter maintains that slavery no longer exists in Europe precisely because "in the course of time, the darkness of pagan superstitions [have been] more fully dissipated, and the morals also of the ruder nations [have been] softened by means of faith working by charity" (*LLB* x). Christian conversion itself, then, erodes the master's absolute power and facilitates the desired "softening" of morals, and both church and state should construct laws to reflect this. For instance, England argues that in the centuries after Christianity became the Roman state religion, Jews were prohibited from holding Christian slaves, under penalty of death, and that slaves who wished to become Christian had to be sold to Christian masters or emancipated (*LLB* 77–95). While these examples do not reject a Christian slavery outright, they do reject the claims of the "polygenist" scientific racism that was beginning to hold sway in the United States and suggest the eventual abolition of slavery is a worthwhile goal.[12] The unspoken implication is clear: those masters who see evidence of religion and morality in their slaves would do well to free them.

As if this were not enough, England also upholds the sanctity of slave marriage. Calling "the liability to separation of those [slaves] married" a "galling affliction in the Christian law, where the Saviour made marriage indissoluble" (*LLB* 99), England condemns the "avaricious or capricious owner [who] cared as little for the marriage bond as he did for the natural tie of affection" (*LLB* 100), selling husbands, wives, and children away from each other. The prohibition of slave marriage could conceivably do away with this problem, but England rejects this as a solution, stating that God ordained marriage for the vast majority of humanity and that forbidding it would only induce "a strong temptation to both master and slave to prefer concubinage to wedlock" (*LLB* 100). To reconcile the competing claims of marriage and obedience to one's master, England harkens back to a policy of the Emperor Justinian: masters may not separate slaves who are already married, but slaves should only be allowed to marry from those on the same "estate." England breezily concludes that while the marriage right is "inalienable, it is like every other to be regulated by restraints, which without the destruction or the serious injury of the right itself, may be found necessary for the good of the community" (*LLB* 105).

Even this qualification, however, has the effect of empowering slaves: the very decision to marry revokes a portion of the master's authority. Many literary and historical testimonies suggest that southern slaveholders often prided themselves on their kindness to their slaves, regarded the forced breakup of slave families as an atrocity, and ostracized members of the community who effected such separations. At the same time, they insisted on the master's right to break up slave marriages. If these marriages have no validity, then a master who can destroy a family yet chooses not to do so enhances his moral standing, but if slave marriages are indissoluble, then they preclude both the exercise and the restraint of the master's will. Moreover, as England's allusion to the temptation of "concubinage" suggests, one consequence of the failure to recognize slave marriage was the sexual exploitation of women slaves and the emergence of a mixed-race slave population. By insisting on the sacredness of slave marriages, England distances the church from the charge that it abets racial amalgamation, while at the same time whittling away at the unacknowledged sexual privileges of masters.

England's letters, then, attempt to steer a course between the demands of Gregory XVI and the need to affirm loyalty to the South. As a characterization of the church's position on slavery, England's case is accurate: one cannot assert the absolute power of masters over their slaves without departing from the accumulation of church teaching. Wittingly or unwittingly, his argument leaves education and marriage as two loopholes through which slaves can wrest a measure of autonomy from their masters. Not surprisingly, the laws in southern states sought to close these loopholes, prohibiting slaves from learning to read and stripping slave marriages of legal validity. If Catholicism were to serve as a more reliable ally to southern planter aspirations, it would require a more thorough and unambiguous justification of slavery than England's. That defense would come in the 1850s in the work of George Fitzhugh and George Frederick Holmes—gentleman intellectuals who, although not Catholic themselves, conceived of a Catholic-inflected redefinition of the South as a more solid ideological basis for its institutions.

❧

Fitzhugh's two most well-known works, *Sociology for the South* (1854) and *Cannibals All!* (1857), attack capitalism and liberalism unrelentingly. Both books categorize free trade, freedom of speech, and universal equality as pernicious modern doctrines, unheard of until John Locke and destined to lead to copious bloodshed. Fitzhugh recommends instead the model of his native Virginia—a society of frank inequality, where the enslavement of blacks ensures their happiness, where all whites possess the rudimentary dignity of freedom, but where only a few whites are judged worthy enough to govern and wield real power.

This rejection of what he calls "free society" does not spring primarily from a belief in the scientific racism of the nineteenth century, for though Fitzhugh believed in the cultural inferiority of blacks, he was a monogenist (that is, he accepted that all human races belonged to the same species) and abhorred what he calls the "doctrine of the 'Types of Mankind.' "[13] Instead Fitzhugh's justification of slavery rests on the conviction that societies are simply patriarchal families writ large. Taking as his model the work of Sir Robert Filmer, Locke's antagonist in the *First Treatise on Government*, Fitzhugh grounds his defense of slavery on the presumption that "fathers do not derive their authority, as heads of families, from the consent of wife and children, nor do they govern their families by their consent."[14] In the same way, government grounds its authority in force and the threat of force, not in the consent of citizens. Filmer, who had derived this principle from God's injunctions to Adam in Genesis, considers patriarchal authority so absolute that even a father's murder of his family cannot be punished. For Fitzhugh, however, the mere threat of violence should suffice: "The negro sees the driver's lash, becomes accustomed to obedient cheerful industry, and is not aware that the lash is the force that impels him" (*CA* 248–49). Indeed, even though he modifies Filmer's position, arguing, for example, that laws protecting slaves from the cruel treatment of masters might be desirable, Fitzhugh preserves the master's power by holding that such restrictions should arise from the masters' own self-interested decision, not from the recognition of the slave's rights.

Such a formulation steps neatly around the curtailments of the master's will that England had conceded while at the same time suggesting that kindness and love toward slaves are the norm rather than the exception. Given the power of life and death over his slaves, the slaveholder who refrains from using it and persuades his entire community to do likewise distinguishes himself as a loving father. In this way Fitzhugh goes far beyond England's defense: he characterizes slavery as "a positive good, not a necessary evil" (*CA* 7) and contrasts the putatively familial relationship between master and slave against the naked exploitation suffered by free laborers of the North within industrial capitalism. More pointedly he argues that in precapitalist Europe, when Catholicism had underwritten the social order, the masses had been protected from such exploitation: "In the palmy days of royalty, of feudal nobility, and of Catholic rule, there were no poor in Europe."[15] The conclusion is obvious: capitalism, Protestantism, and liberal political theory have reinforced each other for centuries, and the results have been disastrous. Indeed all intellectual work dating from after the turn toward modernity is suspect: Fitzhugh asserts that "all books written four hundred or more years ago, are apt to yield useful instruction, whilst those written since that time will generally mislead" (*CA* 53). As Eugene Genovese tartly observes, "Thus did he consign the classic works of Protestantism—always leaving room for exceptions—to the rubbish heap."[16]

Fitzhugh does recognize that in the wake of the American, Haitian, and French Revolutions, his position no longer commands universal assent. What holds such a manifestly unequal society as antebellum Virginia together when alternative social models exist for comparison? Here Fitzhugh identifies religion as the essential glue: "Society can linger on for centuries without slavery; it cannot exist a day without religion."[17] His position, at once utilitarian and elitist, reveres religion not for the truth of its doctrines but for the social harmony that it enforces and underwrites. Like T. S. Eliot, who would endorse a similar program in *The Idea of a Christian Society,* Fitzhugh recommends unquestioning belief for the masses while allowing those in power to entertain private doubts about religion as long as they do not undermine it publicly. Freedom of religion, in short, would be an oxymoron, for only an official religion could guarantee social stability: "Popes and cardinals are not infallible, but society is. Its harmony is its health; and to differ with it is heresy or treason, because social discord inflicts individual misery; and what disturbs and disarranges society, impairs the happiness and well-being of its members." Hence, no freedom of religion, no "Infidels, Skeptics, Millerites, Mormons, Agrarians, Spiritual Rappers, Wakemanites,

Free Negroes" (*CA* 131), or other agitators. As shown by the very proliferation of sects that freedom of religion makes possible, freedom weakens allegiance to totalizing systems of belief, encourages a perception that religion is largely a matter of personal desire, and thus tends inevitably toward the abolition of religion, which in turn leads to the violence and anarchy that Fitzhugh associates with the French Revolution. Accordingly Fitzhugh takes heart in signs that "we are gradually dismissing our political prejudice against religion," for only a reestablishment of official religion can slow the national slide into chaos.[18]

Yet though the logical result of Fitzhugh's thinking would be to endorse Catholicism wholeheartedly, Fitzhugh does not quite go so far. In a chapter of *Cannibals All!* entitled "The Reformation—The Right of Private Judgment," he writes: "The Reformation, like the American Revolution, was originated and conducted to successful issue by wise, good, and practical men, whose intuitive judgments and sagacious instincts enabled them to feel their way through the difficulties that environed them" (*CA* 130). This attempt to paint Protestantism not as a radical break from what preceded it but as a gradualist attempt at reform, however, is disingenuous. For all Fitzhugh's attempt to depict Luther and Calvin as moderate reformers, they were in revolt against the established religious orders of their days—and therefore, from a consistently conservative standpoint, deplorable. Fitzhugh does not convincingly explain how to distinguish between Luther's reformist theses on the church door at Wittenberg and the radical doctrines of the Mormons. In fact when he criticizes the Reformation, he carefully attacks not its doctrines but what he sees as its pernicious but unintended consequence, "the right of private judgment, which speculative philosophers and vain schismatics attempted to engraft upon it, or deduce from it" (*CA* 132). Yet this right, the fountainhead of the liberal society that Fitzhugh castigates, is no mere by-product of the Reformation: the crucial abolition of priests between God and human beings that Luther advocated compels human beings to exercise their "right of private judgment" in the interpretation of scripture—and encourages the extension of this right into other spheres of life. Since Fitzhugh is uninterested in the truth or falsity of religion, logical consistency would require him to decry the Reformation precisely because its social consequences—sectarian wars throughout Europe—have been so bloody and far-reaching. Yet at the same time, his fidelity to tradition would require him to affirm the beliefs and traditions of his own society, which in antebellum Virginia were Protestant when not merely deist.

Why then does Fitzhugh not follow his thinking to its logical conclusion and recommend Catholicism—which, because of its antiquity, hierarchical structure, and claims to absolute authority, is Western Europe's "traditional" religion par excellence? His hesitation seems to have had much to do with his conception of himself as what we might today call an "organic" intellectual in Antonio Gramsci's sense—a thinker who has a duty not just to defend but to embody, insofar as possible, the existing practices and beliefs of his society. But this sense of his public role produced a tension within his work regarding religion, as Genovese recognizes:

> That the South was Protestant rather than Roman Catholic proved to be unfortunate, as Fitzhugh appreciated in his day and perhaps only Allen Tate has appreciated in ours. . . . Fitzhugh did not hide his admiration for Catholicism, nor did many other antebellum Southern intellectuals . . . but he could hardly join the Church. Whatever his private thoughts, as a man intent on leading his section to high ideological and political ground, he could not afford to offend its traditional religious sensibilities. Fitzhugh, an admirer and upholder of tradition, had to embrace a traditional Protestantism when he knew very well that the South needed the very Romanism it so instinctively hated.[19]

Fitzhugh thus stands at the beginning of a tradition within southern writing that would recognize Catholicism as congenial to a conservative ideology but would hesitate to adopt it out of respect for the institutional structures already in place.

Alongside Fitzhugh, the most important southern intellectual to recognize the value of Catholicism to a traditional society was George Frederick Holmes, classical scholar and largely unsuccessful planter. Though Holmes began his career with much dabbling in "infidelity" and even went through a period of enthusiasm for August Comte, he is known today primarily as a staunch defender of the southern slave system and an apologist for Christian orthodoxy. Unlike Fitzhugh, Holmes was in his earlier work an overt critic of Catholicism, and yet even his most stinging rebukes often contained much praise. In "Rome and the Romans," an 1844 essay, for instance, he called the papacy "the most strict and permanent system of ecclesiastical tyranny, that ever cursed any portion of the human race," but he also argued that to the papacy "we owe the revivification of the world," because, among other reasons, "the Catholic church preserved for us Christianity; she cherished the early growth of our modern organization; she was the law to Europe, when Europe would have bent to no other law."[20]

By 1853, however, Holmes had become attracted to Catholicism, both for its glorification of the medieval order (which he seems to have imbibed through French Catholic writers such as Chateaubriand, Joseph de Maistre, and Frederic Ozanam) and for the profundity of Aquinas's *Summa Theologica*.[21] And by 1862, in the midst of the Civil War, Holmes would confess in his unpublished writings that he had "long suspected" that Protestantism stood "absolutely condemned by the decree of Heaven written in the course of history; and Catholicism . . . absolutely sanctioned." Indeed, in the same entry, he would speculate that the intellectual turmoil of the nineteenth century, of which the Civil War was merely one expression, sprang inevitably from "the rejection of spiritual authority" and the "cannonization" [*sic*] of intellect.[22] In other words, his reservations about Protestantism were the same as Fitzhugh's—by enshrining the right of private judgment as an absolute principle, Protestantism had fatally undermined any attempt in the present to preserve or resuscitate a stable social order. And yet, like Fitzhugh, Holmes never converted to Catholicism, despite an obvious affective yearning toward it that owes as much to the Catholic faith of his wife, sister-in-law, and favorite daughter as to Aquinas's rigor.[23]

It would be misleading to regard Fitzhugh and Holmes's positions as simply "medieval," for only their beliefs in the absolute authority of masters, the desirability of Catholic faith, and the superiority of earlier historical epochs mark them as such. Fitzhugh's utterly unromantic belief in the primacy of force—even when mitigated by assertions of familial love between master and dependents—proves jarring to a sensibility raised on Scott's novels and accustomed to view violence through the aestheticized lenses of honor and chivalry. Moreover, unlike some of his successors, Fitzhugh rejected the assumption that industrial development per se was an evil; the problem lay instead in the capitalist system of allegedly free labor within which this development takes place. His contention that "the wit of man can devise no means so effectual to impoverish a country as exclusive agriculture," combined with his praise of the North's standard of living, hardly seems assimilable to the pro-Agrarian stand that a subsequent generation of white southern partisans would take.[24] Even so, by connecting a justification of slavery to the necessity for an absolute religious authority, Fitzhugh and Holmes played a considerable role in the construction of a medievalized, heroic, and southern Catholicism that Twain would ridicule—and around which Allen Tate, Fitzhugh's twentieth-century descendant, would construct a political, critical, and aesthetic practice.

If Walter Scott's novels provided one starting point for the attempt to imagine a conservative southern Catholicism, a still more visceral expression of that desire can be found in the work and mythologization of Abram Ryan, a priest and poet who served briefly as a Confederate chaplain during the war. His jangly verses, notable for their stereotypically romantic *Sehnsucht*, their conventional religious devotions, and their maudlin commemoration of the Confederacy, became popular among white southerners in the last years of Reconstruction and remained so for decades. According to Hannis Taylor's effusive biographical note in *The Library of Southern Literature*, "The lost cause became incarnate in the heart of Father Ryan, who cherished it as his forefathers had cherished the cause of Ireland."[25] "The Conquered Banner," Ryan's signature poem, was set to music and widely recited in southern schools in the manner of Longfellow, while Ryan himself was honored throughout the South in official proclamations and public monuments.[26]

This popularity derives as much from Ryan's biography as from his poems, for he embodied a new figure of the southern hero that combines military heroism, southern partisanship, Catholic mysticism, and romantic, world-weary frailty. A certain amount of conscious self-fashioning was undoubtedly involved: for example, Ryan's use of the name Abram, rather than his baptismal name Abraham, allegedly sprang from a desire not to be confused with "Father Abraham" Lincoln in the public mind.[27] Many of his legend's specific lineaments, however, emerge in the embellishments of his admirers. Taylor's physical description of Ryan summarizes the legend's outlines:

> No man ever looked more like a poet than Father Ryan. A weak, delicate body was crowned with a great leonine head, from which soft brown hair floated down over stooping shoulders. His face was always sad. "In his eyes was the twilight of grief, but in that grief the starlight of a smile." He moved along like an old man of seventy, when he was but little over forty, attracting attention from every passer-by. No personality was ever more marked. There was a magnetism about him that cast a spell upon all who came near him. While he was careless in his dress, almost to the point of slovenliness, his dignity and reserve were impenetrable to all save a few very near to his heart. Over and above all else he showed a contempt for danger, a courage that nothing could daunt. . . . No more heroic or romantic warrior ever fought under the standard of Christ.[28]

This account, which suggests an odd mixture of Faulkner's Jason Compson Sr. and Stonewall Jackson, sketches an obvious model for a southern heroism reeling from its defeat in war. Although the description insists upon Ryan's valor, his courage is noteworthy not just for its heroism on the battlefield but for its expression in a frail, prematurely old body stamped with sadness and a sense of beautiful failure. Ryan becomes an embodiment of the ravaged, mourning South, "slovenly" in its poverty, psychologically "impenetrable" to outsiders, defeated yet unbowed, and given to a longing for past glories that borders on mystic melancholia and anticipates some of the pro-Catholic nostalgia of decadent writers of the late nineteenth century. Ryan's "magnetism," obvious to every bystander, shines through his unimpressive physique, as does his essentially poetic nature. Like the southern heroes that Kreyling catalogs, Ryan's heroism is "self-evident . . . not subject to appeal."[29]

Ryan's peripatetic movements, around which numerous apocryphal stories have accrued, also contribute to his legend. Born in Hagerstown, Maryland, Ryan apparently gave different accounts of his birth to his biographers, so that some early sources list him as a native of Ireland, while others give his birthplace as Norfolk, Virginia. After a childhood spent largely in St. Louis, Ryan was ordained a Vincentian father in 1860, although he would break with this order within two years. For a short time during the war, he served as a parish priest in Peoria, Illinois, leaving to become a Confederate chaplain and then to hold brief stints as parish priest at Edgefield (now part of Nashville) and Knoxville, Tennessee. One widely circulated (and probably false) account also places him in New Orleans, where he reputedly confronted General Butler, the Federal commander of the occupied city, with defiant words.[30] After the war he settled first in Augusta, where he became founding editor of the "unreconstructed" *Banner of the South,* and next in Mobile, where he would live until his semiretirement in 1881. Thereafter he lived for a time in Biloxi and died in a Franciscan monastery in Louisville, Kentucky, in 1886. These wanderings would cement his regional reputation: his refusal to identify with any one location and his differing accounts of his birthplace suggest a desire to fashion himself as a champion of the whole South. Even his brief tenure in the North during the Civil War would redound to his legendary glory. Despite some evidence that he served as a spy for the Confederate government, accounts of Ryan's ministry in Peoria stress his gracious service to his northern parishioners, as do stories of his wartime service that show him ministering to Yankee as well as Confederate wounded—a kind of Confederate counterpart to the "wound dresser" persona fashioned by Walt Whitman during the same period.[31] Such accounts paint Ryan as a paragon of southern virtue who does not shrink from honorable combat when necessary but remembers his pastoral duties and does not seek to harm those who have not attacked him.

Ryan seems to have been something of a renegade priest. Evidence suggests that his break with the Vincentians occurred because he never hid his pro-Southern convictions despite the order's policy of strict neutrality in the Civil War—hardly, it would seem, a wise policy for a priest in Peoria. Indeed his military chaplaincy was never officially sanctioned by the church, and his postwar departure from Augusta was probably precipitated by a quarrel with Bishop Verot of Savannah over the claim of papal infallibility that the First Vatican Council would soon make official dogma: Ryan spoke out in its favor, while Verot opposed it.[32] For all his opposition to his immediate superiors, then, Ryan upheld the patriarchal model that gave the pope absolute authority—a familial principle that former slaveholders, recently deprived of their extended "families" by the Thirteenth Amendment, would have embraced. Such stances figured not just as evidence of firm convictions but as proof that southern and Catholic loyalties were fully compatible.

The strong identification with Ireland running through Ryan's life and work adds a new twist to the discourse of a feudal, Europeanized South. Against accounts of Irish immigrants as semihuman creatures, both brutalized by their work in dark satanic mills and brutal to others, Ryan's treatment of Irishness, imbued with a strong dose of romanticism and love of the land, anticipates such later fictive Irish southerners as Margaret Mitchell's Gerald O'Hara, who voices equal hatred for the British and the North. For Ryan, Ireland is distinguished not just by its famously devout Catholic population but also by its agrarian, pre-industrial condition. Left to their own devices, he implies, the Irish would have continued in patriarchal bliss, close to nature and God alike. The English invaders, however, brought a toxic modernity with them, stripping clans of their land, persecuting the one true church, and unleashing the curses of industrial development and laissez-faire trade that would culminate in the Potato Famine. Ryan's paean to the cause of Irish independence, "Erin's Flag," urges unbending defiance toward the British:

> Take it up! Take it up! from the tyrant's foul tread,
> Let him tear the Green Flag—we will snatch its last shred,
> And beneath it we'll bleed as our forefathers bled,
> And we'll vow by the dust in the graves of our dead,
> And we'll swear by the blood which the Briton has shred [*sic*],

And we'll vow by the wrecks which through Erin he spread,
And we'll swear by the thousands who, famished, unfed,
Died down in the ditches, wild-howling for bread,
And we'll vow by our heroes, whose spirits have fled,
And we'll swear by the bones in each coffinless bed,
That we'll battle the Briton through danger and dread;
That we'll cling to the cause which we glory to wed,
'Till the gleam of our steel and the shock of our lead
Shall prove to our foe that we meant what we said—
That we'll lift up the green, and we'll tear down the red![33]

I have no wish to argue for the aesthetic worth of Ryan's poetry; lines such as these, entirely representative of his work, seem self-evidently awful. As a cultural document, however, "Erin's Flag" displays obvious parallels to the narrative that many white southerners were fabricating to describe their wartime situation. The marauding Yankees "tear the Green Flag" of the South by attacking its agrarian economy and peculiar institution, putting up a "red" flag in its place that could signify both the bloodshed that capitalism unleashes and the specter of socialism, which many southern intellectuals considered the inevitable point toward which liberal capitalist society was tending.[34] Southerners defend themselves by rallying around family ties, attachment to the soil, and honor: the "forefathers" who have become "dust in the graves" and "bones in coffinless bed[s]" underscore the literal inseparability of patriarchal rule and agrarian society. Dispossessed of slaves, livelihood, and crops by the invaders, southerners can invoke the suffering of the Irish Famine as a precursor to their own. Their determination to continue fighting, however, feeds not just on a claim for justice but a desire to vindicate honor: the need "to prove to our foe that we meant what we said" evinces a touchiness not solely motivated by retribution. The casting of the Irish cause as just no matter how the tide of battle turns is evident: the flag boasts "Not a stain on its green, not a blot on its gold" despite the indignities it has suffered, and God's justice will not allow such an unstained emblem to "droop thus forever" (*SP* 5). While the poem ends with a prediction of triumph, its invocation of God's justice cannot erase its catalog of bloodshed. Southerners attempting to claim divine favor in the war effort would have faced a similar quandary. What if the ravages of war are God's punishment for southern sins? To forestall this question, constant, unvarying assertions of justice and determination are needed: hence the poem's insistent anapestic meter, repetition of key words, and monotonous rhyme scheme.

"Erin's Flag," however, offers a rare instance of unmixed optimism in Ryan's work. More characteristically, his poems balance a celebration of southern heroism with its inevitable tragedy. "The Sword of Robert E. Lee," for example, passes through five relentlessly phallic stanzas (each begins with "Forth from its scabbard" or "Out of its scabbard") that sing the triumphs and unimpeachable character of Lee before ending on an elegiac note that puts to rest both the patriarch and his phallus. "In Memoriam: David J. Ryan, C.S.A.," Ryan's most obvious juxtaposition of Catholic themes and imagery with the southern cause, also blends heroism and tragedy, rendering Ryan's slain brother as a sacrificial lamb in lines with the same meter as the *Stabat Mater,* the traditional Catholic hymn that commemorates Mary's vigil at Calvary. Here, though the sacrifice might have some redemptive value, there is no resurrection to follow: the poem ends, like "The Sword of Robert E. Lee," with the heroic figure in eternal sleep. In this, both poems correspond to the usual pattern of postwar southern heroic representation: even in death and defeat, the purity and justice of the hero's cause cannot be gainsaid.

Proclaiming no resurgence of southern independence, many of Ryan's poems suggest that withdrawal from the corrupt world is the best response to disappointment. "The Conquered Banner" makes the point most forcefully, ending on a note of hopelessness for the Confederate partisan: "Touch [the banner] not—unfold it never, / Let it droop there, furled forever, / For its people's hopes are dead!" (*SP* 18). In disavowing further pursuit of southern independence, the poems also embrace suffering and flee into melancholic pleasures. Even such pedestrian passages as this conclusion to "A Thought" take on a larger resonance if they are read as allusions to the South's defeat:

> Life is a burden; bear it;
> Life is a duty; dare it;
> Life is a thorn-crown; wear it,
> > Though it break your heart in twain;
> > > Though the burden crush you down;
> > Close your lips, and hide your pain,
> > > First the cross, and then, the crown.
> > > > (*SP* 83)

While Protestant figures in the postbellum South often interpreted the southern defeat as divine judgment for a great southern sin (Faulkner's obsessive treatment of this position, particularly in *Go Down, Moses,* is well known), Ryan sees this suffering as a sign of merit. Here specifically Catholic attitudes of meditation on suffering and ritualized celebration of martyrdom prove themselves amenable to the religion of the Lost Cause. The very mediation of Catholic faith, then, with its fondness for ritual and monument, promotes displays of southern patriotism closed to less iconographically minded denominations, even as, in its celebration of death, it again suggests an undercurrent of decadence in southern memorial.

As the most partisan and one-dimensional of southern Catholic writers, Ryan became a useful weapon to brandish against the charges—which would become increasingly strident in the first decades of the twentieth century—that Catholics were enemies of the southern way of life, promoters of miscegenation and cultural anarchy. A single incident illustrates Ryan's political significance most clearly. When the Diocese of Nashville began plans to build a high school for boys in the 1920s—at the height of Ku Klux Klan anti-Catholic activity—one priest suggested that the school be named for Ryan, immediately defusing political tensions and preventing a Klan riot.[35] Ryan would be joined in the pantheon of southern poet-priest heroes by John Bannister Tabb (1845–1909), a Virginia convert to Catholicism who had the additional distinction of being a prisoner of war. Tabb's star would never rise as high as Ryan's, in part because his now forgotten poetry has little to say about the South and in part because he lacked Ryan's knack for drama and self-fashioning. The recognition of two certified hero priests, however, would provide a rallying point for popular associations of Catholicism and the South well into the twentieth century.

❧

Aristocratic pretensions, Confederate nostalgia, assertions of absolute authority, veneration of priests—all were equally abhorrent to Mark Twain, whose own work offers the most sustained critique of them among nineteenth-century southern writers. Yet while Twain would have been unmoved by the canonization of Father Ryan (it is easy to imagine Twain lampooning Ryan, perhaps as a masculine version of Emmeline Grangerford), he did celebrate his own brand of heroism that both problematizes and betrays a longing for the kind of transcendent, ahistorical authority associated with white southern heroism. Admittedly, the familiar story of Twain's career traces a path of disillusionment that begins with the arrogant American optimism of *The Innocents Abroad*, progresses through the critiques of American society in such novels as *The Gilded Age* and *Adventures of Huckleberry Finn*, and culminates in the cynicism and misanthropy of *No. 44, The*

Mysterious Stranger—with pointed deflations of southern idées fixes along the way. The man who castigated the horrors of war and idealized a boy who perceives happiness only in flight into the territory can certainly not be accused of supporting the tenets of white southern heroism in any simple or obvious way. Running alongside Twain's critique, however, is a continued hope for exemplary heroic figures, who sanctify particular truths even when they do not conquer. If in such works as *The Innocents Abroad* and *A Connecticut Yankee in King Arthur's Court* Twain pours scorn both on southern heroism and its medievalist and implicitly Catholic underpinnings, in *Personal Recollections of Joan of Arc*, Twain presents, in the figure of Joan, a heroine who affirms Catholicism, medievalism, and political conservatism even as her anachronistic belief in rights and her status as a woman subvert these notions and make Twain's critique all but incoherent.

This argument presumes that Mark Twain can be read as a southern writer—a position that can provoke controversy because of Twain's centrality to the American canon. Barbara Ladd's reminder of Twain's historical positioning is salutary: he "had grown up in a slave state and served, very briefly, as a Confederate irregular during the Civil War." To be sure, he did "in some sense fle[e] the South (as so many southern artists and intellectuals have done)" but would "return again and again to that scene of slavery and loss in and around the Mississippi River, to the displaced slaveholders who dreamed of future wealth and past glories, and to the slaves who were among the victims of those dreams."[36] In the Reconstruction era, these dreams of "past glories" continued to build on associations of the South with a feudal order and would express themselves, as in Ryan's poetry, in a melancholy nostalgia quick to see parallels in a vanished, happy Europe swept out of existence by the calamities of modernity. Nothing marks Twain as more southern than his recurrent and critical focus on these dreams—a focus not limited to his work set in the Mississippi Valley but discernible also in his European-centered texts. To the extent that *The Innocents Abroad*, *A Connecticut Yankee in King Arthur's Court*, and *Personal Recollections of Joan of Arc* all deal with the gullibility and the pain inherent in medieval yearnings, they register as engagements with the terms of southernness as some southern thinkers had been defining it.

Published in 1869, four years after Appomattox and at a moment when the fate of the occupied southern states was still much debated in Congress and the nation at large, *The Innocents Abroad* never alludes to the contemporary sectional antagonism. Though Twain's narrator indulges in many observations at the expense of his fellow travelers, he seems to regard them all as patriotic Unionists and never broaches the subject of the war. The European and Middle Eastern setting of the book serves as an implicit unifying force: thrown together in the midst of strange and backward foreigners, differences between the Americans fall away. Having passed through the Strait of Gibraltar—and thus finding themselves now surrounded by the European, African, and Middle Eastern coasts—the travelers glimpse "a stately ship . . . [a] beautiful stranger" flying the Stars and Stripes. The narrator's swelling emotion encompasses all who see the flag: "Many a one on our decks knew then for the first time how tame a sight his country's flag is at home compared to what it is in a foreign land. To see it is to see a vision of home itself and all its idols, and feel a thrill that would stir a very river of sluggish blood!"[37] The possibility that some of the company may have fought against that flag in the recent past—as Twain himself briefly had—fades to insignificance because the foreignness of the environment promotes an automatic religious feeling, a worship of idols.

The narrator's constant mockery, however, suggests a displacement of the American political scene onto the foreign lands he observes. Almost everywhere he finds ignorance, superstition, and petty tyranny holding sway; almost everywhere he recommends the importation of universal equality and Yankee ingenuity. Disgusted by what he sees of the Middle East, the narrator displays the obvious influence of racist and Christian discourses that associate the Islamic world with sloth, violence, and absolutism. The one nation that escapes the narrator's wholesale condemnation, France, also most closely resembles the United States: having had a revolution that swept away an absolute monarchy and an established church, France continues to tread the path of "the highest modern civilization, progress, and refinement" (*IA* 126). The Ottoman Empire, on the other hand, remains "a degraded, poverty-stricken, miserable, infamous agglomeration of ignorance, crime, and brutality" (*IA* 128).

Between these two extremes lie the countries of Mediterranean Europe: the Portuguese Azores, Italy, and Greece, more exotic and potentially more threatening than the Protestant nations of Britain and Germany but also historically connected to the United States in troubling ways. An American of the period could dismiss the Islamic world as hopelessly benighted but could not so easily ignore the historical ties linking the United States to southern European countries, given the standard narrative of western civilization in which democracy first flourished in ancient Greece and Christianity first established dominion in Rome. The narrator's critique of these lands, then, suggests a certain embarrassment: these people should know better, and in

certain isolated things—the architectural glories of Milan Cathedral, for example—evidence of lost greatness can occasionally be glimpsed, but the effect is only to register the surrounding backwardness more forcefully.
Because Twain at this time embraced the rhetoric of "assimilation," suggesting that newly freed slaves should be incorporated into the body politic
and occasionally expressing kinship with African-Americans and "foreigners," his disdain probably does not spring from a biologically defined racism
that would consider southern Europeans an inferior racial stock.[38] Instead
what these countries have in common is a lack of Protestant Christianity
and a blind reverence for the past, two traits that in Twain's view imply
each other. Here an implicit analogy with the American South becomes evident: just as southerners, sharing common traditions with the North, should
have known better, these Europeans refuse to accept progress and cling to
atavistic modes of thought. Thus Twain's travelogue presents an analysis of
what happens when feudal elements persist in society. Whether intended
or not, he casts light on the contemporary effort to link Catholicism and
southernness.

The first stop on the tour, the Azores, offers as exemplary an agrarian
society as can be found:

> The principal crop is corn, and they raise it and grind it just as their great-
> great-great-grandfathers did. . . . Oxen tread the wheat from the ear, after
> the fashion prevalent in the time of Methuselah. There is not a wheelbarrow
> in the land—they carry every thing on their heads, or on donkeys, or in a
> wicker-bodied cart, whose wheels are solid blocks of wood and whose
> axles turn with the wheel. There is not a modern plow in the islands, or a
> threshing-machine. All attempts to introduce them have failed. The good
> Catholic Portuguese crossed himself and prayed God [*sic*] to shield him from
> all blasphemous desire to know more than his father did before him. (*IA* 55)

This description does not, of course, reflect the system of plantation agriculture that existed in the South. The Old South's export-driven, capitalist,
and in some respects technologically advanced economy bears little resem-
blance to a system that even Fitzhugh would have derided as a sure means
to universal poverty. The rhetoric, however, suggests certain stereotypically
southern "virtues" held to be intimately bound up with feudal institutions.
The passing reference to Methuselah invokes the original patriarchs of Genesis as Azorean forebears, while the unyielding adherence to tradition comments sardonically on the southern claim that everything began to go
downhill when reason usurped custom and authority. Ultimately this stasis

persists in the Azores only because Catholicism maintains its arrogant absolutism, labeling the desire to depart from worn paths "blasphemous."

From the point of view of a Fitzhugh, such a social arrangement—except for the primitive state of farming and the lack of industry—ensures the happiness of all because those in authority wisely look to the care of their inferiors, even when they have no essential obligation to do so. Twain, however, exposes a will to power behind Catholicism untempered by a concern with general welfare. The Jesuit priests of the islands make up a large proportion of the well-to-do; their "humbuggery" includes the attempt to pass off a polished piece of wood "in [an] excellent state of preservation" as a fragment of the True Cross (*IA* 57)—the first of several such hoaxes that the narrator will catalog. Since the people believe in the wood without hesitation and prove their gullibility by leaving money for the repose of their souls, Fitzhugh's assertion that even an arbitrary hierarchy promotes happiness at first seems to have some validity, and the narrator clearly finds this observation disturbing. To avoid the contradiction, he focuses on a belief in human dignity that would prefer freedom, however painful, to a happy degradation. This belief, though, is itself a legacy of Protestantism that even Fitzhugh could not dismiss without contradicting his position.

Jesuit deceptions prove more rampant in Italy, where even the friars pledged to self-mortification "look like consummate famine-breeders . . . all fat and serene" (*IA* 164). Nor do they content themselves with preying on the local population: the vast tourist industry surrounding cathedrals and sacred sites works those wealthy foreigners who might be naive enough to believe in the relics' authenticity. A church that grounds its claims to authority on its unbroken continuity with the apostles, proclaiming its authenticity above all, reveals itself as fake through and through: there are enough bones of St. Denis scattered about "to duplicate him, if necessary" (*IA* 165). Even the rare instances of goodness and simplicity in the church's history become reconstructed as grotesque displays of arrogance and wealth, such as the burial of St. Charles Borroméo, a genuine friend to the poor, in a sarcophagus encrusted with gems. Intended to comment on the saint's greatness, these "gew-gaws" appear merely "poor, cheap, and trivial" (*IA* 178). The constant efforts of priests to show off the "treasures" of cathedrals and to enumerate the financial worth of gold and silver grows not just grotesque but also astonishing: any authority that deprives and brainwashes its followers while making such an undisguised display of the effort required to maintain itself involves a breathtaking contradiction. One wonders what Twain would have made of the effort to restore southern plantations to their

prewar opulence and turn them into tourist attractions, with their chande-
liers and Doric columns more conspicuous than their slave quarters.

If this display of wealth provokes in the narrator indignation and a certain
reluctant wonder, the prominence of death and torture in Catholic sites
moves him to repugnance. While the use of gold and gems to adorn tombs
comes across as merely grotesque, the brutally lifelike crucifixes, sometimes
with actual nails and hammers laid by to increase the verisimilitude, is actively dangerous, particularly to the mental well-being of children (*IA* 208).
The height of this infatuation with death, however, is evident in the Capu-
chin Chapel, whose walls are decorated with the skeletons of dead monks
and whose caretakers fully expect to join their predecessors one day. These
practices emerge as logical consequences of an institution so preoccupied
with its own authority: veneration of one's fathers culminates in a pervasive
morbidity. As Jenny Franchot points out, American tourists to Rome in the
antebellum years dwelled at great length on the ubiquity of death, corpses,
and the aesthetic of excess that Catholic shrines often constructed around
them. Just as Franchot sees in such anti-Catholic discourses a desire "for
North and South alike to imaginatively resist white America's impending
fratricidal violence" by making common cause against Catholic treachery,
Twain's postbellum account attempts to present a unified American front
against the lingering wounds of civil war.[39] The worship of death that so
disturbs his narrator, however, found its analogue in the increasingly necro-
logical commemorations of the southern cause—of which Ryan's work, as
we have seen, provides a good example. Indeed it may be that one powerful
source of "decadent Catholicism" in the South—discussed in detail in
Chapter Three—comes from the apparent love of death and decay that such
tourists noted and then applied to Catholic enclaves in the United States.
Twain would revisit the subject of graveyards in *Life on the Mississippi* when,
after a lengthy description of the above-ground burial vaults found in mostly
Catholic New Orleans, he labels the whole practice of burial and commemoration of the dead "grotesque, ghastly, horrible," and unsanitary—before
proceeding to an argument in favor of cremation.[40]

Read in the context of Reconstruction and the still emerging discourse
that sought to link the South with a feudal, absolutist, and ultimately Catholic order, *The Innocents Abroad* provides assertions of national unity that dis-
place southern nostalgia and heroic fantasies onto a backward, Catholic,
southern Europe. Even if America's distant Catholic antecedents cannot be
disavowed, just as the Civil War cannot be erased from the historical record,
one can still consign it to the past and kill off its lingering remnants through

mockery. The question still remains, though: why do so many fail to recognize these glories and grovel before the arrogance of power? In his travels through rural southern Italy, the narrator finds himself using the language of Fitzhugh and is certainly conscious of the irony:

> We passed through the strangest, funniest, undreampt-of [*sic*] old towns, wedded to the customs and steeped in the dreams of the elder ages, and perfectly unaware that the world turns round! And perfectly indifferent, too, as to whether it turns around or stands still. *They* have nothing to do but eat and sleep and sleep and eat, and toil a little when they can get a friend to stand by and keep them awake. *They* are not paid for thinking—*they* are not paid to fret about the world's concerns. They were not respectable people—they were not worthy people—they were not learned and wise and brilliant people—but in their breasts, all their stupid lives long, resteth a peace that passeth understanding! How can men, calling themselves men, consent to be so degraded and happy. (*IA* 209)

It is difficult not to hear in this passage echoes of the racism of southern paternalism, in which childlike African-Americans, relieved of the necessity of thought by their kind protectors and social betters, spend their lives in a pleasant daze of eating, sleeping, and working. Yet this passage betrays more than an ill-concealed ethnocentrism: it draws attention to the contingency of social orders, the impossibility of justifying any of them by simply arguing their congruence to human nature. To encompass the shock of seeing human beings in such a condition, the narrator makes a reluctant qualification: these "men" must not consider themselves men, for otherwise their behavior is inexplicable. Their complete indifference to matters of fact (the question of whether the world turns, however, being a case in which the "truth" runs counter to one's immediate, empirical common sense) strikes a child of the Enlightenment as incredible. No less than Fitzhugh, Twain shows himself at a loss when forced to explain why the truth of his position is not self-evident. In the aftermath of a war that revealed his nation to be divided, the desire to erase these divisions is understandable but can only be postponed.

~

A Connecticut Yankee in King Arthur's Court, published two full decades after *The Innocents Abroad*, draws the parallel between the South and a Catholic order more clearly. Twain's most obvious target in the novel is, of course, the ethos of chivalry: the climax, which features the electrocution of thousands of knights, seems to a prematurely giddy Hank Morgan "the last stand of the chivalry of England" and the dawn of republican government.[41] Yet as horrifically impressive as this military victory is, the church figures as the silent but undeniable power that introduced slavery, caste, and knighthood into England and maintains them still:

> There you see the hand of that awful power, the Roman Catholic Church. In two or three little centuries it had converted a nation of men to a nation of worms. Before the day of the Church's supremacy in the world, men were men, and held their heads up, and had a man's pride and spirit and independence; and what of greatness and position a person got, he got mainly by achievement, not by birth. But then the Church came to the front, with an axe to grind; and she was wise, subtle, and knew more than one way to skin a cat—or a nation; she invented "divine right of kings," and propped it all around, brick by brick, with the Beatitudes—wrenching them from their good purpose to make them fortify an evil one; she preached (to the commoner,) humility, obedience to superiors, the beauty of self-sacrifice; she preached (to the commoner,) meekness under insult; preached (still to the commoner, always to the commoner,) patience, meanness of spirit, non-resistance under oppression; and she introduced heritable ranks and aristocracies, and taught all the Christian populations of the earth to bow down to them and worship them. (*CY* 100–1)

However historically inaccurate this account (slavery, monarchy, and aristocracy, after all, long predate the establishment of Christianity in Britain and elsewhere in the world), the implication that royal power finally depends upon the church's continued sanction ironically recalls Fitzhugh's assertion that society "cannot exist a day without religion" and the more authoritarian that religion, the better. The church's ultimate authority flows from its dissemination of superstition among the masses and its monopoly on education that restricts literacy to a few dozen priests. Under such a regime, the vast mass of the population consists of "slaves, pure and simple" (*CY* 98): even those who are spared the indignity of iron collars exist only to grovel before church, King, and nobility. The meritocratic ideal that allegedly held sway before Christianity entailed not just the absence of slavery but also a democracy of heroism—any man could become a hero if he demonstrated sufficient intelligence and pluck. Yet while this construction of heroism ran counter to southern figurations of the hero's self-evident, transcendence-bestowing aura, Twain's masculine gendering of the hero, as well as his portrayal of the church as a wily, subtle woman (in keeping with Protestant readings of the church as Whore of Babylon) reveals his inability to give up the sexism of southern heroic ideals. By extension this feminization of the church likewise recalls constructions of the South as female to the North's aggressive but triumphant and logical maleness—and suggests that just as the South required bloody correction to mend its ways, so too will Catholicism and its puppets, monarchy and chivalry.[42]

Like the Italian priests who exploit tourists, the church of Arthurian England maintains its power through a system of spectacle that, if less gaudy and materialistic than that of its descendants, proves just as inauthentic. One of the novel's most memorable sequences involves Morgan's triumph in the "Valley of Holiness," whose reliable traffic in religious pilgrims has been stanched by the drying up of a holy spring. Since it is believed that a previous drought occurred because a monk had the effrontery to bathe in the sacred waters, pilgrims and monks alike maintain a scrupulous bodily dirtiness that exceeds the general lack of hygiene among the masses; indeed Morgan takes a special delight in the introduction of soap, for he believes that "a rudimentary cleanliness" will ultimately "undermine the Church" (*CY* 191). This reveling in filth recalls the preoccupation with death that so disturbed the narrator of *The Innocents Abroad*: the truest measure of the church's diabolical intelligence is its ability to capitalize upon the morbid and the unclean.

To be sure, the monks of the abbey believe in the spring's holiness and do not recognize the economic or ideological implications of its fame: the abbot appeals to Morgan for help because the new and unknown sin that this drought reveals terrifies him. Morgan obliges the abbot, causing the water to flow again by setting off a massive explosion (and humiliating his rival, Merlin, in the process). Despite his self-serving motives for doing so, Morgan evinces real sympathy with the monks and thus draws attention to the systemic and often unintended nature of the church's oppression. He maintains that "not all priests were frauds and self-seekers . . . many, even the great majority . . . were sincere and right-hearted, and devoted to the alleviation of human troubles and sufferings" (*CY* 215). This useful insight has an applicability that extends far beyond a critique of the church per se: just as individual slaveholders might be humane and generous without lessening by one iota the oppression of the system that benefits them, the kindness of individual priests does not finally matter much. Morgan thinks systemically, not in terms of the anomalous individuals whom he respects, and in doing so he reflects his creator's own commitment to observation and theorizing instead of automatic reverence.

Twain makes the parallel between sixth-century Catholic England and the Old South explicit. Sounding rather like W. J. Cash describing the proto-Dorian bond between rich and poor whites in the South, Hank Morgan observes that just as English commoners would betray members of their own class to defend the rights of the king or the local noble when called upon to do so, "the 'poor whites' of our South who were always despised and frequently insulted, by the slave-lords around them, and who owed their base condition simply to the presence of slavery in their midst, were yet pusillanimously ready to side with the slave-lords in all political moves for the upholding and perpetuating of slavery, and did also finally shoulder their muskets and pour out their lives in an effort to prevent the destruction of that very institution which degraded them" (*CY* 387). Most commentators who have remarked on this parallel, however, have assumed that Morgan represents Twain's critique of both Yankee carpetbaggers and nascent New South boosters, whose naive belief in progress ends in senseless holocaust.[43] One could just as easily, however, read the novel's argument as precisely the opposite. Despite Morgan's naiveté, despite his ludicrous attempts to introduce baseball and the stock market into Arthurian England, despite even his bloodthirstiness in the climactic massacre, the claim that these things represent genuine progress cannot be wholly effaced. Just as the victorious North imposed its will upon the South, Morgan's vision finally triumphs—it merely requires thirteen centuries for its realization. That he does not see the transformation himself and dies in a delirium of regret does not change the outcome; it simply indicates once again the relative indifference of "progress" to individuals.

One central conflict in *A Connecticut Yankee* revolves around the question of whether this progress is inevitable or whether the eventual triumph of Enlightenment in Western Europe and America resulted from a chain of contingencies no less foreseeable than the rise of Christianity. Here Morgan's reasoning swings back and forth. At one point he espouses a thorough constructivism, stating baldly that "there is no such thing as nature; what we call by that misleading name is merely heredity and training" (*CY* 217); at another, moved by evidence of pride and dignity in a commoner, he exults that despite all efforts at brainwashing, "a man *is* a man, at bottom. Whole ages of abuse and oppression cannot crush the manhood clear out of him" (*CY* 390). To the extent that he believes the former position, Morgan veers uncomfortably close to the opinions of Fitzhugh, who had no problem with defining society as constructed and who held only that authoritarian constructions made for the greatest general happiness. The more essentialist Morgan, however, who lauds indomitable manhood, still cannot deny that this capacity for manhood is unequally distributed—and that for all their childishness and stupidity, the nobles are the ones who seem to possess it in abundance. Disguised as a peasant, King Arthur ought to be toast— and his kidnapping and enslavement indeed suggest that his kingship derives mainly from his royal garb, not from divine right or an undeniable aura. Yet not only does he demonstrate a sentimentalized heroism "at its last and loftiest possibility, its utmost summit" (*CY* 372) by caring for the family afflicted with smallpox, he also proves himself intelligent despite his lack of learning by following Morgan's discourses so easily. Indeed Morgan opines that "a peasant's cap was no safe disguise. . . . you could know [that head] for a king's, under a diving bell, if you could but hear it work its intellect" (*CY* 353). Here Twain's attraction to a discourse of human nature moves him temporarily toward a conservatism whose claims exceed even Fitzhugh's: the monarchical authority that for Fitzhugh was arbitrary and based in the end only on force becomes for Twain an inherent, irrepressible quality closer to the transcendence of southern heroic representations.[44]

Though his well-documented deism and hostility toward specifically Christian claims would become more pronounced in later years, Twain reveals in *A Connecticut Yankee* an unwillingness to abolish religion altogether.[45] Morgan wishes to disestablish the Catholic church once his power permits it and to take away its means of support, but his countermeasures include the building of secret "Sunday-schools" and the founding of "a complete variety of Protestant congregations" (*CY* 118), which together contribute to general literacy. In fact he insists that "We *must* have a religion—it goes without saying" (*CY* 216). This Christian pluralism of course implies freedom of religion—a prospect that Fitzhugh condemned as the source from which Mormons, free-love advocates, and other enemies of society sprang. No less than Fitzhugh, however, Twain's protagonist suggests that religion of some sort is required for social cohesion and that its doctrines ultimately matter less than its social usefulness. Here too a certain elitism is evident: those who rule (like Morgan) may acknowledge privately the fact that one religion is as good as another, but the masses whose tranquility religion assures had best remain untroubled in their belief. Historically, however, the fragmentation of Christianity and the denial of its absolute power have resulted in gradual secularization and the weakening of any religious claims that purport to be authoritative. Wishing to preserve religion's authority while destroying its political power, Morgan appears less consistent than Fitzhugh, attempting to do what may well be impossible.

In its critique of feudal ideals and its linkage of these ideals with both the Old South and Catholicism, *A Connecticut Yankee in King Arthur's Court* goes considerably beyond *The Innocents Abroad*. Its condemnation of slavery and its promotion of freedom of thought are unambiguous, while its unattractive portrait of noble and clerical power offers a rejoinder to those late nineteenth-century southerners who eulogized the old order's alleged sweetness and light. Perhaps because it engages more forthrightly with southernness, making explicit the analogies that were only faint allusions in the earlier text, *A Connecticut Yankee* also wears its contradictions more prominently. Morgan's faith in universal male equality founders before occasional suspicions that royalty confers superiority after all, while his hostility toward the church evinces a certain confusion about what ought to replace it to guarantee social cohesion and progress. Its critique of nostalgic postbellum southernness is fuller but also more ambivalent, and its investment in heroism remains despite Morgan's own contempt for chivalry. Twain's final extended engagement with Catholicism, in *Personal Recollections of Joan of Arc*, would only deepen these contradictions, valorizing a heroism that at once affirms and subverts the familiar southern model.

❧

Discussions of *Joan of Arc* nearly always begin by noting its uncharacteristic piety. In this late work, written especially for his daughter Susy, the irreverent humorist turns to hagiography, sentimental prose, worship of the Middle Ages, and a one-dimensional characterization that surpasses even his most misogynist stock figures.[46] Though Twain regarded it as his best book, the critical verdict has been unanimous, seeing Joan, in J. D. Stahl's words, as "not a plausible human being, much less a woman."[47] My purpose here is less to dissent from this judgment than to propose that the text's very implausibility and aesthetic flaws reflect on the relationship between southernness and Catholicism discussed so far. The fact that Joan, Twain's most unqualified hero, is a woman already problematizes models of southern heroism, in which women were represented as passive figures on pedestals in need of male protection. That she should perform this heroism in revolt against the clerical order of her time yet proclaim throughout her fidelity to that order adds still another contradiction.

The Hundred Years' War, the historical event that occasions Joan's rise to greatness, foregrounds both the emotional power of nationalism and the pain of a nationalism forced into submission. The novel's French patriots find their identity threatened both by the English, who with the Treaty of

Troyes reduce France to a mere English province, and by the Burgundians, with whom they fight a civil war. Confronted with these threats, the French partisans must devise new strategies of imagining their nation if they are to preserve its conceptual integrity. Yet in doing so they unwittingly comment upon what Benedict Anderson calls a paradox of nationalism: "the objective modernity of nations to the historian's eye vs. their subjective antiquity in the eyes of nationalists."[48] In the opening pages of the novel, Louis de Conte recalls a scene from his childhood in which a begging soldier who has found food and lodging with Joan's family thrills his hosts with talk of "the ancient glories of France," finally topping it off with a rendition of the *Song of Roland*, which moves Joan to cover him with "idolatrous kisses."[49] Such rituals, which belong more to the era of the modern nation-state than to that of the dynastic realm, perform the same function as Ryan's poetry: by rallying around sacred national icons, whether an epic poem or a Confederate general's sword, the community's resolve is strengthened, its consciousness of defeat or tenuousness diminished. Yet just as the Confederacy, the product of an attempted war of independence, could not completely ignore its newness and sometimes resorted to ancient models of feudalism, the French patriots in Twain's novel attempt to draw on a fiction of continuity with ancient times.

Thus far the novel seems to celebrate precisely the kind of hereditary feudal state advocated by Fitzhugh. The France for which Joan and her followers fight is defined both by the French language and by the legitimacy of the king: even though all acknowledge that Charles I is weak, vacillating, and ultimately treacherous, no one questions his claim to the throne. Yet Joan herself, rather than the king, functions as the heroic embodiment of France—indeed de Conte recounts that "the Dwarf" actually calls Joan "France" (*JA* 174)—and neither king nor army have any authority or power without Joan's sanction. As Joan's old comrade the Paladin maintains, "When a person in Joan of Arc's position tells a man he is brave, he *believes* it. . . . in fact to believe yourself brave is to *be* brave. . . ." (*JA* 140). Just as in other nineteenth-century southern novels, heroism is displayed through Joan's instantaneous bestowal of meaning and sacredness on her cause and identity. Yet by fashioning the hero as a young peasant woman rather than a Richard the Lion-Hearted or a Robert E. Lee, Twain's novel destabilizes the definition of the hero in terms of gender and class. A woman in male armor, who never kills anyone but whose impressive sword inspires men to kill, an illiterate rustic whose grasp of military strategy exceeds that of

France's ablest generals, naturally inspires anxiety even in the order that she saves from destruction.

Even as Joan guarantees the authority of France's royal line, she troubles a number of the assumptions that define this authority in the first place. Since the right of kings was held to be established by God, the power of the church should take precedence over the royal power. De Conte states this principle not as a mere theory but as an unquestionable fact: "*The parish priest governs the nation.* What is the King, then, if the parish priest withdraw his support and deny his authority? Merely a shadow and no King; let him resign" (*JA* 261, emphasis in text). Joan's insistence that God has willed Charles I's coronation and France's military triumph are thus necessary to ensure the legitimacy of the whole enterprise. Yet Joan's strongest and most original attachment is neither to king nor church, but to the "Fairy Tree" that stood in her village of Domremy, a vestige of a long-ago pagan past. This tree is the home of fairies who

> did any friendly thing they could for the children, such as keeping the spring always full and clear and cold, and driving away serpents and insects that sting; and so there was never any unkindness between the fairies and the children during more than five hundred years—tradition said a thousand—but only the warmest affection and the most perfect trust and confidence. . . .
>
> Now from time immemorial all children reared in Domremy were called the Children of the Tree; and they loved that name, for it carried with it a mystic privilege not granted to any others of the children of this world: Which was this: whenever one of these came to die, then beyond the vague and formless images drifting through his darkening mind rose soft and rich and fair a vision of the Tree—if all was well with his soul. (*JA* 10)

Here, however, the very continuity with the pagan world of Roman Gaul—itself a desirable trait to emphasize in the construction of a national identity—finds itself at odds with Christianity. A tradition that stretches back a thousand years fulfills the requirement of antiquity that national narratives often invoke, but given the Christian and dynastic underpinnings of France in the fifteenth century, fairies hardly seem the most appropriate forebears to cite. Attempts to reinterpret the tree's significance for Christian purposes—for instance, as an evocation of Christ's death on a cross—inevitably conflict with the older, pagan associations. The people of Domremy, to be sure, are as conservative as can be expected: "Their religion was inherited, their politics the same. . . . a Pope outside of Rome was no Pope at all" (*JA* 7). Once again the problem that had engaged Fitzhugh emerges:

on the one hand, the putative authenticity of religion lies in its capacity for social identification and stability, even when this authenticity takes a pagan form. On the other hand, the very continuity that this authenticity invokes is threatening to a religion whose fundamental claim is about truth rather than utility.

Joan's first conflict with authority, in fact, occurs when the local priest decides to banish the fairies from the Tree, because as "kin to the Fiend" (*JA* 18), they pose a danger to the children who love them. In this instance, Joan defends the fairies' right to live there, for even "Kinsmen of the Fiend have *rights*" (*JA* 20). If her identification with the fairies marks her as pre-Christian, her talk of rights makes her anachronistic, an advocate of eighteenth-century Enlightenment discourses long before they were common currency. Indeed, throughout the novel, Joan makes throwaway statements that suggest a nascent Protestantism—a point that Bernard Shaw would make explicit twenty-four years later in his own *St. Joan*. When a group of scholars attempt to dissuade her from her mission, citing Catholic authorities, she responds: "The Book of God is worth more than all these ye cite, and I stand upon *it*" (*JA* 128, emphasis in text). Her specific injunctions to her army—no profanity, no prostitutes, regular attendance at Mass, and a drastic reduction in the amount of drinking (*JA* 145–46)—even have a distinctly nineteenth-century Protestant American flavor, as Laura E. Skandera-Trombley shrewdly notes when she calls Joan "the archetypal W[omen's] C[hristian] T[emperance] U[nion] reformer."[50] If Joan's destabilizing of gender norms and humble origins are not enough to alarm the church and the aristocracy, her pagan affiliations and Protestant-inflected talk of rights confirm her as a heretic before her time.

The crux of Joan's struggle with the church, the controversy around which the most damning evidence accumulates at her trial, centers on her claim that she did none of her exploits of her own free will, that the voices of St. Michael, St. Catherine, and St. Marguerite have consistently informed her of God's intentions for her. Sounding much like Christ being interrogated by the high priest, Joan utters a veiled threat: "If you were well informed concerning me you would wish me out of your hands. I have done nothing but by revelation" (*JA* 344). This assertion of her own passivity adds a particular difficulty to Twain's efforts to render her heroic. Just as the usual model of the southern hero stresses that hero's congruence with his society, so that he does not create social meaning but instead emerges from and legitimates it, Joan claims that she has done nothing but what is required of her and takes no credit for herself. Yet clearly Twain wants us to admire

Joan while rejecting her interpretation of her activity—that is, to make her heroism creative rather than merely an affirmation of church and king. In his unsuccessful attempt to resolve this problem, Twain exposes the circular nature of claims to a transcendent heroism. If Joan's heroism springs truly from the creative force of her personality, then her endowment of France with a national identity testifies only to her greatness in imagining a community. On the other hand, if Joan is a passive vessel for divine commands, then the transcendent nature of the order is assured, but her own stature diminishes accordingly.[51]

In his prosecution of Joan, Cauchon agrees that Joan is passive but argues that her voices must have come from Satan; any commands issued to her that contradict the will or teachings of the church would count as ipso facto evidence of the voices' malevolence. Here too Joan clings to the church's authority even as she calls it into question, citing the distinction between the Church Triumphant and the Church Militant and maintaining that because the former had sent and directed her, the latter should have no quarrel with her. When her interrogators persist, she submits herself to the highest ecclesiastical authority: "*Take me to the Pope*. I will answer to everything that I ought to" (*JA* 388, emphasis in text). On the one hand, this assertion of the pope's final say proclaims faith in the church's patriarchal structure; on the other, the clear implication that the lesser church authorities can disagree weakens institutional claims of absolute authority. In the end, Joan's positions become logically impossible. Affirming the church even as she is cut off from it, participating in the construction of the French nation even as her actions reveal that construction's tenuousness, espousing latent Protestant and Enlightenment points of view several centuries before their wide dissemination, Joan exposes the contradictions and circular nature of the hero that most narratives seek to conceal.

Though *Personal Recollections of Joan of Arc*, unlike *A Connecticut Yankee*, never draws an explicit parallel between fifteenth-century France and the South, the analogy nevertheless holds. A great general defeated but untarnished, Joan serves essentially the same function for the French that Lee would for white southerners of the late nineteenth century. Twain's critique of the southern order and its construction of heroism, which increasingly looked to Catholicism for support, manages to demystify heroism even as it celebrates it—an approach that indeed makes Joan herself an aesthetic flaw yet reveals through that very failure the contradictions of southern heroism. Finally perhaps one could characterize *Joan of Arc* as a fable of co-optation. The Joan depicted in the novel stands as a voice of self-determination, of freedom, of national identity endowed with religious significance. Though she maintains her fidelity to church teaching, the authorities, recognizing her real threat, silence her. If this were the end of the story, then the reading would be a fairly straightforward account of tragic heroism that could map neatly onto white southern Reconstruction narratives. But as de Conte points out, Joan is rehabilitated. The same church that put her to death begins the long process of claiming her as a saint, a process that would come to full fruition only in the twentieth century. It may be that Twain's heartfelt rejection of both the Old South and Catholicism did not preclude an awareness of their capacity for appropriation, an awareness that even the most subversive elements can be pressed into a reactionary politics. The fact that efforts to marshal Catholicism for the defense of a racist southern order would continue into the twentieth century testifies to Twain's gloomy perceptiveness.

The attempt to construct a southern identity that drew on medieval, Catholic, heroic, and patriarchal sources, contested not just by Twain but by the increase in anti-Catholic rhetoric across the South in the late nineteenth and early twentieth centuries, would receive a boost in 1878 when Pope Leo XIII's encyclical *Quod Apostolici Muneris* appeared. Subtitled "On Socialism," the document rejects not just socialist thought per se but all intellectual and political movements that intend to overthrow governments. Even as the encyclical admits the existence of corrupt and oppressive leaders, it counsels patience, pointing out that the church commands leaders, on pain of damnation, to be kind to the poor and lowly. Proposing a three-tiered hierarchy, the church recognizes civil governments but views them, like Fitzhugh, as large families; the family itself is held to be "the cornerstone of all society and government." At the top of the pyramid, however, is the church itself, whose "salutary power . . . redounds to the right ordering and preservation of every State and kingdom."[52] If the imagined community of the South required a more permanent foundation than the contingencies of history, this assertion of Catholic primacy, easily assimilable to the myth of an organic and happy society, would become more and more attractive to conservative southern intellectuals—and would reach the full extent of its power via the conduit of the Agrarian movement.

The Pleasures of Decadence: Catholicism in Kate Chopin, Carson McCullers, and Anne Rice

Since the 1970s, when Kate Chopin's fiction began to be rediscovered by feminist critics, the initial reception of *The Awakening* has passed into literary history as the story of a great but unsurprising atrocity. According to this narrative, a gifted writer, successful as a local colorist, is effectively silenced when she undertakes her greatest work because her contemporaries, blinded by the pieties of the genteel tradition, cannot recognize its value. In the preface to her first biography of Chopin, Emily Toth describes her own discovery of *The Awakening* in these words: "I . . . was astonished that a woman in 1899 had asked the same questions that we, in the newly revived women's movement, were asking seventy years later. . . . How *had* Kate Chopin known all that in 1899?"[1] Toth's question suggests that Chopin was a splendid anachronism, a genius who would have to wait for the right readers. In other words, it dehistoricizes her, precluding the possibility that her hostile readers may have reacted not out of incomprehension but out of a political and aesthetic opposition that identified in *The Awakening* the same content celebrated by recent critics: the frank portrayal of a woman's desires for autonomy and sexual fulfillment.

To be sure, the novel's early reviews, some of which have become famous in their own right, often used the language of physical and mental illness—a tic that might seem proof of the reviewers' obtuseness. The *Chicago Times-Herald* dismissed the novel as an example of "sex fiction"; the *Los Angeles Sunday Times* labeled it "unhealthily introspective and morbid," and Willa Cather (writing for the *Pittsburgh Leader*) lamented the fact that Edna Pontellier's particular "disease" afflicts "women of strong and fine intuitions."[2] Yet such rhetoric also points toward a dimension of Chopin's work that these reviewers may have understood better than we do—its affinities with the style and sensibility of decadence, that fin de siècle aesthetic most often associated with French and English writers of the late nineteenth and early twentieth centuries.

As a literary-historical phenomenon, decadence is notoriously difficult to define. Not only do many of its characteristics overlap with those of other contemporary terms, including Symbolism, Impressionism, and *la belle époque,* its writers and theorists used the word in a variety of senses. Even so, according to critical consensus, decadence first emerges as a widespread phenomenon in France in the mid-nineteenth century, eventually making its way to England, where it flourishes in the "yellow decade" of the 1890s, and finally coming to color a great deal of western art and literature by the turn of the century, so that in retrospect it seems a harbinger of the emerging Modernist sensibility. Its key figures include Charles Baudelaire, Théophile Gautier, Joris-Karl Huysmans, Algernon Swinburne, Arthur Symons, Aubrey Beardsley, and Oscar Wilde; its indispensable literary forebears include the Marquis de Sade and Edgar Allan Poe.

From the beginning, decadence has had a contradictory aspect. On the one hand, it exemplifies what Robert Sayre and Michael Löwy call "romantic anticapitalism": an outcry against the Enlightenment, the Industrial Revolution, the triumphant but vulgar bourgeoisie, and the modern rationalization of life that follows in capitalism's wake.[3] On the other hand, its most common response to these conditions is less a romantic return to nature than a defiant championing of artifice. Such contradictions point toward the fraught historical context from which decadence emerges in France, which includes the failures of the Revolution of 1848 and the Paris Commune in France; the humiliation of the Franco-Prussian War; demographic decline, particularly in the country; the rise of socialism, feminism, and anarcho-syndicalism as mass movements. Indeed, throughout Europe, much literary, philosophical, and scientific thought in the period from 1870 to 1914 turned to theories of historical decline to account for these upheavals. Scientists such as Francis Galton and Cesar Lombroso saw evidence of decline in industrialization, criminal behavior, and the alleged atavism of certain physical types; critics such as Max Nordau and historians such as Oswald Spengler applied such theories to culture as a whole, finding intellectual and moral degeneration everywhere.[4] Against this backdrop of political and cultural turmoil, decadents both decried and embraced the perceived degeneration of the age, seeking an apolitical escape into art, self-fashioning, and religion that often included a deliberate and highly wrought nostalgia for the past. The cultivation of the artificial, the perverse, and the self-consciously evil (as in, for instance, Baudelaire, Swinburne, and Husymans's periodic involvements with Satanism) functioned as protests against the "laws" of nature and economic development, which were allegedly destroying all that was noble, beautiful, or affective.

In the face of such an obvious retreat from engagement with the world, many have found it easy to conclude that decadence is no more than a massive delusion. In Jennifer Birkett's words, "Decadence is an attempt—and a very successful and entertaining one—to substitute fiction for history. . . . Decadent artists sell their own desires to the populace as the image of a common dream, building on a thin foundation of historical fact the edifice of outrageous but seductive lies which is their own private fantasy."[5] In this sense, decadence has obvious links to the medievalist ideologies that became increasingly attractive to white southerners in the nineteenth century. Even before the Civil War and its destruction of the Old Southern order, white southerners frequently combined paeans to the glories of their premodern social structure with anxiety that it could not long hold out against the capitalist juggernaut. The example of Edgar Allan Poe, whose influence on French decadence is well established, demonstrates that fears of cultural collapse and a simultaneous attraction to it were prevalent in antebellum intellectual life. Indeed in his linking of beauty with terror and death we see an early installment of what Lewis P. Simpson calls the southern "culture of failure"—a culture that ought to be regarded as proto-decadent.[6]

Yet if decadence was a mere fantasy, it was an influential one, with an aesthetic that is relatively easy to identify. According to Ellis Hanson, decadent style

> delights in strange and obscure words, sumptuous exoticism, exquisite sensations, and improbable juxtapositions; it is fraught with disruption, fragmentation, and paradox; it has a tendency to vague and mystical language, a longing to wring from words an enigmatic symbolism or a perverse irony. Decadent writing is also commonly defined by its thematic preoccupation with art—not only literature and painting, but also masquerade, cosmetics, and the sartorial and epigrammatic flamboyance of the dandy. . . .
>
> Most notoriously, the decadents cultivated a fascination with all that was commonly perceived as unnatural or degenerate, with sexual perversity, nervous illness, crime, and disease, all presented in a highly aestheticized context calculated to subvert or, at any rate, to shock conventional morality. Both stylistically and thematically, decadence is an aesthetic in which failure and decay are regarded as seductive, mystical, or beautiful.[7]

One could easily catalog these traits in Chopin's *The Awakening*: representations of consciousness in sumptuous and vaguely mystical terms; the foregrounding of the aesthetic in Edna's painting and Mademoiselle Reisz's music; the conventionally shocking depiction of Edna's adultery; intimations of lesbianism; and a languorous, eroticized account of suicide that corresponds nicely to the decadent valorization of failure. The most perceptive of the novel's early reviewers may well have been the writer for the *Los Angeles Sunday Times* who proposed this comparison: "It is like one of Aubrey Beardsley's hideous but haunting pictures with their disfiguring leer of sensuality, but [which carry] a distinguishing strength and grace and individuality."[8]

Viewing Chopin as a decadent writer allows us to consider three aspects of her work that have not received sufficient attention: homosexuality, Catholicism, and the relation of both to southern literature. As Hanson notes, decadent writers often found the church enormously attractive: "The sheer excess of the Church—its archaic splendor, the weight of its history, the labyrinthine mysteries of its symbolism, the elaborate embroidery of its robes, the elephantine exquisiteness by which it performs its daily miracles—has always made it an aesthetic and fetishistic object of wonder" (*DC* 6). In one respect, this attraction follows the same logic as the medievalist ideology described in Chapter Two: the church as bulwark of beauty and nobility against a sordid, commercialized modern world. Yet decadence adds to this nostalgia a distinctly homoerotic element, and gay and lesbian writers associated with decadence have frequently been drawn to the church because despite its prohibition against homosexual activity, its aesthetic affords congenial space for homoerotic performance. In Eve Kosofsky Sedgwick's words, Catholicism "is famous for giving countless gay and proto-gay children the shock of the possibility of adults who don't marry, of men in dresses, of passionate theatre, of introspective investment, of lives filled with what could, ideally without diminution, be called the work of the fetish."[9] In its conjoining of the aesthetic, the homoerotic, and the religious, decadence carries implications for the rescripting of identity and for a corresponding politics.

Moreover Chopin's representations of a decadent Catholicism have much in common with what Leslie Fiedler describes as a strand of the southern grotesque noted for its "frankly homosexual" sensibility. Fiedler places such writers as Katherine Anne Porter, Eudora Welty, Carson McCullers, and Truman Capote in this tradition but considers them mere epigones of Faulkner:

> In Katherine Anne Porter, the grotesque tensions and masculine vigor of
> Faulkner still largely survive; in Eudora Welty, they tend to disappear among

the more delicate nuances of sensibility; in Carson McCullers, especially after her first book [*The Heart Is a Lonely Hunter*], they have been quite sub-dued; and in Truman Capote, who is the heir of the feminizing Faulknerians, tone and style have been accommodated to notions of chic nurtured by such fashion magazines as *Harper's Bazaar*. . . .

In Faulkner, such writers find a ready-made *paysage moralisé*, through which to move their epicene protagonists, the landscape of the South already endowed with the proper symbolic values of decay and brooding evil. And in Faulkner, they find, too, a fear and distrust of women which they respond to according to their own lights. But it was not until the female intermediaries had begun the grafting of Jamesian sensibility onto the South-ern gothic stem, that the true Magnolia Blossom or Southern homosexual style could be produced: pseudo-magical, pseudo-religious, pseudo-gothic.[10]

We need not subscribe to Fiedler's sexist and homophobic opinion of these writers to recognize the heuristic value of the southern grotesque or to ac-knowledge its affinity with transgressive constructions of sexuality and gen-der. More recent critics from Mab Segrest to Patricia Yaeger have productively focused on the southern grotesque, examining how its tropes register the historically specific oppression of women, African-Americans, and gays and lesbians in the South, starting from similar premises yet reach-ing conclusions very different from Fiedler's.[11] And indeed the spectacle of a South haunted by defeat, by the ghosts of racial atrocities, and by a fantasy of past cultural glory also suggests a continuity between the medievalist longings of the nineteenth-century southern writers discussed in Chapter Two—longings which, as Twain suggested, sometimes came to the edge of necrophilia—and associations of Catholicism with decadence. If failure is indeed beautiful to a decadent, then the ruined, faux-aristocratic South be-comes a splendid backdrop for all manner of aesthetic and erotic practice. Chopin's introduction of decadent *Catholic* tropes into southern literature thus adds a homoerotic, "French" strand of decadence to preoccupations with the past and with death already well established in southern literature. While subsequent practitioners of southern grotesque do not always invoke the Catholic tropes imagined by Chopin—indeed, many ignore religion al-together—decadent Catholicism, when it appears in such works, compli-cates their meaning in ways not yet fully appreciated.

Chopin's decadent sensibilities were fundamentally ambivalent. Her de-light in the aesthetics and erotics of Catholicism was tempered by her fidel-ity to literary and commonsense realism (a trait that she shared with the

New England local colorists), a belief in the naturalness of heterosexuality, and a consequent conclusion that homoeroticism could flourish in the church only because of the church's skill in shutting out reality. Nevertheless her work draws upon the European fin de siècle tradition of Catholic decadence and inaugurates a new representation of Catholic identity in southern literature. Just as associations between the church and miscegenation were deployed by Catholic and non-Catholic writers across the political spectrum in the South, figures of a decadent and often homoerotic southern Catholicism signified in multiple ways and became linked to other preoccupations, including fear of miscegenation, nostalgia for an aristocratic order, and, more provocatively, the emergence of new forms of sexual identity. The decadent Catholicism that Chopin regarded with wary attraction would become a source of anxiety for some writers, of delight for others, and of fascination for nearly all who considered it.

Chopin would develop her portrayal of Catholic decadence most fully in the short stories of *A Vocation and a Voice,* establishing a fundamental tension between subversive homoerotic pleasure and the unyielding reality of the southern social order, with its codes of honor, gentility, and silence about sex. However subversive Catholic decadence may be, Chopin's work suggests that it will not go unpunished by the white conservative South, even as some of its preoccupations with loss and death spring from the same sources as southern medievalist ideology. Indeed, even its most fervent exemplars will stand accused of being unnatural, will believe themselves to be so, and will therefore be doomed to a good deal of suffering along with their ecstasy. Later writers such as Carson McCullers and Anne Rice would expand upon this range of references, linking a decadent Catholicism to that fluid sexuality that we would today call "queer" (in *The Member of the Wedding),* to miscegenation, and to fantasies of aristocratic privilege (in *The Feast of All Saints*). Yet through all of these associations, the double-edged quality of decadent Catholicism would persist: pleasure and terror, life and death.

❧

Baptized a Catholic and educated for many years in a school operated by the Sisters of the Sacred Heart, Chopin maintained a vexed relation to the church all her life. Although she ceased practicing her religion after the death of her mother, criticized the church's prohibition against divorce, and was known to read books placed on the infamous *Index,* her fiction abounds in Catholic characters, references, and imagery.[12] Chopin's early work treats Catholicism dismissively, as a system of petty legalisms that would be ridiculous were it not for its power to make people miserable. Sometimes she extends sympathy toward unhappy folk who cannot obtain divorces because of the church, as in *At Fault* and "Madame Célestin's Divorce"; at other times, she pours scorn upon hypocrites like Belle Worthington, the society matron in *At Fault* whose Catholicism is merely a means of keeping proper appearances." In either case, the church's purported absurdity comes to the foreground.

This absurdity, however, gives way in Chopin's later work to a preoccupation with Catholic decadence, a reluctant but wondering sense that however unreasonable the church may be, its pleasures cannot be denied. Chopin certainly read some of the major English and French decadent writers (above all, Guy de Maupassant, whose stories she sometimes translated), and her St. Louis salon, known for its unconventional literary tastes, included such regulars as the journalist Billy Reedy, known for his hatred of censorship and his defense of Oscar Wilde against bigotry. A story such as "An Egyptian Cigarette," with its descriptions of a drug-induced hallucinatory state and Orientalist luxury that recall Flaubert's *Salammbô,* displays just how thoroughly Chopin absorbed a decadent ethos from her reading.[13] Yet there is also a "homegrown" dimension to her decadence that reflects her familiarity with a distinctly French variety of American Catholicism and a greater appreciation for the church's erotic and aesthetic potential than the dominant Irish-American model of Catholicism would allow. As Charles Morris has noted, the Irish clergy—which became dominant within the American Catholic church during the nineteenth century—emphasized an almost Jansenist hatred of bodily pleasures and the material world more generally.[14] This model of Catholicism, however, proved less widespread in the South, and the reputation of New Orleans, St. Louis, and other Catholic cities in the South as centers of vice and hedonism certainly sprang in part from a more tolerant attitude on the part of French Catholicism toward pleasures of various kinds and a less rigorous enforcement of moral strictures—a tolerance that in some places led to conflicts between Irish and French Catholics.[15] At the same time, the association of this bacchanalian atmosphere with decay and mental illness recalls nineteenth-century conceptions of the church as morbid and diseased, developed in works as different as Twain's *The Innocents Abroad,* Nathaniel Hawthorne's *The Marble Faun,* and Harold Frederic's *The Damnation of Theron Ware.* Chopin's decadent characters, who display intense eroticism, questionable mental health, and in one case a preoccupation with death, repeat many of the traits that had so troubled Twain but provoke fascination rather than disgust and xenophobia.

The Awakening combines Chopin's earlier treatment of Catholicism with her emphasis on decadence. The novel's most obvious Catholic figure, the rosary-wielding "lady in black" who follows Edna and Robert, may invite mockery for her nit-picking view of the doctrine of indulgences, but elsewhere in the novel, Catholicism is aligned with the erotic and the aesthetic. Edna is of Kentucky Presbyterian origins, and her marriage to Léonce Pontellier takes place in part because the "violent opposition of her father and her sister Margaret to marriage with a Catholic" strengthens her resolve.[16] The Creole culture that Catholicism imbues signifies for Edna both exoticism and an occasionally shocking freedom: she is impressed "most forcibly" by the "entire absence of prudery" that Creole women display in conversation, a degree of freedom "incomprehensible" to her Protestant upbringing.[17] Indeed Edna's marriage arguably constitutes the first step toward her "awakening," because it removes her from the more repressive milieu of her birth and situates her in an environment more conducive to the pursuit of desire. The intimations of lesbianism that some critics have discussed in the novel, consistently associated with art and with the sea, likewise emerge in a milieu colored by the pervasive influence of Creole Catholicism.[18]

Chopin's use of Catholic decadence is most evident, however, in *A Vocation and a Voice*, her final collection of short stories, which was scheduled for publication in 1900 but withdrawn before it went to press.[19] Particularly in "Lilacs," "Two Portraits (The Nun and the Wanton)," and the title story, the church functions as a luxuriant and seductive spectacle that provides shelter for unconventional sexualities despite its official rhetoric and discipline. Moreover, from the very beginning, tropes of Catholic decadence in southern literature become intertwined with tropes of miscegenation: particularly in "Two Portraits," transgressive sexuality and racial indeterminacy come together in a powerful way.

In *A Vocation and a Voice*, the primary sites of decadent Catholicism are the convent and the monastery, long established in a variety of literary traditions as havens for the outcast (in Catholic devotional literature and Louisiana local color stories), as prisons within which abusive acts occur (in the gothic), or as hotbeds of sexual deviancy. Chopin's stories draw on all of these associations, but the deviancy resonates most strongly. As Joanne Glasgow has argued, many late nineteenth- and early twentieth-century lesbians, including Radclyffe Hall and Alice B. Toklas, converted to Catholicism precisely because, according to their reading of Catholic doctrine, the erasure of female sexuality within the church allowed lesbians to be invisible and therefore undisturbed.[20] This understanding of women's sexuality perhaps explains why, as Hanson points out, the convent figures as a place "either sadistic or lesbian" in novels stretching at least as far back as Denis Diderot's *La Religeuse*, and the nun as "a curiously eroticized figure" (*DC* 32). Even if the church's teaching on sex precludes an official recognition of women's sexuality (a questionable but understandable interpretation), it also affords the opportunities of silence and secrecy—opportunities acknowledged in the genre that Hanson calls "Western nun fantasies" (*DC* 32).

That Chopin herself perceived the potential eroticism of convent life is suggested by a remarkable diary entry of 22 June 1894, which records a visit with Liza Miltenberger, an old classmate who had become a nun:

> Those nuns seem to retain or gain a certain beauty with their advancing years which we women of the world are strangers to. . . . The conditions under which these women live are such as keep them young and fresh in heart and in visage. One day—usually one hey-day of youth they kneel before the altar of a God whom they have learned to worship, and they give them- selves wholly—body and spirit into his keeping. They have only to remain faithful through the years, these modern Psyches, to the lover who lavishes all his precious gifts upon them in the darkness—the most precious of which is perpetual youth.

Chopin goes on to call Liza's existence "a phantasmagoria" that lacks any foundation in reality, but this passage betrays a reluctant attraction toward the convent's aesthetic and sexual delights.[21] The divine "lover in the dark- ness" who keeps these women young and beautiful may be only a substitute for the joys of physical love, but just as in many decadent works where sex is less about bodies entwined than about intoxicating flights of fancy, Chopin voices a suspicion that such "insubstantial" love may be preferable to the real thing. The realization that celibacy does not necessarily preclude an intense sexuality is at the heart of Chopin's treatment of decadent Ca- tholicism. Even as she refrains from embracing the mélange of Catholicism, sex, art, and mysticism that she records, she cannot deny its power and wonder.

"Lilacs," the least overtly sexual of the three stories, depicts a friendship between two women: Adrienne Farival, a wealthy Parisian who has become famous as the singer and dancer "La Petite Gilberta," and the chaste and cloistered Sister Agathe. Adrienne's life, comfortable but disreputable, is a veritable catalog of decadent clichés: we encounter her at home, reclining in a negligee, surveying a space littered with musical scores and "astonishing-looking garments," tossing hothouse roses against the face of her servant Sophie, and indulging in wine, cigarettes, and the attentions of her "manager."[22] This glimpse into her life, however, occurs only after she has spent two weeks visiting the nuns at her old convent school. Each spring she makes this pilgrimage in order to relieve her periodic and stereotypically decadent ennui. As she tells Sister Agathe, the first scent of lilac blossoms awakens in her nostalgia for the convent: "I bec[o]me like an *enragée*; nothing could [keep] me back" (*VV* 135). For Adrienne, the lilacs evoke innocence, purity, and timelessness, unlike the sensual roses that she keeps at home. She brings a bouquet of lilacs with her each year, as well as an expensive gift—a crucifix, or fine lace, or a jeweled necklace for the statue of the Blessed Virgin.

Adrienne is deceived, however, by appearances, for at least one nun experiences desires for someone more concrete than a divine lover in the darkness. Most of Sister Agathe's expressions of affection for Adrienne appear unremarkable and would not have aroused suspicion, especially if, as Glasgow argues, women's sexuality in a convent would have been largely invisible. Sister Agathe links arms with Adrienne, holds her hands, and strokes them. The two women sleep in the same room, but Sister Agathe "disrobe[s] noiselessly" and "glide[s] into bed without having revealed, in the faint candlelight, as much as a shadow of herself" (*VV* 137–38). Even so, despite her careful chastity, she displays moments of real erotic passion. When she first greets Adrienne, the narrator comments, "What embraces, in which the lilacs were crushed between them! What ardent kisses! What pink flushes of happiness mounting the cheeks of the two women" (*VV* 132). The pointed crushing of the lilacs in this embrace suggests the falseness of the story's symbol of innocence.

When Adrienne returns a year later for her next visit, she is met by an unfamiliar nun who returns the expensive gifts and denies her entry. A letter attached to the parcel informs her that she is no longer welcome, and she reacts in a fashion appropriate to the innocence that she has been seeking, weeping "with the abandonment of a little child" (*VV* 145). Though the Mother Superior has learned of Adrienne's true occupation through a detective whom Sophie hired to follow her, it is likely that Sister Agathe's desires have also been discovered. Apparently informed of Adrienne's unsuccessful visit, Sister Agathe kneels beside a bed, "her face . . . pressed deep in the pillow in her efforts to smother the sobs that convulsed her frame" (*VV*

145). The story ends with another nun sweeping up the lilacs that Adrienne leaves on the doorstep, as if to remove any traces of innocence within.

Although the Mother Superior prevents the entry of worldliness into the holy precincts, the story functions as an ironic commentary on Adrienne's belief in the purity of convent life. Indeed Adrienne and the Mother Superior are allied in their desire to keep the two worlds separate, for Adrienne leaves no forwarding address when she visits and does not tell her servant where she is going. While her exclusion from the convent pains her, Adrienne is too conscious of her own deception to react with righteous anger to the ban and interprets it as an act of "seeming cruelty" because "she did not dare to say injustice" (*VV* 145). The decadent inhabitant of the demimonde retains her belief in innocence, but miserable Sister Agathe, locked away from her beloved, knows better.

"Lilacs," then, both acknowledges the existence of homoerotic desire within the church and the need to silence it. A later story, however, provides a conflation of desire and religion whose more pointedly decadent tropes culminate in ecstatic masochism. "Two Portraits," written in May 1895, was never published during Chopin's lifetime, perhaps because its frank sensuality went beyond anything else that Chopin had written. Although Chopin exhibits in this story the same fidelity to an intractable "reality" that she expressed in dismissing Liza Miltenberger's life, her protagonist's disturbing but erotic exaltation resonates more strongly than any reservations about it.

Chopin's subtitle for "Two Portraits" is "The Wanton and the Nun." In fact "the wanton and the nun" are the same person, and the two portraits refer to the two sections of the story, which may be read either as successive stages of the protagonist's life or as different fictive possibilities for her. The first section begins: "Alberta having not looked very long into life, had not looked very far. She put out her hands to touch things that pleased her and her lips to kiss them" (*VV* 45). The protagonist is thus introduced as a girl whose ability to enjoy innocent sensual pleasures depends on her inability to delay gratification. Alberta is fond of her "mama who was not really her mama" (*VV* 45)—a pointed hint of shameful origins—despite the fact that this woman alternates showers of affection with vicious beatings. Alberta grows up surrounded by transient visitors, among whom the women who praise her beauty and the art students who like to paint her nude stand out most clearly in her mind. After her mother commits suicide, Alberta goes to live with a couple who stop the beatings because they understand that "Alberta's body was too beautiful to be beaten—it was made for love" (*VV*

46). There is, then, the clear suggestion that Alberta's mother is a prostitute and that Alberta is being trained unawares to carry on the profession. Moreover, while the descriptive markers that might reveal Alberta's race are ambiguous—she is described only as having "dark eyes" and a "thin and white" face (*VV* 50)—there is also the hint that her wantonness is a result of mixed race, coded as a kind of instinctive knowledge: "She did not lack for instruction in the wiles—the ways of stirring a man's desire and holding it. Yet she did not need instruction—the secret was in her blood and looked out of her passionate, wanton eyes and showed in every motion of her seductive body" (*VV* 47). In fact as Alberta's "career" proceeds and she takes to giving and withholding her favors in order to become wealthy—a strategy that suggests a quadroon woman entertaining offers of *plaçage*—she becomes more aggressive, carrying a knife with her and reflecting that should she ever become old and ugly, she has the means to kill herself. If on the one hand Alberta is trained to become a prostitute, Chopin also strikes a familiar note of biological racism that associates women of mixed blood with sexual voracity and violence.

Yet the second section of the story begins exactly like the first, suggesting that Alberta's career as nun is no different: "Alberta having not looked very long into life, had not looked very far. She put out her hands to touch things that pleased her, and her lips to kiss them" (*VV* 48). Discovered by a "very holy woman" who reveals God to her in the profusion and loveliness of nature, Alberta becomes absorbed in spiritual joys, rejects the sordidness of her life, and enters the "convent . . . whose atmosphere of chastity, poverty, and obedience penetrates to the soul through benumbed senses" (*VV* 48). Once there, however, she experiences intensely eroticized visions:

> The first of them came to her when she was wrapped in suffering, in quivering contemplation of the bleeding and agonizing Christ. Oh, the dear God! Who loved her beyond the power of man to describe, to conceive. The God-Man, the Man-God, suffering, bleeding, dying for her, Alberta, a worm upon the earth; dying that she might be saved from sin and transplanted among the heavenly delights. Oh, if she might die for him in return!
>
> . . .
>
> She pressed her lips upon the bleeding wounds and the Divine Blood transfigured her. The Virgin Mary enfolded her in her mantle. She could not describe in words the ecstasy; the taste of the Divine love which only the souls of the transplanted could endure in its awful and complete intensity. She, Alberta, had received this sign of Divine favor; this foretaste of heavenly bliss. (*VV* 50)

Such intoxication echoes Chopin's description of Liza Miltenberger and her "divine lover." Yet this experience, for all its purported spirituality, fixes on the flesh: it is less a bodiless communion of souls than a ménage à trois involving Alberta, the Virgin Mary, and a crucified Christ whose gory wounds feminize him, foreground his carnality, and provide a powerful site for cathexis. Moreover, the masochism of Alberta's vision suggests how Catholicism both fosters and formally prohibits such ecstasy: the pleasure is undeniable but so is the necessity of self-abasement. Chopin would undoubtedly consider Alberta's visions "a phantasmagoria"; the implicit disapproval directed against one who "has not looked very far into life," as well as a distaste for masochism, is unmistakable. Yet in this passage, perhaps the most stereotypically "decadent" in all Chopin, the force of this disapproval dwindles. Alberta's implicitly mixed-race background suggests the convergence of two separate constructions of southern Catholicism: the church welcomes both the child of miscegenation and the decadent.

"A Vocation and a Voice," Chopin's longest short story, also connects the church to intense but fundamentally unreal pleasure. Here, however, Chopin's picture of decadence is more critical: heterosexual desire is presented as essential and authentic, while the church's ability to foster homoeroticism is linked to its suppression of reality. The protagonist, a boy from the Irish ghetto of St. Louis, oscillates between his love for the church and his desire for Suzima, an itinerant fortune-teller with a beautiful singing voice. Upon meeting Suzima and her violent husband, Gutro, the boy impulsively decides to travel south with them, encouraged by a "vague sense of being unessential which always dwelt with him, and which permitted him, at that moment, to abandon himself completely to the novelty and charm of his surroundings" (*VV* 3). As an orphan on the brink of puberty, the boy has not yet settled upon a firm sexual identity and is consequently able to move among various possibilities, yielding to their "charm." Initially his appearance and manners are distinctly feminine: he speaks with "the high, treble voice of a girl"; his hair is "longer than the prevailing fashion demanded"; and his eyes are "dark and quiet . . . not alert and seeking mischief, as the eyes of boys usually are" (*VV* 2). His journey southward, however, awakens a heterosexual desire in him that is associated with his appreciation of nature. Observing the countryside, "[h]e felt as if he had been transplanted into another sphere, into a native element from which he had all along been excluded. The sight of the country was beautiful to him and his whole being expanded in the space and splendor of it" (*VV* 10). The full extent of this "expansion" becomes evident, however, only when he encounters Suzima naked and seated upon a rock and becomes over-whelmed with desire. His heterosexuality is presented as innate, requiring only the right stimulus to awaken it.

The boy's initial girlishness manifests itself in his fondness for the specta-cle and mysticism of Catholicism. He loves serving at Mass, dressing in ele-gant vestments that would be "a sin" anywhere else, and reciting the hieratic Latin phrases that he cannot speak outside the church building (*VV* 18). Indeed when Suzima, Gutro, and the boy settle down for a break from their wandering existence in Louisiana, the boy introduces himself to the local priest, who is pleased to find a boy "who did not have to be coaxed, cajoled, almost lassoed and dragged in to do service at the Holy Sacrifice!" (*VV* 17). Although sufficiently impressed by the figure the boy cuts in his vestments, Suzima sees them less as an expression of mysticism and beauty than as a good financial angle. Her shrewd grasp of the economic potential of Catholicism, at odds with the boy's unwillingness to sully the sacred mys-teries with too much of the world, reinforces her symbolic role as the prin-ciple of the real, firmly grounded in need, nature, and heterosexuality. By contrast, the boy's feminized investment in the church depends upon his love of the unknowable, the indistinct, and the transcendent. The only ex-periences that approximate his religious ecstasies are his nighttime walks in complete darkness (*VV* 14–15)—an apt figure for a life of fantasy.

The boy interprets his attraction to Suzima and subsequent sexual rela-tionship with her as temptations that undo him. When Gutro moves to strike her one day, the boy reacts with rage and nearly kills him. Instantly he feels remorse: "He had never dreamed of a devil lurking unknown to him, in his blood, that would some day blind him, disable his will, and di-rect his hands to deeds of violence. . . . He shrank from trusting himself with this being alone" (*VV* 31–32). Aware that only his desire could have awakened such an impulse, he deserts the couple and flees to a monastery, intending to renounce the world of female temptresses forever. His flight, however, also entails a thoroughgoing sexual transformation:

> Brother Ludovic was so strong, so stalwart, that the boys of the institution often wished he might be permitted to give an exhibition of his prowess or to enter a contest of some sort whereby they might shine in the reflected honor of his achievements. Some said it all came of sleeping with open windows, winter and summer, because he could not abide the confinement of four walls. Others thought it came of chopping trees. For when he wielded his axe, which was twice the size of any other man's, the forest

resounded with the blows. He was not one to dilly-dally about the grape vines or the flower beds, like a woman, mincing with a hoe. He had begun that way, they told each other, but he was soon away in the forest felling trees and out in the fields breaking the stubborn lands. So he had grown to be the young marvel of strength who now excited their youthful imaginations and commanded their respect. (*VV* 32–33)

This portrayal of clerical life—the monk as Paul Bunyan—suggests not a specter of aesthetic decadence but a communal version of "holy marriage of males" identified by Fiedler as an omnipresent trope in American literature.[23] Unlike the enclosed and feminizing space of the church building, the monastery figures here as a wilderness that the community of affectionate men both subdue and revel in. The absence of women not only prevents Brother Ludovic from becoming "soft" but also signifies to him the overcoming of moral imperfection, made visible in his bodily transformation. Life in the monastery is divided among religious contemplation, education of the boys, and hard physical labor, all of which shut out heterosexual temptations and give him the peace of largely dreamless sleep (*VV* 34). Indeed so great is Brother Ludovic's antipathy to the outside world of women that his greatest dream is "to build, with his own hands, a solid stone wall around the 'Refuge'" (*VV* 34)—a dream he pursues with single-minded ferocity.

The story ends, however, with a rejection of this blissful monastic homoeroticism and a return to essential heterosexuality. The collapse of this model might be found in its misguided attempt to reconcile "nature" with homoeroticism: as Brother Ludovic's plans for the stone wall suggest, even in a community of men, nature has to be shut out and dominated, lest the incitement to lust that women bring prevail. Just after a young monk remarks jokingly but significantly that the proposed stone wall will make the monastery a "prison," Brother Ludovic hears the sound of a woman's voice singing and leaves his work to pursue it. If the end of the story is read as its logical end, then Chopin's final judgment on Catholic homoeroticism would seem negative: no matter what form gay desire takes, whether effeminate decadence or aggressively masculine camaraderie, it will eventually yield to heterosexuality if not confined in the hothouse of a monastery. In this sense, Chopin demonstrates her fidelity to the realist conventions of the local color fiction for which she became known: decadence appears as a part of the larger exotic fabric but does not finally disrupt the social order. Nevertheless, Chopin's identification of the church with unconventional sexual desires establishes it as one protector of individuals with these desires. What Chopin would characterize as "reality" is, after all, painful—and however reluctant her praise of the church, the stories of *A Vocation and a Voice* formulate a construction of Catholicism as potentially "queer" that would recur in southern literature for decades. When transplanted from Chopin's exotic settings of France and Louisiana to the more Anglo-Celtic world of the white small-town South, however, these tropes of a decadent Catholicism come to signify not just the potential for intense pleasure but also a sense of palpable dread.

꽃

For Chopin the primary problem with a decadent Catholicism is not its affirmation of pleasure but its willful denial of reality. Later southern writers, however, would return to many of the same tropes that Chopin had developed while focusing more equally on their delights and terrors. As Harper Lee's Miss Maudie Atkinson memorably put it in *To Kill a Mockingbird*, significant numbers of twentieth-century southern Protestants have subscribed to the belief that "anything that's pleasure is a sin."[24] This standpoint, close in some respects to the Jansenist-influenced Irish Catholicism that dominated the U.S. church in the North, condemned expressions of Catholic decadence not just for their homoerotic resonances but for their flamboyant aestheticism, appreciation of fleshly pleasures, and multiplicity of sexual objects and desires. Viewed through this lens, Catholicism becomes seductive but terrifying: it promises exotic, "foreign," pleasures in which sex, death, and aesthetic delight are intermingled, but the price for such pleasures may be one's soul.

The nativist resurgence of the 1910s and 1920s contributed greatly to the association of Catholicism with indecent and decadent pleasures. The same kinds of lurid anti-Catholic propaganda that had circulated in the North during the 1840s—accounts of women immured and victimized in convents, papal strategies for world domination—now found an eager audience in the South, and political figures such as Tom Watson (a leading power broker in Georgia politics and a two-time candidate for the presidency under the Populist Party) often turned to anti-Catholicism to further political power. Beginning in 1910, for instance, Watson's *Jeffersonian Weekly* devoted many articles to the sinister power of priests in the South, and while some of them emphasized the church's collusion with miscegenation, others revived fears of sexual abuse in the confessional and connected this to priestly enjoyment of other pleasures, as in this example:

Through his questions, the priest learns which of his fair penitents are tempted to indulge in sexual inclinations. Remember that the priest is often a powerfully sexed man, who lives on rich food, drinks red wine, and does no manual labor. He is alone with a beautiful, well-shaped young woman who tells him that she is tormented by carnal desire. Her low voice is in his ear; the rustle of her skirts and the scent of her hair kindle flames. She will never tell what he says or does. She believes that he cannot sin. She believes that *he* can forgive *her* sin. She has been taught that in obeying *him,* she is serving God.[25]

As C. Vann Woodward has maintained, Watson's grievance against Catholicism was primarily political, for in Georgia, church leaders had thrown their support to the Republican Party in 1896.[26] Yet his instinct for sensationalism as a means to political power dovetailed well with increasing Protestant suspicion of the church that would persist well beyond this political moment. We need only compare Watson's diatribe with this somewhat tongue-in-cheek portrayal of Catholicism in Yazoo City, Mississippi, in Willie Morris's 1967 memoir *North Toward Home* to see how widespread and long-lasting such associations were:

> And there was the Catholic church, a big, damp, ominous place not far from our church. It was a frightening place for a child, and when you walked by it, even in broad daylight, you always felt the compulsion to walk a little faster. They even said the priest, Father Hunter, had drunk a whole beer right out of the can at a ceremony to raise money for a new convent. One afternoon three of us, working up our courage through dares, walked right into the Catholic church, peered down the long aisle and saw the statues in that brooding darkness, smelled the sweet foreign odors, and found the whole secret business so awesome that the common Puritan dread hit us simultaneously, and there was a mad running away such as you never saw. Yet we came back, not only to the Catholic church but to a Catholic funeral . . . and as I sat in the pew watching those strange rituals and hearing those solemn litanies, I was full of such terror I could hardly stay there, not only for [my Catholic friend] Strawberry's death but for a God-in-death so different from mine that he had to be serving another constituency altogether.[27]

For the young Willie Morris and his friends, the Catholic church is linked both to open and unabashed sensuality—the consumption of alcohol, the "sweet foreign odors," the suggestive but indistinctly understood "secret business"—and a terror of death and the unknown. His "Puritan dread" reacts not just against the pleasures of homoeroticism that Chopin had illustrated but against the more fundamental animus against pleasure that Miss Maudie Atkinson identifies, in which sin and death are always lurking. Morris's portrayal, one might say, draws both on the portrait of a necrophilic Catholicism that Twain had condemned and on the secret pleasures glimpsed in Chopin's fiction. As in Watson's account—but with a saving, ironic awareness—terror and titillation go hand in hand.

I propose that the word "queer" accounts for the full range of contradictory pleasures and terrors evoked by Catholicism here and elsewhere in later southern literature, including but not limited to the overtly homoerotic. As Sedgwick has argued, "queer" implies "the open mesh of possibilities, gaps, overlaps, dissonances and resonances, lapses and excesses of meaning when the constituent elements of anyone's gender, of anyone's sexuality aren't made (or *can't be* made) to signify monolithically."[28] Insofar as Catholicism encourages such "excesses," it functions both as a source of potential freedom and as a terrifying specter of the dissolution of the self. If its decadent solemnity sends boys fleeing in terror, its imaginative possibilities also become, in the hands of other southern writers, affirmations of pleasure and religious devotion alike.

Interestingly enough, these affirmations and terrors appeared both in the work of conservative, Agrarian-influenced writers such as Caroline Gordon (whose religio-aesthetic theory of fiction and treatment of decadence is examined in Chapter Four) and writers identified with the southern liberal tradition, such as Lillian Smith and Carson McCullers—neither of whom was herself Catholic and both of whom have been claimed by contemporary lesbian critics as forebears. Smith's critique of the Jim Crow South, *Killers of the Dream,* examines in great detail the animus against pleasure and paranoid drive to conform that imbued the white South's religious and cultural life, yet it does draw one significant distinction within white southern religion: "I separate Protestant from Catholic just here not because the training of Catholic children was less severe but because the Catholic child was given more adequate compensations for its renunciations than were given little Protestants."[29] Though Smith does not explain what these "compensations" were, her import is clear: now matter how thoroughly Catholics may have been indoctrinated, they were permitted to enjoy some pleasures and received a more satisfactory explanation of why others were to be renounced.

McCullers, however, went beyond Smith both in her appreciation of Catholicism and her association of it with queer pleasures. In her 1959 essay

"The Flowering Dream: Notes on Writing," McCullers describes a childhood encounter with Catholicism as a key event in her life:

> When I was a child of about four, I was walking with my nurse past a convent. For once, the convent doors were open. And I saw the children eating ice-cream cones, playing on iron swings, and I watched, fascinated. I wanted to go in, but my nurse said no, I was not Catholic. The next day, the gate was shut. But, year by year, I thought of what was going on, of this wonderful party, where I was shut out. I wanted to climb the wall, but I was too little. I beat on the wall once, and I knew all the time that there was a marvelous party going on, but I couldn't get in.[30]

The convent is, most of the time, forbidding and locked shut, a place that suggests Gothic associations of torture, brainwashing, and plans for world domination. Yet as the young Lula Carson Smith's glimpse of the marvelous "party" within shows, the convent also represents a rare place where pleasure can be enjoyed without compunction. This double vision of Catholicism as threat to the social order and as delight to those queer enough to see it is easily assimilable to the southern grotesque, evoking at once the terror of the exotic and the primacy of desire.

In her early novels, McCullers's allusions to Catholicism swing easily between common associations with fear and queer sexuality. In *The Heart Is a Lonely Hunter,* Mick Kelly tells Spareribs that "Catholics buy a pistol for a baby as soon as it's born. Some day the Catholics mean to start a war and kill everybody else."[31] And in *Reflections in a Golden Eye,* Captain Penderton, suffering from repressed homosexual desire for Private Williams, yearns for an imagined monastic and homosocial camaraderie that he associates with the Catholic Middle Ages: "His imaginings of the barracks were flavored by this medievalist predilection."[32] While Mick repeats the fears of the church that had been common throughout the Protestant South in the 1930s, Penderton combines southern medievalism with intimations of Catholic homoeroticism into a painful amalgam. McCullers's most interesting treatment of Catholicism, however, occurs in *The Member of the Wedding,* a novel that locates the church as one—but by no means the only—site in which queer sexuality can define itself in the South with relative freedom.

Many feminist critics have regarded *The Member of the Wedding* with ambivalence, describing it as a bildungsroman in which a free-spirited and creative adolescent girl is forced to adopt the stifling conventions of southern womanhood.[33] Such readings often refer to McCullers's own struggles with her sexuality—which has been celebrated by some as lesbian and described by others as devoid of physical desire altogether. Yet as Rachel Adams has pointed out, the protean sexualities adopted by both Frankie and John Henry over the course of the novel are better described by the term "queer" than by "lesbian" or "homoerotic."[34] The multiple roles that Frankie adopts in the course of the novel include not just the presexual tomboy, the lesbian, and the caricature of southern femininity but also the Catholic decadent, a role more frequently associated with gay male than lesbian sexuality. The mutability of these identities, as well as the fact that none finally prove dominant, constitutes the novel's most solid claim to queerness.

In reading Frankie as a character whose sexual identity is constantly shifting, I do not mean to imply that Frankie always consciously adopts particular roles. As Judith Butler has argued, the intelligibility of gender roles inheres in their repetition of recognizable performances, which become intelligible only within specific cultural contexts: "As in other ritual social dramas, the action of gender requires a performance that is *repeated*. This repetition is at once a reenactment and reexperiencing of a set of meanings already socially established; and it is the mundane and ritualized form of their legitimation."[35] Accordingly individual subjects do not exist prior to their performances; the performances themselves construct subjects as "male," "female," "straight," or "gay." Strictly speaking, then, Frankie's intentions may be irrelevant. Even so, the novel provides evidence that Frankie delights in the mutability of sexual identity and, like her even queerer cousin John Henry, regrets the fact that it is not socially sanctioned: "She planned [her ideal world] so that people could instantly change back and forth from boys to girls, whichever way they felt like and wanted."[36] To consider Frankie a decadent gay man, then, entails nothing more than the observation that at certain points in the novel she behaves in ways that signify within such a context. Although these constructions are historically specific, sometimes resonating with particular force in the context of her small southern hometown, they remain comprehensible in our own historical moment.

⤳

The instability of Frankie's sexuality is evident in the first words that she speaks in the novel: "It is so very queer" (*MW* 4). As Lori J. Kenschaft explains, the word "queer" was, in 1946, "a code word known to many 'in the life' but few outside; it was used frequently to identify oneself to another discreetly, under the public eye but without public knowledge. . . ."[37] Yet while "queer" may mark the novel's openness to lesbian interpretations, as

Kenschaft suggests, the word's signification becomes even less fixed as the novel progresses. On the one hand, it retains its connotations of homosexuality, understood in the novel as gender inversion—that is, the discrepancy between the gender of one's inner being and the sex of one's body. It also refers, however, to most of the novel's depictions of heterosexuality, beginning with Frankie's unspecified "queer sin" (*MW* 30) with Barney MacKean. "Queer" thus illustrates the iterability that Butler describes: it repeats its familiar meaning of "homosexual," but it also extends its meaning to other kinds of relationships and signifies not only in accordance with 1940s definitions of the word but also with our own.

Frankie's "queer sin" is one of several events that precipitate her plunge into sexual confusion. The first, her banishment from her father's bed, springs directly from her emergence into puberty. Although Mr. Addams uses decidedly unfeminine language to describe Frankie, calling her a "great big long-legged twelve-year-old blunderbuss" (*MW* 29), he nevertheless registers in his "rejection" of her the cultural demand that she become sexually normative. Frightened and aggrieved by his rejection, Frankie responds with theft, violence, and sexual experimentation, stealing a knife from Sears Roebuck, shooting pistol cartridges, and engaging in her "queer sin." She resists becoming feminine through the stereotypically masculine activities of shooting and knife throwing, fantasizing about joining the army and fighting Germans (like Captain Penderton, she admires the camaraderie of soldiers but seems less consciously aware than he of the army's homoerotic undercurrents), and usurping her father's power by stealing his pistol. In this context, the characterization of her actions with Barney as "queer" makes sense: if Frankie performs masculinity, then sexual activity with Barney certainly counts as "queer." At the same time, however, the encounter alluded to remains ostensibly heterosexual—and thus also highlights the instability and flux associated with contemporary notions of queerness.

Frankie comes to believe that all sexual activity corresponds to this model—in other words, that all sex is sordid and tinged with violence. She therefore reacts to intimations of heterosexual behavior with the same loathing, dismissing overheard descriptions of coitus as "nasty lies about married people" (*MW* 14) and pretending that her glimpse of the Marlowes' lovemaking revealed only "a common fit" (*MW* 47). Against these revelations, Frankie idealizes the wedding of her brother and his bride as a sexless union of souls, a *"we of me"* (*MW* 50, emphasis in text) defined by spiritual communion rather than erotic intimacy. Even here, however, her disgust for sex prevents her from seeing just how queer she is, since her desire to become a "member of the wedding" manages to be incestuous, bisexual, and full of disdain for the physical all at once. Only after she fights off a soldier who attempts to rape her does she connect her earlier sexual experiences: "There slanted across her mind twisted remembrances of a common fit in the front room, basement remarks, and nasty Barney; but she did not let these separate glimpses fall together, and the word she repeated was 'crazy'" (*MW* 165). This remark suggests that the common denominator of Frankie's sexual life is its mutability, its queerness, its ability to correspond to different sexual roles. If Frankie is not yet ready to pursue the implications of this truth—and her substitution of the more pointedly disapproving word "crazy" for "queer" here, as well as her willful failure to connect these events, would suggest as much—she has nevertheless become momentarily aware of them.

The contention that Frankie finally succumbs to the ideology of southern womanhood—a conclusion reached by many feminist critics of the novel—rests upon a set of assumptions about the novel's tripartite structure. In Part One, Frankie's rebellion against the patriarchal order takes the form of boyish clothing and behavior; in Part Two, F. Jasmine's transgressive potential expresses itself in a parodic display of femininity that reveals both its dangers and its constructedness. When, therefore, Frankie adopts the more prosaic name "Frances" and ceases to perform so theatrically in Part Three, many readers conclude that she has reached a synthesis of her two former attitudes: a stable, permanent, and oppressive femininity congruent with the demands of her culture. In this view, the novel enacts a closed dialectic: the ending is privileged as the result toward which the narrative logic has been marching. And indeed Part Three offers evidence that queer sexuality will not be tolerated: Frankie is ejected from the wedding; her effort to run away is thwarted by a police officer; and John Henry, the novel's queerest character, dies a painful death from meningitis.

Such evidence of Frankie's submission, however, should be considered alongside the new identity that she develops in Part Three, which includes friendship with Mary Littlejohn and a newfound appreciation for art, poetry, and Roman Catholicism. The convergence of these interests suggests that despite the undeniable blows she has suffered, Frankie retains much of her queerness. The passage describing her relationship with Mary is worth quoting at length:

> Mary was coming at five o'clock to take dinner, spend the night, and
> ride in the van to the new house tomorrow. Mary collected pictures of great

masters and pasted them in an art book. They read poets like Tennyson together; and Mary was going to be a great painter and Frances a great poet—or else the foremost authority on radar. . . . When Frances was sixteen and Mary eighteen, they were going around the world together. Frances placed the sandwiches on a plate, along with eight chocolates and some salted nuts; this was to be a midnight feast, eaten in the bed at twelve o'clock. . . .

Berenice could not appreciate Michelangelo or poetry, let alone Mary Littlejohn. There had at first been words between them on the subject. Berenice had spoken of Mary as being lumpy and marshmallow-white, and Frances had defended her fiercely. Mary had long braids that she could very nearly sit on, braids of a woven mixture of corn-yellow and brown, fastened at the ends with rubber bands, and, on occasions, ribbons. She had brown eyes with yellow eyelashes, and her dimpled hands tapered at the fingers to little pink blobs of flesh, as Mary bit her nails. The Littlejohns were Catholics, and even on this point Berenice was all of a sudden narrow-minded [*sic*], saying that Roman Catholics worshiped Graven Images and wanted the Pope to rule the world. But for Frances this difference was a touch of final strangeness, silent terror, that completed the wonder of her love. (*MW* 190–91)

Interpreters who view Frankie's development in Part Three as a surrender to gender norms tend to contrast her new interests unfavorably with her earlier ones. Louise Westling argues that once, Frankie wrote her own plays; now she "gushes sentimental nonsense about the Great Masters." For Barbara A. White, Frankie's former ambitions of "flying planes, of being able to switch genders whenever she wished, of joining the wedding, were protests against the secondary status of women ," but "her new dreams are socially acceptable and easily within her reach." Even Patricia Yaeger, who discerns a more pointed political critique in the novel, concedes that Frankie must "grow up" and "sublimate her desire for John Henry's quirkiness within the ordinary high jinks of Mary *Littlejohn,* her new-minted friend."[38] These readings, however, overlook the homoerotic overtones of the relationship: the clitoral implications of Mary Littlejohn's surname; the allusion to a "midnight feast, eaten in the bed"; the imagery of the grotesque (Mary's "lumpy and marshmallow-white" skin and "pink blobs of flesh"). Moreover, in addition to these distinctly lesbian hints, elements of male homoeroticism are also evident: Frances's exclamation "I am just mad about Michelangelo" (*MW* 190) both alludes to and mocks T. S. Eliot's "The

Love Song of J. Alfred Prufrock" and evokes what Camille Paglia has called Michelangelo's "obsessive theme [of] glorified maleness . . . [which] drives femaleness out of existence."[39] Tennyson, although less obviously assimilable to a homoerotic or decadent aesthetic, displays glimpses of decadent preoccupations in some of his most popular poems: the hermetic but ultimately self-destructive pleasures of art in "The Lady of Shallot"; the languorous, hallucinatory delights of "The Lotos Eaters"; the elegiac commemoration of love between men in "In Memoriam." Mary and Frances's desire to travel around the world together and become great artists thus brings together several elements of a paradigm of gay male aestheticism. Mary's Catholicism becomes especially significant here, connecting this aestheticism to the church's elaborate rituals, sumptuous architecture, traditions of mysticism, homosocial communities of clergy, and sensuality at once ecstatic, erotic, and, as Robert S. Phillips has observed, implicitly gothic.[40] When Frankie thinks of Mary's Catholicism as "a final touch of strangeness, silent terror, that completed the wonder of her love," she expresses this sentiment precisely.

The novel's portrayal of a decadent, homoerotic Catholicism does not go unchallenged, although the challenge takes the form of the much more specific Protestant complaint, voiced by Berenice, that Catholics worship "Graven Images." Just as the nurse in McCullers's essay prohibits the young child from investigating Catholicism and its pleasures, Berenice, as Frankie's guardian and chief moral teacher, registers her objections to Mary and her faith. The charge of idolatry is inseparable from this Protestant animus against pleasure, for attention to the aesthetic delights of religious art presumes an inability to focus on God and purely spiritual joys. Interestingly enough, Berenice proves elsewhere in the novel to be a connoisseur of sexual pleasure: she speaks thrillingly of her first marriage to Ludie Freeman and claims that she will not marry T. T. Williams, her current suitor, because "he don't make [her] shiver none" (*MW* 113). Yet she is also adamant in her support for heterosexuality, "insisting that the law of human sex was exactly right just as it was and could in no way be improved" (*MW* 118). Given her familiarity with the vicissitudes of Frankie's sexuality, Berenice seems to intuit the homoerotic potential of Frankie's friendship with Mary and to cloak her real objections to that friendship with the code words of Catholicism and graven images. Berenice's other purported objection to Catholicism, her assertion that the pope wants to rule the world, can be viewed in similar terms: the triumph of Catholicism would entail the dethroning of compulsory heterosexuality and an end to the southern way of life.

Although Frankie's relationship with Mary signifies in several respects as that of a gay male couple, it would be misleading to argue that at this point in the novel Frankie simply "becomes" a gay man. As suggested above, some aspects of Frankie's relationship with Mary also suggest lesbian desires. Moreover, even at this late point in the novel, Frankie clings to some of her earlier enthusiasms and gender identifications: she cannot decide, for example, whether to become a poet or retain her "tomboyish" dream of becoming "the foremost authority on radar" (*MW* 191). Even her choice of "Frances" as her preferred name retains some ambiguity, since it is a homophone for the masculine name "Francis," and its gender only becomes evident when the word is written. In other words, the fundamental point of Frankie's queerness is its failure to be reduced to unified sexual identities, even at those textual moments when one particular identity seems dominant over others. Frankie's shifting identities of straight woman, tomboy, lesbian, and gay man continue at the end of the novel, repeating themselves, but always with a difference.

For the same reasons, it would be problematic to impose a pattern of development, so crucial to the definition of the bildungsroman, on *The Member of the Wedding*. Identities and enthusiasms in the novel do not replace each other in stages of increasing emotional maturity or regression; they recur and multiply, fixing upon new objects of desire. Frankie's emotional "development" in the novel may be limited to the mere—and, given the silence surrounding sexuality in her southern milieu, necessarily incomplete—recognition on her part that this queerness need not be a reason for self-loathing. Whereas before she had regarded the Freaks at the fair with terrified self-recognition, she will now no longer visit them with Mary because "Mrs. Littlejohn said it was morbid to gaze at Freaks" (*MW* 193). One could, of course, read this prohibition as Mrs. Littlejohn's attempt to prevent Mary and Frances from seeing alternate possibilities of identity. Yet the disappearance of the Freaks from the novel may also appear in a positive light, as Frances replacing a "freakish" self-image of sexual identity with others that are healthier.[41] Such "development," however, implies no trajectory toward higher or more morally advanced stages. Frances's last words in the novel, "I am simply mad about—" (*MW* 195), interrupted by the arrival of Mary Littlejohn, underscore this point, because the expected repetition—"I am simply mad about Michelangelo"—fails to happen and leaves the novel with a structural lack of closure. Any object, any new conjunction of sexual identities, may take the place of Michelangelo, filling the gap in the sentence, and then yield to something new. The novel ends not with a stable sexual identity, straight or gay, but with a gesture toward the possibility of endless desires and identifications. Among this proliferation of queer identifications, Catholicism takes its place.

꧁

Decadence, androgyny, and queerness have long been hallmarks of Anne Rice's popular gothic novels, in which queer, philosophizing vampires invent new sexual identities and ponder perennial religious and philosophical questions against a backdrop often permeated with Catholic resonances.[42] Rice's most specific treatment of Catholicism and decadence in a southern context, however, occurs in her lesser-known historical novel *The Feast of All Saints*. Set among the *gens de couleur libres* of New Orleans in the 1840s, *The Feast of All Saints* is meticulously researched, drawing heavily on the work of Creole historians such as Rodolphe Lucien Desdunes and even incorporating into its plot the publication of *L'album littéraire,* the literary journal that preceded *Les Cenelles*. Indeed Rice has characterized the novel as a reclamation project, an attempt to publicize the largely unknown history of the *gens de couleur libres,* to compare them to the unsung but blessed dead who are commemorated on All Saints' Day. The desire to recover a forgotten history marks Rice's novel as a product of the late 1970s, a complement to such fictional and nonfictional excavations of the African-American past as Alex Haley's *Roots,* Gayl Jones's *Corregidora,* and David Bradley's *The Chaneysville Incident*. It is also, perhaps, a product of its time in its overwrought and highly sexualized prose, an apt pop-culture product in a decade that saw the resurgence of the word *decadence* as both an opprobrium and a term of praise.[43] Unlike these novels, however, *The Feast of All Saints* also addresses the cultural ramifications of decadence, miscegenation, and Catholicism in the South, bringing the central concerns of this book to perhaps the widest audience.

As Chapter One argues, the historical *gens de couleur libres* distinguished themselves carefully from both whites and blacks, emphasizing on the one hand their unique social position and on the other the universality of their Catholicism to preserve their racial privileges. Rice's novel presents their strategy fairly accurately, stressing the disdain that her characters feel for the slaves around them (some of whom are their property), even as they must acknowledge their own origins in a slave system. Rice also, however, complicates this picture of racial division by portraying class divisions within the *gens de couleur libres*. One group, consisting largely of the women who have been *placées* and their children, guard their wealth jealously and aspire to the luxurious, decadent way of life that they associate with the white planter class. A second group, represented primarily by the Lermontant family, is solidly middle class, emphasizing the value and dignity of work and adhering rigidly to the social mores that have enabled it to survive. Finally, a third group, whom we meet only during an interval in the country, consists of wealthy landowners who own plantations, trace their genealogies back to Haiti, and succeed to a greater extent than the other groups in shutting out the white world altogether.

The novel's protagonist, Marcel St.-Marie, is the son of Cécile, a *placée,* and Philippe Ferronaire, a planter who has provided for his mistress and child for many years. Having been indulged all his life by his father, Marcel expects to emigrate to France one day for an education and a chance to become famous. His idol, Cristophe, is the pride of the *gens de couleur libres* community, a man who left for Paris and became famous both for his enormously successful novel, *Nuits de Charlotte,* and for the tales of his extravagant debauchery. When Cristophe returns to New Orleans to establish a school for the *gens de couleur libres,* Marcel quickly becomes both friend and pupil of Cristophe and lover to Cristophe's beautiful but deranged mother, Juliet Mercier. The odd life of this threesome, which combines rigorous study and love of art with sex, drunkenness, and homoerotic tension (Cristophe has had male lovers and eventually confesses his attraction to Marcel), plays out a decadent fantasy that is enabled entirely by their class position. That Marcel's own father is barely literate (but enjoys the novelty of having a "scholar" for a son) is ironic, since Marcel's fantasies of aristocratic, cultured elegance are entirely dependent upon him.

Because of their privileges, both Marcel and Cristophe can afford to strike unconventional, Byronic attitudes marked with the stamp of the putatively aristocratic. Their world is characterized by passion, grand gestures, whimsy, an occasional desire to "slum" among the lower classes, and a typically romantic contempt for propriety. Cristophe, for example, decides to admit his slave Bubbles to class, an egalitarian affirmation that results in the desertion of nearly all of his pupils, members of what Cristophe calls the "[d]amned insufferable bourgeoisie!"[44] Similarly Marcel's own impulsive nature, his tendency toward preoccupied fugue states, and apparent inability to resist sexual temptation figure in the novel as a sign of wild, aristocratic freedom. Both men fancy themselves criminals, lost souls, and Cristophe in particular can access "an unnatural state in which all things leapt out at him, beautiful or tragic, and seemed somehow sublime" (*FAS* 259). That Marcel's own sister Marie, who is light-skinned enough to pass for white, is being groomed to be a *placée* herself—in part so that her financial support may help to pay for Marcel's travel—is of little concern to him.

Politically the novel's sympathies are with the unglamorous Lermontants, who run a funeral home and oppose to the intoxication of desire a stolid common sense that does not shrink from Machiavellian tactics when necessary. The Lermontant way is vindicated: Marcel's friend Richard Lermontant, after a long struggle with his father, finally gets to marry Marie St.-Marie and take the trip to France that Marcel so yearns for. Marcel, on the other hand, discovers that his father's debts prevent him from traveling to France, and when he confronts his father, he is beaten across the face with a whip. Yet if his aristocratic fantasy proves unable to sustain itself, neither the prospect of living among his prosperous, landowning relatives in the country nor the possibility of aligning himself with the slaves' struggles proves a viable alternative. Indeed Lisette, the St.-Maries' slave (and Marcel's half-sister), gets her revenge on her beautiful sister by dragging her to a *voodooienne*, who drugs her and then allows five white men to rape her. If the decadent indulgence of the aristocrats depends upon unhappiness, sexual exploitation, and violence, and alliance with the slaves is impossible, then only middle-class doggedness and insistence on propriety can carry the day.

It could be argued that Rice's novel is fundamentally dishonest, that we see this triumph of middle-class values only after we have been titillated by the passion and extravagance of Marcel's world. Indeed the unabashed linkage of sex with luxury and with violence may even suggest an eroticization of masochism and, more disturbingly, of the slaveholding order itself. We see one interracial liaison, between Vincent Dazincourt and Anna Bella Monroe, critiqued only after we have seen how hot the sex is, and we see Cristophe, who has reveled in his contempt for social nicety, refuse to sleep with Marcel even though he desires him. Perhaps this contradiction is unavoidable, given Rice's stated desire to recover and celebrate the history of the *gens de couleur libres*—after all, any celebration of their achievement would also have to acknowledge their privileges, their complicity in injustice, and the difficulty of assimilating them into a progressive narrative of African-American identity. If *The Feast of All Saints* asks us to dwell on the horrors of slavery and *plaçage*, it also seduces us with images of sexual transgression that depend on aristocratic privilege.

As in *Les Cenelles,* the world of *The Feast of All Saints* is imbued with Catholic imagery and practice, yet there is also a considerable difference.

First, though members of all social classes adhere to the forms of Catholicism, attending Mass and receiving the sacraments, attraction to Catholicism is much more pronounced among the aristocrats, although here it is primarily a focus of aesthetic and sexual delight, not a system of belief. When he finds himself tormented by desire and unable to act, Marcel enjoys sitting "in the rear pew of the Cathedral, staring at every detail of the statues and paintings" (*FAS* 13). His sister Marie, having fallen in love with Richard Lermontant, compares her desire for him with her emotions on the day of her first Communion: "That Christ was with her, inside of her, had been the only thought in her mind as she walked down the aisle" (*FAS* 200). And Cristophe, whose studies and experiences have led him to atheism, nevertheless signifies as culturally Catholic. Indeed the narrator underscores the permanence of Catholic influence on the novel's characters: "There is a saying in the Catholic Church: 'Give me a child until he's six years old and I'll give you a Catholic forever'" (*FAS* 327). Only Anna Bella Monroe, the outsider, the "American" free woman of color who has found herself in this largely French world and who has converted to Catholicism, seems to understand the role religion plays in everyone's life: though devoted to the Virgin Mary and pained by the fact that her life of sin prevents her from receiving Communion, she lacks a "heartfelt religious conviction" because the church seems to her "ornate and alien at times of real trouble . . . a luxury like the lace she'd learned to make, the French language she had acquired" (*FAS* 333–34). Catholicism is everywhere, but primarily as part of a general fabric of luxury, a beautiful object that is implicated in its adherents' grand passions but not to be taken too seriously. As part of an aristocratic, decadent way of life, it is opposed to the *voudun* that the slaves in the novel practice, though to maintain this opposition the *gens de couleur libres* must deny the fact that *voudun* itself contains Catholic elements. When Marie, about to be drugged by the priestess, is distracted by "a statue of the Virgin on that altar" adorned with "the dead skin of a snake" (*FAS* 561), her premonition of terror seems directly related to the fact that this formerly aesthetic object has been placed in a context where it might wield real and terrifying power. If *The Feast of All Saints* reveals how thoroughly Catholicism had come to signify both miscegenation and decadence, it also exposes the class fantasy evident in these associations. In the end, the *gens de couleur libres* of Rice's novel are not so different from those white southerners of the nineteenth century with medievalist longings, for whom Catholicism signified above all as a guarantee of their continued rule and their way of life.

By linking Catholicism with homoeroticism, the aesthetic, and the mystical, Chopin contributed greatly to the later development of Catholic representations in southern literature. Even as these representations persisted through the twentieth century, they took on new resonances in later writers, becoming intertwined with more familiar instances of the southern grotesque, with queer formations of sexuality, and with fantasies of aristocratic privilege. Because these representations of Catholicism evoke both pleasure and dread, disease and vitality, life and death, the question of how they function politically remains open. Ellis Hanson argues that the possibilities of decadent Catholicism still resonate within gay communities, and he attempts to valorize its aesthetic, against a range of Marxist and cultural materialist arguments that regard the aesthetic and Catholicism alike as so much mystification. To the extent that Chopin, McCullers, and Rice's portrayals of decadent Catholicism glory in an eroticized aesthetic, they would seem to support Hanson's project here. But it is worth remembering that even at their most decadent, these writers display a disturbing eroticization of power. The masochistic fantasies of Chopin's Alberta, the touch of "terror" that Frankie retains toward Mary Littlejohn, the connection between Catholicism and sexual victimization in *The Feast of All Saints* would seem more in keeping with Camille Paglia's vision of sex and art alike as irreducibly hierarchical and shot through with the will to dominate. In this respect, representations of decadent Catholicism trouble our conventional notions of southern literature and identity but present problems of their own. Like the southern grotesque, which has been read both as a mark of patriarchal power triumphant and as a defiant reminder of what that southern culture has repressed, decadent Catholicism has multiple valences—and evaluations of its political potential should not take the form of broad generalizations. We ignore the particularity of individual cases at our peril. We can, however, agree with Bertram Wyatt-Brown's judgment that by challenging the received ideology of the white South, borrowing from the more introspective and decadent models of Continental fiction, Chopin proved herself one of "the first 'moderns' of southern literature" and bequeathed to her successors a richer sense of fiction's potential for representing erotic and affective life.[45]

4   *Agrarian Catholics: The Catholic Turn in Southern Literature*

Is Flannery O'Connor best viewed as a southern writer or as a Catholic writer? This question may appear willfully reductive, but it marks a divide that refuses to go away. Even after several decades of attention to her work, O'Connor's critics can be grouped into those who read her primarily through a theological lens (often casting themselves as faithful exegetes or rebellious doubters) and those who focus primarily on her regional identification. If theological readings tend to dilute the cultural specificity of O'Connor's work (and to become old quickly, as Michael Kreyling has complained), "southern" readings of O'Connor tend to reduce her religious concerns to a mere by-product of the South's "Christ-haunted" cultural context.[1] Implicit in both kinds of readings is the notion that O'Connor is an anomalous figure, central both to southern and Catholic literary traditions but comfortably situated in neither.

O'Connor, however, saw her identities as southerner and Catholic neither as complementary nor as merely additive. In "The Catholic Novelist in the Protestant South," she asserted that "the" southern Catholic novelist

> will feel a good deal more kinship with backwoods prophets and shouting fundamentalists than he will with those politer elements for whom the supernatural is an embarrassment. . . . His interest and sympathy may well go—as I know my own does—directly to those aspects of Southern life where the religious feeling is most intense and where its most outward forms are furthest from the Catholic, and most revealing of a need that only the Church can fill. . . . [He] discovers that it is with these aspects of Southern life that he has a feeling of kinship strong enough to spur him to write. . . . The Catholic novelist in the South will bolster the South's best traditions, for they are the same as his own.[2]

By identifying the "best traditions" of the South and the church as "the same," O'Connor suggests that we should not be deceived by the wide-spread anti-Catholicism of the twentieth-century Protestant South. This is a surprising claim, not least because O'Connor's fiction seldom depicts Catholicism: her characters, nearly always Protestant, associate the church (when they think of it at all) with sinister foreigners and the Whore of Babylon. And her few Catholic characters, such as the lapsed boy who accompanies Haze Motes to a whorehouse in *Wise Blood,* the cruel but ridiculous schoolgirls of "A Temple of the Holy Ghost," or the annoying priest in "The Enduring Chill" who harangues Asbury for missing Mass, rarely inspire admiration. Unless one resorts to anagogical interpretations dictated largely by O'Connor's stated intentions, one finds little evidence in her fiction that southern and Catholic traditions are "the same."

This paradox is nowhere more striking than in "The Displaced Person," O'Connor's most extended representation of Catholicism.[3] Guizac, the Polish refugee who becomes a tenant farmer in Georgia, arrives on a farm that functions as a microcosm of the South. The three chief social classes are represented: the white ruling class in the figure of Mrs. McIntyre; the poor whites in her tenant farmers, the Shortleys; and the black laborers tied to the land in Astor and Sulk. Though these classes resent each other, they have reached an equilibrium, certain of their places within the social order and comfortably confirmed in their prejudices. Mrs. McIntyre "knows," for instance, that "all Negroes would steal" and that "white trash thinks anybody is rich who can afford to hire people as sorry as they are," while Mrs. Shortley "knows" that "if Mrs. McIntyre had considered her trash, they couldn't have talked about trashy people together."[4] Like Jesus, who, according to The Misfit in "A Good Man Is Hard to Find," "thrown everything off balance," Guizac disrupts the functioning of the system.[5] A diligent and apparently selfless worker who actually needs to be told that Negroes will steal, Guizac cannot be tolerated and suffers a symbolic crucifixion when his backbone is crushed by a tractor.

Mrs. Shortley, the first character to become suspicious of Guizac, associates him with the atrocities of the Holocaust:

> [She] recalled a newsreel she had seen once of a small room piled high with bodies of dead naked people all in a heap, their arms and legs tangled together, a head thrust in here, a head there, a foot, a knee, a part that should have been covered up sticking out, a hand raised clutching nothing. . . .
> This was the kind of thing that was happening every day in Europe where they had not advanced as in this country, and watching from her vantage point, Mrs. Shortley had the sudden intuition that [the Guizacs], like rats with typhoid fleas, could have carried all those murderous ways over the water with them directly to this place. (*DP* 196)

Although Mrs. Shortley's fear centers first on the violence, rampant sexuality, and disease that she projects onto Europe, she soon comes to believe that Guizac's Catholicism looms as the great evil behind the rest: "Mrs. Shortley looked at the priest and was reminded that these people did not have an advanced religion. There was no telling what all they believed since none of the foolishness had been reformed out of it. Again she saw the room piled high with bodies" (*DP* 197–98). She regards Guizac as less dangerous than the priest who brought him, believing that the priest intends to populate the farm with displaced Polish refugees and to deprive the poor whites and blacks of home and livelihood. She therefore works to turn Astor and Sulk against Guizac by presenting herself as their advocate. In this sense, the threat of Catholicism is associated with the removal of African-Americans—leaving the southern elite without cheap labor and the southern poor whites without a class to look down on.

Mrs. McIntyre, however, only begins to suspect Guizac when she learns that he is trying to raise money for his sixteen-year-old cousin to come to America—and that in return for contributions to this fund from Sulk, Guizac will allow Sulk to marry her. When a horrified Mrs. McIntyre confronts Guizac about this plan, he responds with nonchalance, "She no care black" (*DP* 223). Just as in the work of the *Les Cenelles* poets, Cable, King, and Dunbar-Nelson, Catholicism is associated with miscegenation, although here the horror is unambiguous. Mrs. Shortley's fear of depopulation yields to something far worse: a Catholicism that violates the South's central taboo, striking at the heart of white southern identity.

"The Displaced Person" does not, to be sure, endorse the views of Mrs. McIntyre or Mrs. Shortley; in fact O'Connor underscores Guizac's role as a Christ figure in the most heavy-handed manner: "Christ was just another D.P." (*DP* 229). She also emphasizes the collective responsibility for his death: Mrs. McIntyre, Mr. Shortley, and one of the black characters have the opportunity to warn Guizac but choose not to do so, and their exchange of glances "froze them in collusion forever" (*DP* 234). If O'Connor's most admirable Catholic is symbolically put to death by the collective South, her equation of southern and Catholic "traditions" seems more counterintuitive than ever.

How, then, to account for this claim? O'Connor's dual identification is most productively considered within the context of a concerted effort during the years after the Second World War to redefine southern literature in specifically Catholic terms—an effort that revives the association of the church with a medieval order that Fitzhugh and Holmes had suggested but theorizes this association in much more detail. The primary architects of this movement were Allen Tate, the poet and ex-Agrarian cultural critic, and his wife, Caroline Gordon, the novelist and short story writer. On 26 November 1947, Gordon converted to Catholicism, and three years later, Tate followed her into the church. Although both had cultivated an interest in Catholicism that dates back to the late 1920s, they resisted making categorical claims about the relation between Catholicism and southern literature until after their conversions—and after Agrarianism was defunct as a political movement. By identifying Catholicism with the structures of southern society itself, Tate provided the theoretical grounding for this redefinition of southern literature. Gordon, applying her new faith to her practice as a writer, developed a theory of fiction as an inherently Catholic medium. O'Connor, who became Gordon's protégée in 1951 when she began sending drafts of her work to the older woman for critical commentary, was strongly influenced by Gordon's ideas about the nature and purpose of southern and Catholic fiction and would come to characterize her own fictional project in similar terms.

Tate and Gordon's conversions are often usefully considered as belated events in the Catholic Revival, that early twentieth-century literary and theological movement that resuscitated Thomist thought and included such international figures as G. K. Chesterton, Georges Bernanos, and Jacques Maritain. And indeed the influence of Catholic Revival thinkers on both Tate and Gordon is indisputable.[6] This influence, however, should be viewed within the specifically southern context that Tate and Gordon inhabited and seen as a response to the failure of Agrarian politics. By 1945, with industrial capitalism firmly entrenched in the South and public confidence in the state renewed by victory in war, the frankly reactionary platform of the Agrarians had lost much of its credibility. Many Agrarians and their younger followers took refuge from their political defeat in English departments, where, as New Critics, they sought to preserve their authority and their ideology through the construction of a southern literary canon.[7] In *Three Catholic Writers of the Modern South*, one of the few studies of Catholic influence on southern literature, Robert H. Brinkmeyer Jr. considers Tate, Gordon, and Walker Percy and argues that their turn to the church responded to the same historical exigencies that had undermined the Agrarian program:

> When Tate, Gordon, and Percy grew up and entered the rapidly changing world of modern society, they found their value systems, indeed,

their identities, under extreme challenge. In what to them must have seemed a shockingly short time, they stepped from a society rooted in myth and tradition into one preoccupied with history and science. The order and stability of their community-based world view gave way before new theories of psychology and sociology that spurned traditional values and morality. Positivism pervaded almost all levels of thinking, even theology. Here was Nietzsche's "weightless" society, bereft of supernatural frameworks of meaning and strict moral guideposts.[8]

Yet while Brinkmeyer's argument is basically correct, his biographical approach depicts the three writers' engagements with modernity and faith primarily as individual struggles rather than as part of a concerted literary and theoretical strategy. He opposes southernness to Catholicism and implies that Tate, Gordon, and Percy ultimately had to leave the former behind: "Though all three saw their southern identities as a way to define themselves against the modern world, at the same time they recognized that this definition was resistance, not transcendence. They turned to the Church to restore myth, meaning, and mystery to what they saw as a morally irresponsible modern world."[9] I would argue, however, that neither Tate nor Gordon abandoned the "resistance" of a southern identity when they migrated to Catholicism. On the contrary, they suggested that they were better able to realize an Agrarian artistic vision because they did not confuse religion with history or myth. Despite the obvious affinities of their project with New Criticism, their work more accurately constitutes an *alternative* to the New Critical retreat into the universities, an attempt to preserve the iconicity of southern literature beyond all historical change by investing it with the authority of an absolutist faith. In particular both Gordon and O'Connor challenge the New Critical dogma of the intentional fallacy, suggesting that their own Christian intentions, even if not grasped by the reader in the process of reading, ought to stand as the interpretive last word. O'Connor's equation of southern and Catholic traditions, then, is best seen as part of this effort to base southern literature on a transcendent foundation.

The twentieth-century attempt to ground southern literature in a "feudal" Catholicism begins with Tate's Agrarian essay "Remarks on the Southern Religion," moves through his more complex treatment of Catholicism in his novel *The Fathers*, and achieves a new authority when Gordon and Tate convert to Catholicism, thus staking their literary integrity on this definition of southern Catholicism. One by-product of Tate and Gordon's efforts is a uniquely Catholic theory of fiction, developed largely by Gordon and put into practice in her novels of the 1950s, *The Strange Children* and *The Malefactors,* and adapted by O'Connor in her own fictional theory and practice. For all the cogency of Tate and Gordon's arguments, however, their association of Catholicism with a conservative southern ideology weathered several challenges, from the surprising implicit critique of a feudal Catholicism in Margaret Mitchell's *Gone with the Wind* to the continuing associations of the church with miscegenation and decadence, both of which appear in Tate and Gordon's fiction and disrupt the coherence of their theories. Their attempt to categorize southern literature as essentially Catholic, always historically dubious, lost much of its force in 1965. That year saw not only the posthumous publication of O'Connor's last book of stories, *Everything That Rises Must Converge,* but also the end of the Second Vatican Council—an event that demonstrated that the Catholic church was no more immune than the South to historical change.

꙳

The story of how many of the former Fugitive poets became the Agrarians in the late 1920s—a story in which the ridicule heaped on southerners in the wake of the Scopes "monkey trial" at Dayton, Tennessee, in 1925 looms large—is well known. Given the origins of their project in a visceral defense of southern Protestant fundamentalism, it should come as no surprise that religion was one of the Agrarians' chief concerns, and their desire to include an account of it in their theories of southern economics, history, and culture is evident throughout *I'll Take My Stand.* As Paul K. Conkin reports, they were united in their "opposition to new or soft or humanistic and naturalistic religions" and favored, like Fitzhugh, an orthodox faith with a sharply defined doctrinal authority.[10] Since the South—except for southern Louisiana—was largely Protestant, the Agrarian allegiance to tradition would logically call for some form of Protestantism. Embracing a single denomination, however, would exclude much of the southern religious experience, while upholding a generic Protestantism would run the risk of doctrinal "softness." Rather than specify any creed, Ransom's "Statement of Principles" at the beginning of *I'll Take My Stand* proposes a definition of religion broad enough for all the contributors to endorse: "Religion is our submission to the general intention of a nature that is fairly inscrutable; it is the sense of our role as creatures within it."[11] Because this definition is not necessarily Christian, let alone Protestant, it conveys the Agrarians' fierce antihumanism but fails to meet the desired doctrinal rigor. Tate's contribution to the symposium, which tries to define religion more precisely, points up its inadequacy.

"Remarks on the Southern Religion" is a dense and puzzling essay, made all the more so by Tate's insistence that its project is impossible, that to discuss religion at all "is a piece of violence, a betrayal of the religious essence undertaken for its own good."[12] Tate contends that religion apprehends objects holistically without dividing them into concrete and abstract properties. Using the illustration of a horse, he holds that religion would not separate the horse into "(1) that part of him which he has in common with other horses, or that more general part which he shares with other quadrupeds or with the more general vertebrates; and . . . (2) that power of the horse which he shares with horsepower in general, of pushing or pulling another object." On the contrary, religion "pretends to place the horse before us as he is" (*RSR* 156–57). Since the very exercise of reason destroys the holistic image, religion must be impervious to rational analysis. Moreover, religion is authentic only insofar as individuals experience it spontaneously, from within a particular place and tradition.

Two important points follow from this definition. The first is that religion asserts itself as a *factual* discourse, maintaining that "the horse as it is" exists even if it is beyond the power of language to describe it. Religion is therefore to be distinguished from myth, which remains a fiction, even if it points obliquely to certain historical or moral truths. If Christianity, for example, were to admit that "Adonis is able to compete with Christ," then it would become one of those "half-religions that are no religions at all, but quite simply a decision passed on the utility, the workableness, of the religious objects with respect to the practical aims of society" (*RSR* 162–63). Part of Tate's difficulty in making his case, as he admits, lies in his inability to hold the beliefs that he finds so desirable; the "religion" he would urge on the South exists for him in "the condition of fairy story and myth" (*RSR* 156). Like Fitzhugh, Tate insists on the centrality of religion to the South, but unlike Fitzhugh, he is tormented by the contradiction between his defense of belief and his lack of it.

Tate's second point is that authentic religion always has a mutually reinforcing relationship with its society's social and economic structures. Indeed he claims that "economic conviction is the secular image of religion" (*RSR* 168). This relationship never developed in the Old South, however, because of certain historical accidents. The South began with the "Jamestown project" (*RSR* 166), "a capitalistic enterprise undertaken by Europeans who were already convinced adherents of large-scale exploitation of nature, not to support a stable religious order, but to advance the interests of trade as an end in itself" (*RSR* 167). In terms that recall Max Weber's *The Protestant Ethic and the Spirit of Capitalism*, Tate holds that a capitalist Jamestown would inevitably profess Protestantism, "a non-agrarian and trading religion; hardly a religion at all, but a result of secular ambition" (*RSR* 168). Thanks to the warm climate and fertile soil, however, which made a slave economy possible, the southern economy soon reverted to feudal and agrarian structures, without a corresponding change in religion. Protestantism, Tate suggests, was perfectly suited to the liberal and capitalist North but alien to the developing order in the South. As a result, the South's subsequent economic and social troubles were all but inevitable. Near the end of the essay, Tate even declares, with apparent ingenuousness, that "The South would not have been defeated had it possessed a sufficient faith in its own kind of God" (*RSR* 174). The political activity of the Agrarians, then, becomes a self-defeating attempt to create the South's God. For if the South never had a proper religion, then the call to reappropriate the southern tradition—already problematic because it implies intellectual distance from that tradition—is fatally flawed. Tate's enigmatic remark that the tradition must therefore be taken "by violence" (*RSR* 174) suggests desperation. In fact, the subtext of "Remarks on the Southern Religion" might be summarized: since the South lacks a proper religion on which to base its tradition, the Agrarians will have to settle for myth as a poor substitute.

Like Fitzhugh, Tate assumes that because Catholicism is historically linked to a feudal order, it would have been a more genuine southern religion. In a letter to Ransom dated 27 July 1929, in which he discusses his ideas for *I'll Take My Stand*, Tate makes this assumption explicit, even as he acknowledges that in doing so he seems to distort southern history:

> The Southernism that I am more and more concerned with would probably issue, if successful, in something superficially very dissimilar to the order our fathers swayed in 1850. The truth is one, yet its garments change with fashion. It makes little difference to me what clothes the truth wears. As you say, we need a stable order. . . .
>
> I do not see any of us as the founder of a religion. The remote source of the old Southern mind was undoubtedly Catholicism—or at least High Church-ism—in spite of the Methodist and Baptist zeal of the Old South—and perhaps something could be done toward showing that the old Southerners were historically Catholic all the time. If that could be done, we have a starting point. For, as [Charles] Maurras says, we need a "master idea." I

cannot agree with his implication that we must manufacture the idea our-selves.[13]

Here, then, is an early hint of Tate's conversion more than two decades later. His impatience with the form the "truth" takes is not, as it might appear, an admission than any myth will do as long as it points to the truth. If that were the case, then it would be more effective either to resurrect the "Southernism" of the 1850s or to "manufacture" a new "master idea." But as the course of southern history after Jamestown shows, changing society (and adopting new myths) does not necessarily change religion. Rather, Tate predicts that only the rediscovery of an authentic, feudal Catholicism will result in the creation of a "stable order."

Catholicism's feudal affinities include not just its friendliness to hierarchy but also its adherence to what Ransom called in *God without Thunder* a "fun-damentalist" faith, an authoritatively stated body of belief that had no truck with humanist, progressive, or tentatively proffered doctrines.[14] Actually during the first decades of the twentieth century, the Vatican hierarchy pro-duced a number of documents reaffirming the church's opposition to "Modernism"—a term encompassing any attempt to arrive at knowledge of the divine solely through personal experience, delimited reason, or any other avenue outside the teachings of the church. The most important of these, Pope Pius X's 1907 encyclical *Pascendi dominici gregis*, unequivocally rejects the principle that "in a living religion everything is subject to change, and must in fact be changed."[15] Refusing to endorse the view that doctrine can evolve with the times, Pius X's encyclical complements Tate's theories nicely, suggesting that only a religion so opposed to change would have re-sisted the "fall" from feudalism into capitalism that proved the fountainhead of the South's confusion.

Tate's claim that the Old South was unknowingly Catholic, however, is dubious even according to the terms of his argument. His contention that southern society after Jamestown was feudal repeats a common failure to distinguish feudalism from slavery. The essential feature of capitalism for Tate, as for earlier southern theorists, is its use of wage labor. Since neither feudalism nor slavery is a wage system of labor, the logic goes, both must be less exploitative and profit-driven.[16] Slavery, however, supported not a subsistence economy devoted to leisure and religion but a capitalist econ-omy whose principal crops—sugar, tobacco, and cotton—were luxury goods exported to international markets. Far from betokening a retreat from capitalism, as Tate asserts, slavery contributed to capitalism's development in the South.[17] In truth Tate would have been more consistent had he identified Protestantism as the South's authentic religion.

Unfortunately for Tate, the other Agrarians were less determined to establish a single religion for the South, and most saw no problem with regarding even the most demanding orthodoxies as necessary fictions. That is to say, they did not insist, as Tate did, on a fundamental distinction between myth and religion. Nevertheless, they acknowledged the attraction of Catholicism as a doctrinally rigorous creed with anticapitalist affinities and forged alliances with Catholic intellectuals. The second of the two Agrarian symposia, *Who Owns America?*, became a joint project with anti-industrialist Catholic leaders, many of whom identified with the English Distributist movement of Hilaire Belloc and G. K. Chesterton.[18] Dorothy Day, the publisher of the *Catholic Worker* magazine, also pledged support to the cause and became a close friend to Tate and Gordon. Yet despite this apparent broadening of its political base, Agrarianism was already on the wane, and Conkin suggests that the dilution of the straight Agrarian line in *Who Owns America?* may have hastened this decline.[19] The collaboration with Catholics, however, confirmed Tate's attraction to Rome and drew him nearer to embracing Catholicism as the last hope for southern authenticity.

As Tate became more involved with Catholic intellectuals, his poetry grew increasingly religious in theme, wrestling more and more with the difficulties of belief and unbelief. Only in his 1938 novel *The Fathers*, however, does Tate represent Catholicism directly—and here it appears, surprisingly, allied with rootlessness, lack of tradition, and delusion. The novel's two families embody an almost schematic opposition of worldviews: the Buchans of northern Virginia represent the traditions of the eighteenth-century squirearchy, which include honor, rationalism, a respect for tradition, and love of the land, while the urban Poseys, dwelling in Georgetown, represent modern alienation from family and the soil coupled with a typically Romantic lust for movement, activity, passion, and abstraction. The novel does at one point suggest that George Posey has abandoned his family's Catholicism and suffers from this unmooring: "In a world in which all men were like him, George would not have suffered—and he did suffer—the shock of communion with a world that he could not recover; while that world existed, its piety, its order, its elaborate rigamarole—his own forfeited heritage—teased him like a nightmare."[20] Yet if George's "forfeited heritage" refers to the church, then its grammatical apposition with "its elaborate rigamarole" hardly seems affirmative. Here Lacy Buchan, the narrator, seems to adopt the view of most Agrarians concerning religion: while religious conviction may afford the benefits of "piety," "order," and a "heritage," it remains a fiction that keener intellects may recognize as necessary but no less fictive.

Other members of the Posey family, however—who have not apparently "forfeited" their heritage—remain claustrophobically isolated from both each other and the larger world. Lacy speaks of the "world of closed upstairs rooms" that the Poseys inhabit (*TF* 182) and details the incipient madness of such family members as Aunt Milly and Mr. Jarman. Catholicism provides few, if any, of the benefits that flow from authentic religion; Lacy exasperatedly remarks at one point that its ritual does no more than prevent the Poseys from "throw[ing] one another at death into the river (*TF* 256). In other words, Catholicism restrains the Poseys' essential savageness, which would otherwise brutally deny the ties of family, place, and affection, but works no further civilizing effects on their lives.

Why, then, would Tate present Catholicism so negatively precisely when he was moving toward the church himself? The explanation surely involves more than Tate's inability to believe as of yet. After all, by 1938 Tate had accepted the desirability of belief and committed himself to its defense: why then does his portrait of believers prove so disturbing? I would argue that in *The Fathers*, Tate's ongoing attempt to construct Catholicism as the grounding for a conservative vision of southernness collides with the widespread association between Catholicism and miscegenation. Even though Catholicism colors the Poseys' existence, the church's only direct intervention into their lives occurs when the specter of miscegenation rears its head.

Halfway through the novel, young Jane Posey, with whom Lacy is in love, is found unconscious in her room, and circumstantial evidence suggests that she has been raped by Yellow Jim, a family slave who is also George Posey's half brother. White supremacy demands restitution for this crime, and Semmes Buchan, Jane's fiancé and Lacy's brother, determines to kill Jim. As for Jane herself, she is whisked away to the convent at once. Father Monahan, encountering Lacy the next day, explains that "the girl can never be the bride of any man." Tellingly Father Monahan anticipates an objection to his plan: staring at Lacy with "heavy beads of sweat on his forehead," he declares, "We've got to keep life simple. That is a practical reason for saving the human soul" (*TF* 236). Even if Jane does not want to go into the convent, even if Jim's guilt is not certain, the priest avows that there is no socially sanctioned alternative for Jane. Any other course of action would create needless complexity, confuse others, and render the business of saving souls more difficult. Monahan's certainty recalls Cable's Père

Jerome and the nuns of Dunbar-Nelson's "Sister Josepha." Like them he holds that when evidence of miscegenation appears, whether in the form of children abandoned by a white father or white women allegedly raped by black men, the church is there to protect its victims. The lack of any objection to his plan suggests that the church's connection with miscegenation would have remained familiar to white southerners as late as 1938.

Yet if the church first appears as a cleanup crew, containing the toxic effects of miscegenation by confining them to convents, a further plot development in *The Fathers* complicates this picture. When Susan Posey, sister to Semmes and Lacy Buchan and wife to George Posey, discovers the plan to kill Yellow Jim, she forbids it, saying, "George Posey, if you allow my brother to shoot your brother for you, I will never see you again" (*TF* 253). In identifying Yellow Jim as George's brother, Susan both reveals the double standard that applies to miscegenation and exposes the essential Posey savagery: George's willingness to kill his half brother appears monstrous, in implicit contradistinction to the Buchan reverence for family, even if George's kinship with Yellow Jim is not publicly acknowledged. The claim of consanguinity here should outweigh the social demand for vengeance, even if that familial claim is itself based on a previous act of rape that went unpunished. To the extent that Catholicism accepts this double standard, allowing Jim to be killed in the interests of "keeping life simple" while George Posey's father lived unharmed, it contributes to the problem it would seem to contain: some forms of miscegenation go unchecked, while others demand "justice" and determine young women's lives. It is ironic that Jim's final action before he is killed by Semmes is to cross himself, since Father Monahan's professed need to save souls seems to find a black man in his position utterly expendable.

Tate's representation of Catholicism in *The Fathers*, then, questions the extent to which southern identity and the church can overlap. Even as he became increasingly attracted to the metaphysical grounding for "southernness" that the church might afford, his account of a church that acquiesces in one form of miscegenation and quietly mops up the effects of another hardly recommends itself to a white southern society invested above all in racial "purity." If the linkage between Catholicism and miscegenation precludes any simple equation of "southernness" and Catholicism, then Tate's conversion in 1950 must have entailed the de-emphasizing of race as a constituent of southern identity. Michael Kreyling has observed that the Agrarians, with the exception of Robert Penn Warren, refused to address or acknowledge issues of race in their polemics and apologetics, even as white supremacy remained an essential subtext of their ideology and aims.[21] Tate's own commentary on racial issues during the 1930s indicated all too clearly that his vision of southern community included a reflexive white supremacy—as when, in his review of the 1934 collection *Culture in the South*, he wrote:

> I argue it this way: the white race seems determined to rule the Negro race in its midst; I belong to the white race; therefore I intend to support white rule. Lynching is a symptom of weak, inefficient rule; but you can't destroy lynching by *fiat* or social agitation; lynching will disappear when the white race is satisfied that its supremacy will not be questioned in social crises.[22]

Tate's defense all but admits that actual lynchings usually had everything to do with the maintenance of white supremacy and nothing to do with crimes of rape against women.

It is striking, however, that even without giving Yellow Jim's execution the full symbolic overdetermination of lynchings that involve hanging, castration, and fire, Tate feels compelled to cite the probability of rape as the justification for Yellow Jim's death. Furthermore Yellow Jim's status as a slave who has run away and thus tasted freedom conforms to a familiar racist logic that white southerners often promoted in the years after emancipation. In Robyn Wiegman's words, "While the slavery period often envisioned the Uncle Tom figure as the signification of the 'positive good' of a system that protected and cared for its black 'children,' once emancipated, these children became virile men who wanted for themselves the ultimate symbol of white civilization: the white woman."[23] The Poseys' Catholicism presented in *The Fathers* may be silent before the injustice of lynching, but to the extent that it has tolerated miscegenation at all—and then allowed Yellow Jim back into the family after freedom has made him dangerous—it has already wrought damage by promoting what Tate calls "inefficient rule."

By 1950, however, Tate had converted to Catholicism and in subsequent decades maintained his membership in a church that provided increasing if inconsistent support for the civil rights movement. At the same time, he did not abandon his claim to southernness, as a letter of 1 January 1952 to Walker Percy indicates:

> When Andrew Lytle says he can't join the Catholic Church because it isn't in the Southern tradition, what he ought to mean is that the South has no tradition without the Church; for the thing that we all still cherish in the South was originally and fundamentally Catholic Christianity. Andrew's

position is sheer idolatry—worship of a golden calf, mere secularism—and alas his views are more representative today than yours or mine—or yours and mine. Twenty years ago I knew that religion was the key to the South (as it is to everything else) but I didn't see far enough then.[24]

From within his new faith, then, Tate declares that his fellow ex-Agrarians are in the throes of delusion, worshiping a myth of southern history rather than God. In this way, he constructs a new position of authority for himself as both the successor to and the fulfillment of the Agrarian legacy. At the same time, however, he remained an avowed Catholic and southerner even when in February 1956 Archbishop Joseph Rummel of New Orleans issued a pastoral letter in which he condemned racial segregation as "morally wrong and sinful" and urged compliance with the injunctions of *Brown v. Board of Education*.[25] Indeed by 1962, just as the Second Vatican Council was beginning to stir, Tate would write to the still vehemently segregationist Donald Davidson that despite his lingering discomfort, he was now "in favor of Negro rights," including both voting rights and integration. While in the 1930s Tate may have been uncomfortable with Catholic attitudes toward white supremacy because of their implications for southern identity, the Catholic Tate no longer invoked race and displayed a new confidence: he spent much of the decade as a polemical defender of Catholicism, high culture, and the cold war, purged of the ironies and self-consciousness that had given his earlier work a genuine complexity.

Yet for all Tate's avowed confidence, his influence on the spiritual and political life of the culture at large remained negligible. Despite his stated ambition to become a spokesperson for the revival of Catholic humanism, Tate found himself not more but less engaged with the Zeitgeist after his conversion, as he admitted in an address delivered at the University of Minnesota on 1 May 1952: "While the politician, in his cynical innocence, uses society, the man of letters disdainfully, or perhaps even absentmindedly, withdraws from it. . . . I have drawn in outline the melancholy portrait of the man who stands before you."[26] Tate's withdrawal even entailed the end of his poetic career, for after the three terza rima poems of 1952–53, "The Maimed Man," "The Swimmers," and "The Buried Lake," Tate published almost no more poetry. Brinkmeyer, recalling Tate's fondness for the Yeatsian epigram that "poetry results from our quarrels with ourselves, while rhetoric grows from our quarrels with others," argues convincingly that Tate's conversion had "resolved the tensions and problems that for so long had fired his creative genius" and thus deprived him of any need to write poems.[27] Having come to believe in his equation of the southern and Catholic worldviews, Tate lapsed into serene poetic silence. It would be left to Gordon and O'Connor to explore the possibilities of a consciously southern and Catholic literature.

꙳

During the same decade that Tate promoted Agrarian politics, flirted with Distributism, and worked through the notion of Catholicism as a feudal, fundamentalist, and quintessentially southern religion, an implicit critique of his ideas appeared in a surprising source: Margaret Mitchell's *Gone with the Wind*, the most popular of southern novels. Contemporary southern reviewers of the novel largely agreed that *Gone with the Wind* did not reward close scrutiny: the leftist Lillian Smith, for instance, called it a "curious puffball . . . rolled in sugary sentimentality," while Caroline Gordon, at the opposite end of the political spectrum, described it as "half a dozen of the best plots in the world wrapped up with the Civil War as cellophane."[28] Historicist criticism of the last two decades, however, has begun to question this belief, examining the novel's depiction of race relations and gender roles, its interpretation of the Civil War and Reconstruction, and its treatment of the tensions between Old and New South ideologies.[29] Yet oddly enough, religion has gone unnoticed—a lack of attention all the more striking when one considers that Scarlett O'Hara, one of the most well-known southern icons, is Catholic.

Mitchell, whose career as a journalist kept her informed about contemporary political debates, probably knew of the Agrarians' interest in religion and their collaboration with Catholic intellectuals. Her own opinions, however, suggest that she would have been enamored of neither the Agrarians' neo-Confederate nostalgia nor their attraction to Catholicism. Although baptized a Catholic, Mitchell lost her faith at an early age and maintained until the end of her life a skeptical and scornful attitude toward the church.[30] Moreover even though her authorship of *Gone with the Wind* led many to view her as an apologist for the Old South, Mitchell considered herself "a product of the Jazz Age . . . who preachers said would go to hell or be hanged before . . . thirty" and expressed embarrassment at finding herself called "the incarnate spirit of the old South."[31] Given these attitudes, it is not surprising that Mitchell's depiction of Old Southern Catholicism in *Gone with the Wind* is less affirmative than the praise of the "feudal religion" voiced by Tate. Where Tate depicts Catholicism as a great unifying force, untroubled by skepticism or internal conflicts, Mitchell presents a Catholicism divided along class and ethnic lines, a field in which different political impulses compete for supremacy.

Nevertheless, the perception of Catholicism as a feudal religion does find its way into *Gone with the Wind* in the figure of Ellen O'Hara, the epitome of aristocratic blood and conduct. As a native of Savannah (an old, refined city contrasted in the novel with the youth and crudity of Atlanta), a descendant of wealthy French planters fled to America from Haiti, and the embodiment of paternalist noblesse oblige, Ellen fulfills many of the obvious requirements of the southern lady. What makes her unusual, however, is the extent to which her actions are informed by her religion. Her program of training her daughters in the ways of ladyhood includes instruction in Catholic belief and practice, and one of her most important duties is to preside over the family's nightly praying of the Rosary—a display of piety that spurs Scarlett to sacrilegious admiration and prompts remorse for her sins when nothing else can. Most significantly Ellen displays the depth of her religious faith by threatening to become a nun as a young woman unless her parents allow her to marry Gerald O'Hara. Although her threat is rooted in anger— she wishes to escape her parents, who have driven away her beau, Philippe Robillard—her refusal to consider any other alternative evinces a deep-seated belief that women must devote themselves entirely to either their family or the church. Her youngest daughter, Carreen, later carries on this belief when, prevented from marrying Brent Tarleton by his death in the war, she enters the convent at Charleston. Throughout her life, Ellen never questions the teachings of the church and always acts as if her choices are predetermined. She displays, in short, the character of "fundamentalism" that Tate and Ransom prized so highly—an unswerving, never-challenged orthodoxy.

Viewed against Ellen's piety and nobility, Gerald O'Hara comes across as neither particularly feudal nor particularly Catholic. Although his family had once owned land before their dispossession by the forces of William of Orange, Gerald himself was born into poverty, and his famous paean to land as "the only thing in this world that lasts" reveals less his distant claim to aristocracy than the "deep hunger of an Irishman who has been a tenant."[32] Even more commonplace than his origins is his start in America: he begins work as a clerk in his brothers' store in Savannah, a calling for which the self-described planters of Georgia would have had only contempt. Gerald is, as the narrator states, a "self-made man" (*GWTW* 42)—or, in the cruder characterization of Rhett Butler, a "smart Mick on the make" (*GWTW* 902). Lacking the cultivated indolence of Savannah society, Gerald displays instead the bourgeois virtues of tenacity and forthrightness. When he seizes the opportunity to win Tara by besting a less skillful opponent in a poker game, Gerald becomes an exemplar of the American trajectory of "rags to riches"—a narrative for which the Agrarians would have felt only contempt.

Gerald is depicted as inferior to his wife not only because of his class position, but also because he lacks her personal piety. Although described as a "staunch Catholic" (*GWTW* 281), his faith consists largely of an identification with his Ireland and hatred for England, and matches Ellen's neither in depth of conviction nor rigor of practice. Where Ellen is calm, virtuous, and self-denying, Gerald is voluble, shrewd, and self-indulgent. This is not to deny that Gerald possesses, as the narrator states, "the tenderest of hearts" (*GWTW* 30); his purchase of Prissy to keep Dilsey from grieving reveals as much. Unlike Ellen's kindnesses, however, which are demanded by her religion and her class position, Gerald's acts of beneficence are spontaneous outbursts of feeling. As with George Posey of *The Fathers*, Gerald's emotions are always "personal," unrestrained by the dictates of social or ethical codes. If southern Catholicism is to be measured, as Tate suggests, by the strength of its feudal and fundamentalist characteristics, then Gerald emerges as only marginally Catholic.

Although Scarlett oscillates between her parents' two styles of Catholicism, her deepest sympathies are with Gerald's energetic go-getterism. To be sure, she continues to idolize her mother and to suffer attacks of "an active Catholic conscience" (*GWTW* 946) until the end of the novel. Yet her actions, from her marriage of convenience to Frank Kennedy to her use of convict labor in her sawmill, indicate that she regards her mother's religion, with its rigorous moral code, as an obstacle to survival in the new world of Reconstruction. As Richard King has pointed out, *Gone with the Wind* "exemplifies the historical consciousness underlying the 'New South creed.'"[33] The boosters of the New South, like Scarlett herself, venerated the old antebellum order but had no desire to return to it. In the New South, religion could be taken or left—and would be left if it interfered too much with the pursuit of success.

Gerald's funeral marks the breakdown of the synthesis between southern aristocracy and Catholicism. The death of the O'Hara patriarch coincides with the announcement of Suellen's marriage to the "cracker" Will Benteen—a transgression of class boundaries that would have been unthinkable before the war. Just as the marriage compromises the O'Haras' class position, the funeral compromises their Catholicism. Unable to procure a priest, Ashley Wilkes takes charge of the service. In an act of withering irony, he demonstrates that even Ellen's devout, unquestioning faith must now take a backseat to the prejudices of his neighbors:

> When Ashley came to the part of the prayers concerning the souls in Purgatory, which Carreen had marked for him to read, he abruptly closed the book. Only Carreen noticed the omission and looked up puzzled, as he began the Lord's Prayer. Ashley knew that half the people present had never heard of Purgatory and those who had would take it as a personal affront, if he insinuated, even in prayer, that so fine a man as Mr. O'Hara had not gone straight to Heaven. So, in deference to public opinion, he skipped all mention of Purgatory. (*GWTW* 708)

Ashley then continues with the prayers from the Episcopalian service. Although these prayers reassure the mourners, they also constitute an unwitting insult to Gerald: "Sturdy Baptists and Methodists all, [the mourners] thought it the Catholic ceremony and immediately rearranged their first opinion that the Catholic services were cold and Popish. Scarlett and Suellen were equally ignorant and thought the words comforting and beautiful. Only Melanie and Carreen realized that a devoutly Catholic Irishman was being laid to rest by the Church of England's service" (*GWTW* 709). Carreen takes her indignation at this insult with her into the convent; Scarlett remains oblivious to it. This quiet foregoing of distinct Catholic practice at so important a moment suggests that Catholicism has conceded too much to the demands of north Georgia etiquette and become an empty ritual. Only Carreen preserves something of the old, uncompromised faith, but the novel invites us to share Scarlett's judgment that Carreen's flight into the convent is also a flight from reality.

Scarlett O'Hara finally appears as an oddly appropriate figure to represent the crisis of religious belief that Tate describes in "Remarks on the Southern Religion." Like many white southerners of the 1930s, she finds herself torn between the affirmation of old traditions and the embrace of a New South ethos fully committed to modernization, capitalism, and the priority of ends over means. Where Tate and the Agrarians urged the recovery of old forms and old-time religion, Scarlett—whose faith is already marked by class and ethnic division—elects to march into the brave new world. Tomorrow is another day indeed.

❧

The expression of a consciously Catholic, southern, and Agrarian literature, suggested by Tate in the 1930s, would not emerge until after Caroline Gor-

don converted to Catholicism in 1947. Like her husband, Gordon first became interested in the church because she found it congenial to the
conservative and antimodern traditions of the Old South. Writing to her
friend Sally Wood in 1930, during the first flush of Agrarian activity, she
declared that it would be best if "all of us that can turn Catholic at once."[34]
Although she attributed her conversion to many factors, she gave particular
credit to her experience as a writer. In a letter to Brainard Cheney, she
wrote: "I am a Catholic, I suspect, because I was first a fiction writer. If I
hadn't worked at writing fiction for so long I doubt if I'd have made it into
the Church, but working at writing fiction all those years taught me how
god-like a trade it is. We are actually trying to do what God did: make our
word flesh and make it live among men."[35] This statement suggests that she
was answering the theoretical problem that Tate had raised two decades before: how to reconcile authentic belief with the intellect.

Tate's horse in "Remarks on the Southern Religion" could not be depicted because rational language would destroy its wholeness. Gordon,
however, theorizes that fiction is a religious form of language, a means of
doing justice to the whole horse. Following the French theologian Jacques
Maritain, Gordon holds that the fiction writer perceives the indivisibility of
the abstract Logos from the materiality of art and so has a great advantage in
understanding and making manifest the analogous indissolubility of God
and humanity in Jesus. In Maritain's words, "The [work of art] is the fruit
of a spiritual marriage uniting the activity of the artist to the passivity of a
given matter."[36] Fiction, then, is an inherently Christian undertaking, and
its materiality aligns it with the icons, sacraments, and devotions of Catholicism. Rather like Mikhail Bakhtin, whose foregrounding of the novel affirms its "lowly" and all-embracing nature, Gordon privileges fiction as the
medium most capable of expressing the profusion of God's creation and
love: as she tells Walker Percy, "the piling of detail upon detail" characteristic of fiction is the surest means of conveying the mystery of incarnation.[37]

Despite a number of similarities between Gordon's theory of fiction and
some of the tenets of the emerging New Criticism, the differences between
them are finally more striking. Her championing of fiction itself differs from
the New Critics' preference for the relative austerity of poetry. And even
though, as Paul Giles observes, "the New Critical fascination with pun and
paradox can be seen not just as a dedication to the independent artistic arti-
fact but also as the functioning of a specifically Christian cultural ideology,"
most New Critics were unambiguous in their statements about the separation of religion and literature, from Cleanth Brooks's assertion that "*literature*

is not a surrogate for religion" (emphasis in text) to W. K. Wimsatt's more rue-
ful claim that we must not expect poetry to serve as myth or religion, "to
do the things it did best in the pre-Homeric age."[38] Therefore, even though
her emphasis on the inherent good of fictional works often recalls the New
Critical valorization of form, Gordon's belief that fiction reveals not only
patterns of order and meaning but transcendent Christian truths goes far beyond what most New Critics maintained and may have even smacked of
heresy to some. Most fundamentally, however, at a time when Wimsatt and
Beardsley's "intentional fallacy" was becoming a piece of critical dogma,
Gordon's position on readerly interpretation of fiction tries to have it both
ways. The text itself, if successfully executed, reveals its Catholic message,
but if readers in their spiritual blindness fail to see the truth, then the author's stated intentions become the interpretive last word. Like O'Connor,
Gordon was ultimately an intentionalist who asserted the priority of her intentions in her fiction over any competing readings.

Gordon's characterization of fiction writing as a Catholic enterprise
never wanders far from her assumption that spirit and matter are inseparable.
Accordingly she criticizes many Catholic writers who oppose the two, assume a didactic stance, and end by producing mere propaganda. As Anita J.
Gandolfo points out, the phrase "Catholic novel" in the pre-Vatican II
United States was almost an oxymoron, for such works were usually "sublit-
erary parochial publication" judged on the basis of their "value as an evan-
gelizing force" and therefore "inimical" to the "inherently dialogic"
interaction with the world that properly distinguishes novels.[39] Within this
historical context, Gordon's definition provides a means of placing non-
Catholic literary works of merit under a Catholic, or at least Christian, rubric. Significantly she argues in a letter to Percy in the fall of 1952 that James
Joyce and W. B. Yeats are "better Christians . . . than Mauriac, Bernanos,
and Greene, partly because their work is based on the natural order, while
[the latter writers] reject the natural order and thereby land in Manichean
despair."[40] While Gordon's position has a coherent logic, it is vulnerable to
the same charge of distortion that Tate faced in his attempt to identify the
southern religion as Catholicism. After all if even Yeats can pass for a Christian writer, then what does a non-Christian writer look like? Gordon's
claim, however, only echoes Maritain's even more extraordinary assertion
that the best pre-Christian art, whether "Egyptian, Greek, or Chinese," is
"already Christian" whenever it "has attained a certain degree of grandeur
and purity."[41]

Given such a broad definition, which makes nearly all good artists unknowing Christians, it is not immediately clear why southern writers should have any claim to distinction. Yet despite her debt to Maritain, Gordon also presents her Catholic theory of literature as one realization of the Agrarian ideology. Having grown up on a farm, unlike all the Agrarians except Andrew Lytle, she sympathized with the Agrarians' beliefs and platform, although she also suspected that "the boys" did not have enough firsthand knowledge of farm life to be convincing leaders.[42] Her novels of the 1930s, *Penhally; Aleck Maury, Sportsman; None Shall Look Back;* and *The Garden of Adonis*, were warmly embraced by the Agrarians, with the character of Aleck Maury receiving special commendation as a prototypical Agrarian hero.[43] As Agrarian politics went into decline and Gordon herself entered her Catholic phase, however, she came to believe that certain brands of Catholic activism—most notably Dorothy Day's Catholic Worker movement—were more effective and authentic expressions of Agrarianism. Writing to Percy in the summer of 1952, Gordon relates that Day has established a lay apostolate whose members maintain rural hostels where daily Mass is celebrated. In effect Day and her associate Peter Maurin "have succeeded in doing what the Agrarians talked about."[44] Day's efforts appear, thinly disguised, in Gordon's novel *The Malefactors* as the "Green Revolution," a movement of clergy and lay Catholics who run farms and soup kitchens and maintain that "people ought to live in communal villages and go out and work the land."[45] While it may be unclear how Gordon's fictive revolution fulfills the specifics of the Agrarian agenda, her implication that an explicitly Catholic Agrarian platform would have succeeded is unmistakable.

Gordon's short story "The Presence," published soon after her conversion in 1948, marks her first conscious attempt to create a southern and Catholic literary work. In this story, Aleck Maury makes his final appearance, at the age of seventy-five. Ailing, lonely, contemptuous of the modern world and prone to self-pity, Maury suddenly remembers the death of his aunt. He had been present when, in the midst of praying the Hail Mary, she had cried out, apparently looking at a point over his shoulder. Maury, who was thirteen at the time, had not thought much of the event. Now, however, facing death, he wonders what it was his aunt saw, and the text ends with the suggestion that he might convert to Catholicism just in the nick of time. Indeed the last sentence of the story, which shifts into free indirect discourse, completes his aunt's prayer: "Holy Mary, Mother of God, pray for us sinners, now and at the *hour* . . . of our death."[46]

Since Maury was well established as an Agrarian hero when Gordon wrote "The Presence," it seems likely that she intended to portray Catholicism as the logical fulfillment of Agrarianism and to show that without the church, the Agrarian approach to religious questions remained confused. The young Maury's confusion of the Virgin Mary with jealous Juno in the story, for instance, suggests Gordon's disapproval of the Agrarians' attempt to fudge the distinction between myth and religion. At the same time, however, Gordon omits an actual conversion from the story and so avoids a straightforward happy ending. This absence of a conversion would continue in her subsequent fictional works, and while it would rescue them from the appearance of didacticism, it would also make her intentions less clear. Gordon no doubt believed, if her statements about the incarnational nature of fiction are taken at their word, that the work itself embodied the Catholic message and had no need to be more explicit. But without more pointed clues—and especially given the paucity of Catholics in her work—the problem of how readers are to discern the Catholic message remains.

Gordon's *The Strange Children*, the first of her postconversion novels, exemplifies this problem of interpretation. In one sense, the novel reworks the theme of "The Presence." Nine-year-old Lucy Lewis, Aleck Maury's granddaughter, lives on her parents' farm in conditions that suggest the Agrarian ideal. The ideal, however, is soon revealed to be empty. A portrait of Stonewall Jackson hangs on the wall, but his eyes stare "unseeingly" and he looks "like an old man"; Lucy's father treats the southern tradition only as something to pillage for his writing, and even Yankees like Tubby McCollum have been able to exploit southern myths for gain, commodifying the Civil War to the point where a publisher is willing to pay "twenty-five thousand just for the title" of an epic poem.[47] Lucy's mother has "got more fool ideas than any white woman [Lucy] ever saw" (*TSC* 89), and daily life on the farm consists mainly of vapid social calls from neighbors, drunken binges and hangovers, and desultory talk about the MacDonoughs, the Lewises' poor white tenants. During the time span of the novel, two friends of Lucy's father, Tubby McCollum and Kevin Reardon, are visiting, and Lucy is faced with the question of which of the two men is a better role model. Since McCollum is not only a Yankee but an adulterer and a man who patronizes the MacDonoughs' religious faith, while Reardon is a Catholic convert who is about to give his fortune to a Trappist monastery, in one sense there is little doubt as to what the outcome will be. The unusually perceptive Lucy chooses Reardon and affirms her choice by returning a crucifix that she had stolen from him.

Yet despite this conclusion, there is much in *The Strange Children* that obscures Gordon's Catholic intentions. Using the Jamesian device of the central intelligence, Gordon presents the action from Lucy's youthful and sometimes naive point of view, thus compelling readers to revise their judgments continuously. Furthermore Reardon remains an exotic, even mysterious figure who cannot be regarded as simply affirmative, and much of the "positive" depiction of religion in the novel flows not from him but from the evangelical, snake-handling MacDonoughs, whose sincerity of faith is beyond question: "When Mr. MacDonough or Mrs. MacDonough said 'Jesus' you felt as if He were in the next room" (*TSC* 108). Finally the outcome at the close of the novel is left suspended, just as it was in "The Presence." Lucy does not become Catholic, and the final word in the novel is given to her father, Stephen, in the form of an abrupt epiphany:

> He raised his eyes to the sky. . . . A Perseid fell, trailing its golden dust, and then another: little meteors that had been falling through space for God knows how many years. But the other stars that shone so high and cold would fall, too, like rotten fruit—when the heavens were rolled up like a scroll and the earth reeled to and fro like a drunkard and men called upon the mountains to fall upon them and hide them from the wrath to come. This very hill upon which he stood would shake. The river which lapped it so gently might turn and, raging against it, tear it from its green base and hurl it toward the sea. But there would be no sea! . . .
>
> He thought of another man [Reardon], the friend of his youth, who only a few minutes ago had left his house without farewell. He had considered him the most gifted of all his intimates. Always when he thought of that friend a light had seemed to play about his head. He saw him standing now at the edge of a desert that he must cross: if he turned and looked back his face would be featureless, his eye sockets blank. Stephen Lewis thought of days, of years that they had spent together. He saw that those days, those years had been moving toward this moment and he wondered what moment was being prepared for him and for his wife and his child, and he groaned, so loud that the woman and the child stared at him, wondering too. (*TSC* 302–3)

This passage, with its apocalyptic imagery and its emphasis on the crucial importance of "this moment," illustrates, like numerous similar endings in Flannery O'Connor's fiction, a sudden and overwhelming descent of divine grace. Even a figure as unappealing as Stephen Lewis, Gordon implies, can receive the freely bestowed gift of grace and realize in that moment that he or she can "cross the desert" into the life of the church. But while Lewis's epiphany clearly supports such a religious reading, its lack of more explicit clues suggests to more secularly minded readers only that Lewis recognizes the distance between himself and Reardon. In short, readers without any knowledge of Gordon's theoretical premises may miss her didactic message entirely, while readers with such knowledge are apt to find the novel forced and predictable.

As if to prevent misreadings, Gordon turns in her next novel, *The Malefactors*, to a more blatant manipulation of Catholic symbols and ends the novel with the clear suggestion of an imminent conversion. The protagonist, Tom Claiborne, who in some respects resembles Tate, is presented as a victim of modernity—a poet suffering from writer's block, middle-aged malaise, and alienation from his wife and friends. Though a Tennessean by birth, Claiborne has spent much of his life in flight from his southern roots, living first among the expatriates in Paris, where he befriended the homosexual and suicidal poet Horne Watts (clearly modeled on Hart Crane), and later in Pennsylvania, where he settled with his wife, Vera, on a farm to create a superficial Agrarian facsimile on northern soil. Claiborne seeks to rejuvenate his life through alcohol, adultery, and finally separation from Vera—all of which predictably fail.

At the same time, Claiborne finds himself confronted with Catholic images and teachings wherever he turns. Sometimes these confrontations are oblique, such as when he overhears a farmer, a member of the Dunkard Brethren Church, condemn the artificial insemination of cattle as sinful because "It's against Nature . . . A man has got to live according to Nature—if he lives right" (*TM* 66). Although the farmer is not Catholic, his disapproval inevitably conjures up familiar Catholic injunctions against human artificial insemination and birth control.[48] At other times, however, the possibility of his conversion to Catholicism is put to him explicitly. He discovers that Catherine Pollard, an old friend who had converted after he had once told her in ironic exasperation to join the church, has become an enthusiastic worker in the Catholic-Agrarian "Green Revolution." Later he meets Joseph Tardieu, the founder of the movement, who has gone mad from a stroke but remains lucid enough to urge Claiborne to read Augustine (*TM* 227). Perhaps the oddest confrontation occurs when he meets Sister Immaculata, an Irish nun who accuses him of being "in a state of invincible ignorance" (*TM* 234) but predicts that he will convert. When Claiborne seeks out Vera again, he learns that she too has converted and become a nurse to the rapidly deteriorating Tardieu, and this discovery provokes panic in him.

The pattern quickly becomes obvious: the church is a kind of Hound of Heaven, and the more Claiborne flees it, the more relentlessly it pursues him.

Claiborne's own conversion experience springs from a dream in which Watts leads him through a cave to the praying figure of Catherine Pollard. After meeting with Catherine and learning that she has had the same dream, he drives away to reconcile himself with Vera, for as Catherine tells him, "a wife is subject to her husband, as the Church is subject to Christ" (*TM* 311). This antifeminist sentiment underscores again the traditionalism that had led her to the church in the first place. While such an opinion might seem a poor advertisement for Gordon's project to many readers, the proposition that Claiborne, having resisted all the appeals of the church until that point, would allow a rather banal dream to change his mind strains credibility nearly to the breaking point. As in *The Strange Children*, Gordon's attempt to depict the gratuitous and inscrutable workings of grace simply fails to convince.

Even more striking, however, is the affinity between Catholicism and homosexuality in *The Malefactors*—the same rich stew of decadence, homo-eroticism, and artistic production that we see in the work of Chopin, Mc-Cullers, and Rice, centered in Gordon's novel on the figure of Horne Watts. While Gordon's politics are overtly antifeminist and reactionary, her belief in the incarnational properties of art leads her to defend a figure opposed to conventional Catholic piety—a promiscuous gay poet who dabbles in alchemy, suffers from erotic cravings for blood, and finally commits suicide. This anomaly has gone unacknowledged by the novel's few critical defenders. Brainard Cheney's 1971 essay in the *Sewanee Review*, for example, looks back with nostalgia to the triumphant preconciliar Catholicism portrayed in the novel and deplores what relativism and science have wrought since then:

> But that was fifteen years ago!—when all of us converts were young in the Church and sainthood was a romantic, if not immediate, prospect, and the new Thomism buttressed us against scientific nihilism. A man could hang a St. Christopher's medal on the rear-view mirror of his car with some assurance of driving to Church in safety, there to hear, in the ancient and universal tongue of the Church, a mass chanted in Gregorian style and to see, at the sound of the bells, the body of Christ elevated, in all its medieval mystery. That was before Pope John XXIII opened the window to let a little fresh air into the Church and in came the Vatican Councils [*sic*]. That

was before the computer had brought the prospect of peace (and priests) to married life, without of course abolishing the divorce courts; and the pill had removed the prospect of marriage as a necessity altogether. The DNA code had not yet become our new language of life, nor had cybernetics yet robbed it of its last alternative, the test tube replaced the womb, and cryogenics put heaven on ice. . . .

But Miss Gordon, I say, is not yesterday's prophet, but tomorrow's. . . . Let me then, with a few tags, characterize this hour of the Age. The hour of Behaviorism's ambiguous triumph; the incoherent climax of the adolescent existentialism of our universities. The hour when our shrill and raucous ghetto rhetoric is answered by Little Sir Echo; when God is dead and his incarnation has reached the limits of scientific and vulgar speculation. It is my guess—the eleventh hour of our interregnum.[49]

Cheney's tirade against American life in the 1970s, although accurate enough in its characterization of Gordon's purposes and beliefs, is also stereotypically decadent in its awe before the glories of the Latin liturgy, the pomp and mystery of the Eucharist. Cheney does not, however, extend the same appreciation to the novel's presentation of Horne Watts, who is valorized as a man in search of God. To be sure, Cheney acknowledges Crane as the model for Watts, even pointing out that the title of Watts's major poem, *Pontifex,* alludes to *The Bridge.* The problematic aspect of Watts's presence in an aggressively Catholic novel, however, seems to elude Cheney. The novel's other gay character, the painter Max Shull, seems a better advertisement for Catholic piety, for although he had once been Watts's lover, he has since moved to a small cottage, resolved to conquer his homosexual desires, and begun work on a mural for the walls of Sister Immaculata's chapel. Nevertheless, it is Watts rather than Shull who receives clerical blessing. The novel's strenuous efforts to recuperate Watts for Catholicism suggest a greater acceptance of homosexuality in Gordon's work than one would expect—and make even more explicit the connections among Catholicism, decadence, queerness, and the aesthetic that Chopin and McCullers had examined.

The most significant defense of Watts occurs during a conversation between Sister Immaculata and Claiborne, whose friendship with Watts has always been strained by his jealousy of Watts's superior poetic craft. Sister Immaculata is at work on a book called *Companions in the Blood,* in which she compares Watts's life and achievement—including his bizarre experiments in alchemy and vampirism—to that of St. Catherine of Siena. Clai-

borne, to whom she appeals for biographical information about Watts, finds
her thesis ludicrous. As he explains to her,

> "I saw [Watts] frequently and he evidently underwent a period of moral
> degradation which may have been connected with his homosexuality. An
> erotic craving for blood was one of his symptoms. Miranda Proctor wrote
> me that when he visited her she had to ask her gardener to keep his fourteen-
> year-old boy out of the way; Horne attacked him once, with a knife. I've
> got a letter somewhere in which he says that he suspects that his powers are
> failing him but that he feels that they would come back—if only he could
> see blood. Enough blood was the way he put it."
>
> [Sister Immaculata] sighed deeply. "Ah, yes. Enough to inebriate him.
> That's all he asked for. That's all any of us ask for. Enough of the Blood of
> Christ to inebriate us."
>
> "Horne asked for about a quart of whisky a day too," he said.
>
> "I come from the Old Country," she said. "The men of me [*sic*] family
> are all drunkards. It takes the power of whisky to still a man's longing for the
> Blood of Christ."
>
> "Maybe it takes more of the blood of Christ to inebriate homosexuals
> than it does ordinary men," he said with a laugh.
>
> "They've an extraordinary longing for it," she said, "and a place in the
> Kingdom. Our Lord Himself said the last word on that: Some men are born
> eunuchs, some men are made eunuchs by men and some become eunuchs
> for the sake of the Kingdom of God." (*TM* 235–36)

Many contemporary readers, of course, will find Sister Immaculata's conflation of gay men with "eunuchs" objectionable. Yet the fact that Watts
himself had once uttered the same scriptural quotation—albeit in a very different context (*TM* 121)—suggests an eerie coincidence intended to point
up the inscrutable nature of divine grace.

Claiborne's attempt to focus on the corporeality of Watts's desires—his
need for alcohol, his pedophilic tendencies—becomes transmuted and aestheticized by Sister Immaculata into expressions of longing for the divine.
His vampirism, itself a common trope of decadence and degeneration, does
not faze Sister Immaculata in the least and becomes instead a sign of his
thirst for the redemptive power of Christ's blood. When Claiborne goes on
to express his own repugnance for homosexuality, she upbraids him: "And
what makes you think that you—or I—are so much better than they were?
When it comes to love, we're all like eunuchs in the presence of the Bride-
groom" (*TM* 237). Even Watts's suicide, traditionally viewed as a cause of

certain damnation, is reinterpreted as his way of "abandoning [him]sel[f] to God's mercy" (*TM* 242). When Claiborne concludes the interview by asking, "You think, then, that because he was a gifted poet God will forgive him for taking his own life?" (*TM* 242), Sister Immaculata does not deign to respond. Like the career of Oscar Wilde—another famously decadent poet who at the end of his life embraced Catholicism—Watts's suggests that the cult of the decadent male artist, bent on dissipating himself as he pursues his vision, is the truest paradigm for religious yearning and redemption. Watts's final appearance in the novel, as the agent of grace who leads his old friend Claiborne to Catholicism by appearing in a dream, would suggest that his erotic thirst for the "Blood" has not gone unquenched. A biographical reading of the novel might speculate that Gordon's treatment of Watts is her wishful means of "saving" Hart Crane, whom she and Tate admired. Nevertheless, given the unflinching presentation and juxtaposition of both militant Catholicism and rampant decadence in *The Malefactors*, one could make the somewhat tongue-in-cheek claim that it is among the "queerest" of southern novels. This queerness disrupts Gordon's wish to ground a reactionary worldview in the church, just as Tate's early presentation of Catholicism in *The Fathers* found itself confronting the destabilizing issue of miscegenation.

Unlike her earlier work, Gordon's fiction of the 1950s has received only lukewarm praise from southernist literary critics. M. E. Bradford, for instance, finds these novels "not so impressive as their predecessors" and insists that "Gordon's most accomplished fiction reflects the values and concerns of her Agrarian phase." Such a reception is perhaps understandable in light of the inconsistencies and sweeping generalizations that were, as I have argued, inherent in Gordon's new Catholic definition of literature itself. But it should also be emphasized that these readers were, for the most part, New Critics and that the model of literature that Gordon advanced through her fiction challenged their position. When Bradford goes on to praise Gordon's earlier novels because they embody principles that were "hers by birthright and inheritance, not by association," he reveals his own preference for the Agrarian shibboleths of myth and tradition over religion, implicitly faulting Gordon's Catholicism because it is not part of her "birthright and inheritance."[50] Gordon's theory of fiction, however, makes the opposing argument that without Catholicism, southern literature can neither transcend history nor lay any claim to authenticity.

In 1951 Flannery O'Connor sent a draft of her novel *Wise Blood* to Caroline Gordon for critical commentary, thus initiating a relationship with the older writer that would last until the end of her life. Though this mentoring relationship has been criticized as "dysfunctional" by critics who hold Gordon responsible for destroying O'Connor's original "female-sexed voice" and causing her to identify with masculinist ideologies, we should guard against the reductivism of assuming that Gordon and O'Connor's theological concerns were little more than a cover for the expression of ill-concealed misogyny.[51] From Gordon, O'Connor learned not just fictional craft and a greater identification with masculine roles but also an entire religio-aesthetic theory of fiction. Many of O'Connor's theoretical pronouncements derive from Gordon's statements about the incarnational and inherently Catholic nature of fiction, which in turn can be traced back to Tate's attempt to ground southern literature in an orthodox and feudal Catholicism. Both Tate's attempt to revive a nineteenth-century southern medievalism through the church and Gordon's sacramental aesthetic are implicated in particular notions of gender but certainly not reducible to them.

The fact that Gordon was a convert to Catholicism rather than a "cradle Catholic" probably made her more amenable to the aesthetics of Maritain than she would have been otherwise. As James J. Thompson notes, American Catholicism has been deeply marked by a Jansenist strain wary of the aesthetic. This Jansenism, associated with Irish priests who arrived in the 1840s, dominated the American Church well into the twentieth century and tended to use the promotion of piety as the chief criterion for judging literature.[52] Lacking any firsthand experience of this Jansenism, Gordon turned toward the more intellectual tradition of French Catholicism, which saw no contradiction between aesthetic appreciation and the moral teachings of the church. O'Connor, however, was born into this atmosphere of suspicion toward art—what she once called the "novena-rosary tradition" with its "nice vapid-Catholic distrust of finding God in action of any range and depth"—and regarded her own success with fiction as a necessary escape from such attitudes: "you have to save yourself from it someway or dry up."[53] Though O'Connor's determination to become a writer is clear long before she became acquainted with Gordon, to the extent that Gordon provided her with a rationale for abandoning the "novena-rosary tradition" without regret, she contributed to O'Connor's development. Moreover Gordon's insistence on the incarnational aspect of fiction provides a gloss on O'Connor's puzzling statement in "The Catholic Writer in the Protestant South" that the best southern and Catholic traditions are "the same." Just as Gordon would employ Protestant characters such as the MacDonoughs in *The Strange Children* to advance a professedly Catholic message,

O'Connor would argue that Catholic fiction "can't be categorized by sub-ject matter" and that any work devoted to the specificity of place, the won-der of incarnation, qualifies.[54]

O'Connor would also display Gordon's tendency toward shocking and portentous reversals at the end of her works. Just as *The Strange Children* and *The Malefactors* end with abrupt epiphanies intended to reveal the workings of divine grace, O'Connor would present the descent of grace in sudden, unexpected, and often violent terms—and both writers would justify these practices by appealing to the gratuitous, inscrutable nature of that grace and the irreducibly material ways it makes itself known. Furthermore, because this understanding of grace presents a stumbling block for many of O'Con-nor's readers, who see nihilism and mayhem in her endings, O'Connor, like Gordon, ultimately endorses intentionalism in interpretation, setting readers who "misread" her straight and insisting on the priority of her theological aims. O'Connor's sympathy with the hierarchical structure of the South and her belief in and her treatment of the workings of divine grace all suggest that she more properly belongs in Tate and Gordon's paradigm of southern and Catholic literature rather than among the anti-intentionalist and myth-oriented ranks of the New Critics.

The attempt of Gordon and Tate to carve out a Catholic definition of southern literature in the 1940s and 1950s represents a break within the old Agrarian movement, an effort to present an alternative to the New Critical model of southern literature that the other ex-Agrarians were building in American universities. Its desire to place southern literature beyond the rav-ages of history, in the timeless realm of the absolute, would be taken up both in their own later works and in the work of O'Connor, although at times their constructions of Catholicism became entangled with competing con-structions of the church with very different political resonances. Even though O'Connor's critical reputation has far eclipsed that of Gordon and Tate, any effort to restore her to contemporary historical context must ac-knowledge the crucial influence of these immediate mentors on her fiction and her declared southern Catholic identity.

≈

If O'Connor's death put an end to the literary production of this con-sciously southern and Catholic movement, the Second Vatican Council (1962–65) undermined the philosophical assumptions on which it was based. One result of these changes would be the highly visible role that many of the Catholic clergy played in the civil rights movement, as the church's new emphases on individual rights and ecumenism carried the day. If, as many white southerners at the time maintained, including such ex-Agrarians as Davidson, one's attitude toward the civil rights movement served as a litmus test for southernness, then Vatican II made it increasingly difficult for one to be both southern and Catholic.

For Tate, having come to Catholicism to fortify the southern tradition against the onslaught of modernity, Vatican II was a bewildering and unwelcome event that seemed to disavow the Church's raison d'être. Tate had asserted in "Remarks on the Southern Religion" that any religion that tried to accommodate itself to secular values would lose its distinctness and legitimacy, and he had not changed his position. "If the Ecumenical movement is merely a levelling [*sic*] process towards 20th century rationalism, it will fail," he wrote to Gordon on 12 November 1963.[55] Although he never renounced Catholicism, made an uncomfortable peace with the cause of civil rights, and received the last rites of the church when he died in 1979, his sense of alienation from the church grew more pronounced as preconciliar attitudes and practices disappeared.

Gordon, on the other hand, became more visibly devout in the years after Vatican II, but she continued to identify with the preconciliar church and with reactionary political positions. As her biographer Nancylee Novell Jonza reports,

> She deplored the use of the vernacular in the Catholic church, and she declared women ought not be allowed to vote. She also disapproved of the zip code: "this computerization of human beings" would be "a step toward the gas chambers of the future," she said. She even raged against structural grammar. "It is my sober and long considered conclusion that this movement is a new sort of Communist front, one that goes deeper underground in a way than any of them has ever gone," she said. "Destroying a people's language is a pretty effective way of brain-washing them."[56]

Bizarre as such ideas may be, however, they contain undeniable traces of Agrarian ideology. If particularity in written language is a virtue and bureaucratic regimentation an unmitigated evil, then zip codes and structural grammar might indeed be deplorable developments. Gordon's clinging to traditional Catholicism partakes of the same attitude, but the church in which she found herself was busily affirming the use of the vernacular and had no objection to zip codes, structural grammar, or women voting. Gordon died in 1981 without completing her most ambitious project, a two-part novel tentatively called *Behold My Trembling Heart*. One part of the novel, *The Narrow Heart*, was to be an autobiographical narrative interspersed with episodes from the lives of certain ancestors who had been involved with public figures. The other part, published in 1972 as *The Glory of Hera*, was a reworking of the myth of Heracles. Gordon's proposed plan, although vague, suggests that she wished to reveal an archetypal structure common to both the Greek myth and the autobiographical narrative: "The lower pattern [the Greek material] winds serpent-wise through the upper pattern of action and deals with the archetypal world which the present-day Jungians and the archaic Greek inform us lies at the very bottom of every human consciousness."[57]

The clearest hint of the role that Catholicism would have played in this massive work is a chapter from the unfinished "upper pattern," published in 1977 under the title "A Walk with the Accuser." This strange story, set in sixteenth-century Paris, depicts a midnight theological debate between Jean Cauvin, later John Calvin, and a stranger described only as "The Shadow." In a move that was probably suggested to her by O'Connor's use of the devil in *The Violent Bear It Away*, Gordon identifies the "Shadow" in a brief introduction to the story as the Devil, "shown in the act of deceiving the young Frenchman."[58] As a result of their debate, Calvin will later deliver one of his rivals, Michael Servetus, to the Inquisition to be burned at the stake. In one sense, the story shows Gordon's defense of Catholicism at its most extreme. By suggesting that Presbyterianism has a satanic origin, she attacks the ecumenism of postconciliar Catholicism, and although she implicitly condemns Calvin for handing Servetus over, she presents no corresponding condemnation against the inquisitors who put him to death for promoting heresy. On the basis of "A Walk with the Accuser" alone, readers might believe that Gordon's Catholicism had become fanatical.

This story, however, sits uneasily alongside the absence of Catholicism in *The Glory of Hera*. Brinkmeyer argues that in *The Glory of Hera*, Gordon returns to Maritain's theory that works of art need not be explicitly Christian to be considered Christian and portrays Heracles as a precursor to Christ. But Gordon's interest in Jung during this period complicates this explanation. Maritain's theory allows for a Christian interpretation of the Heracles myth but never implies that Christ and Heracles are interchangeable. Jungian theory, however, would treat Christ and Heracles as mere local variations on the same archetype, neither of which can be considered superior. By referring to Jung in her descriptions of her project, Gordon comes perilously close to admitting that Heracles can compete with Christ and therefore, as Tate had argued in "Remarks on the Southern Religion," depriving Christianity of its legitimacy. Even in "A Walk with the Accuser," Gordon's naming of the Devil as the "Shadow" suggests an unwitting equation between Jungian psychoanalysis and Catholic theology. Since it seems unlikely that Gordon intended such an interpretation, it may be kinder to her, her own statements notwithstanding, to conclude with Ashley Brown that *The Glory of Hera* is simply "a comedy of manners with the gods for characters" rather than a Christian allegory.[59] I would argue that the dichotomy between the fierce religiosity of "A Walk with the Accuser" and the explicitly Jungian concerns of *The Glory of Hera* reflects Gordon's own confusion within the postconciliar church. Wishing to defend Catholicism with inquisitorial zeal, Gordon discovers that in a modernized church, her old ideas about fiction as a Catholic enterprise are even less evident than before—and that her best hope in defending the church must now spring from such secular sources as Jungian theory. As for the relations between the South, Catholicism, and fiction, the incompleteness of *Behold My Trembling Heart* precludes any guesses as to what position Gordon would have taken. In any event, her old project of defining southern literature in Catholic terms, as a means of preserving a medievalist identity for the South and of affirming a sacramental definition of fiction, had lost its dubious coherence—and with its collapse came the last gasp of an Agrarian Catholicism.

5   *Toward Catholicism as Lifestyle: Walker Percy, John Kennedy Toole, and Rebecca Wells*

During the decade from 1955 to 1965, the civil rights movement emerged as a major political force in the South, and despite fierce resistance from southern whites, it began to achieve success. The Civil Rights Act of 1964 and the Voting Rights Act of 1965 abolished de jure racial segregation and ensured black southerners' right to vote, thus sounding the death knell of what many had long identified as the "southern way of life." For American Catholics, too, these were years of upheaval: John F. Kennedy's election as president in 1960 was followed swiftly by the Second Vatican Council, which precipitated, in Peter Huff's words, "the modernization of basic dogmas, the democratization of church structures, the liberalization of canon law, and the 'de-Romanization' of Catholicism itself."[1] And for white southern Catholics, who were digesting these changes just as their bishops were trying (without much intensity of effort or success) to convert them to an integrationist politics, the times were heady and bewildering. Entire systems of social and religious practice were questioned and rejected, with breathtaking speed. Meanwhile the rapid expansion of a consumer-based economy and its new media—above all, television—contributed to a new individualism that increasingly came to view such practices as lifestyle choices rather than marks of an essential identity. Neither South nor church nor nation would ever be the same.

Against this backdrop of political, religious, and cultural change, Walker Percy began his career as a writer, publishing his first important essay, "Stoicism in the South," in 1957 and his first novel, *The Moviegoer,* in 1961. Although a bona fide member of the southern gentry, boasting such famous relatives as his uncle, the planter-poet and memoirist William Alexander Percy, the younger Percy was also a committed integrationist and a convert to Catholicism. Biographical accounts of his 1947 conversion often stress his pursuit of metaphysical certainty—a journey that began with his loss of faith both in the stoic paternalism of his uncle and in the positivism of his medical studies and ended with his finally arriving at Catholicism after a roundabout, highly intellectual passage through Dostoevsky, Kierkegaard, and the French existentialists. In this respect, Percy's trajectory resembles Tate's: both were attracted by the church's doctrinal rigor and absolute claims. Yet whereas Tate's horror of abstraction often suggests an implicit irrationalism, a refusal to believe that faith and reason share any common ground, Percy's more complex position—described by Paul Giles as "Kierkegaard confronting Aquinas"—involves a seemingly contradictory affirmation both of the absurdity of faith and of its rational, systematic nature.[2] Moreover Percy's rationalism allows him to reject the medievalism implicit in Tate's vision of the church and to argue that intellectual defenders of a medieval ethos had merely superimposed a quasi-feudal and fundamentally stoic code upon a skeletal Christian framework. Hence Percy's critique of his "Uncle Will" in "Stoicism in the South": the chivalric Catholic veneer imposed on a feudal ideology by Walter Scott and others is bogus, "a Christianity . . . aestheticized by medieval trappings and a chivalry . . . abstracted from its sacramental setting."[3]

"Stoicism in the South," however, should not be seen merely in personal terms as the first installment of Percy's quarrel with his uncle: it is also an intervention in the racial and religious politics of the time. First appearing just months after Archbishop Rummel's pastoral letter declaring segregation sinful, "Stoicism in the South" argues that white southern ideology's greatest flaw is its failure to recognize the equality of African-Americans: "What the Stoic sees as the insolence of his former charge—and this is what he can't tolerate, the Negro's demanding his rights instead of being thankful for the squire's generosity—is in the Christian scheme the sacred right which must be accorded the individual, whether deemed insolent or not."[4] However well-intentioned Uncle Will's racial paternalism (abundantly on display in his memoir, *Lanterns on the Levee*) may have been, it must be rejected by a Catholicism defined by the equality of all fallen human beings. Percy's thinking reflects the influence of J. H. Fichter and Louis Twomey, two Jesuit priests from Loyola University in New Orleans who had given him his religious instruction and who had been active in interracial and progressive causes for some time, earning a good deal of hostility from many white Catholic southerners. (In fact Fichter's 1951 sociological study of a middle-class New Orleans parish, *Southern Parish,* had been so critical of the parishioners' racism and perfunctory religious practice that Fichter had been vilified by large segments of Catholic clergy and laity alike.)[5] But though support for integration was a minority position among white southern Catholics, it increasingly reflected the official position of Catholic bishops and provided a foretaste of the more fundamental transformations of Vatican II. Percy's conversion from paternalist white supremacy to a moderate liberalism went hand in hand with his religious conversion, as even his atheist friend Shelby Foote admitted.[6]

The most familiar reading of Percy's career refers only indirectly to his involvement in the political and religious transformations of his time. Instead, it casts him as a prophet in the wilderness, imploring readers to turn away from the empty consumerism and false gods of modernity—including, to be sure, white supremacist ideology—and toward the abundant life of the church. Instead of conflating the South with the church, as Tate and Gordon had attempted to do, Percy makes a deliberate choice between them. Having seen through the artificial barriers imposed by a racist social order, Percy's wayfaring protagonists are at liberty to perceive the sacramental grandeur of creation, the Hopkinsesque moments in which God's glory shines through the ordinariness of the world.[7] Yet for all his proselytizing impulses, the salvation of souls barely registers as a concern in his novels, while his representations of Catholicism have less to do with either eternity or sacramentalism than with the problem of living in interesting times. Percy's often-remarked apocalyptic strain—expressed by characters who fantasize about starting the world over again after some catastrophe—bespeaks less a desire for heaven than a wish to cleanse the world of its intractable historical follies.

At a number of key moments, Percy's protagonists—usually scions of a distinguished family brought up, like Percy himself, in the traditions of southern honor and noblesse oblige—turn yearningly toward the church. The stoic, paternalist ideology that once defined them has become incredible in a rapidly changing South, and their crises of identity are matters of anguish and high seriousness. Meanwhile the Catholics around them go on displaying traits that have, until now, struck them as frivolous: an indifference to metaphysical questions and heroic longings, a love of home comforts and fleshly pleasures, and a refusal to take themselves too seriously. Even if the protagonist is, like *The Moviegoer*'s Binx Bolling, nominally Catholic, he distinguishes between himself and these happy souls who wear their faith lightly. Their relentlessly ordinary way of life seems more enduring than his own, and he might be tempted to call himself (in a phrase that Lewis P. Simpson uses to describe Percy) "a survivor of a world that has ended."[8]

The most tormented of these protagonists, Lance Lamar from *Lancelot,* reflects on this contrast as he looks through his window in the Center for

Aberrant Behavior on All Souls' Day and watches the women scrubbing tombs in Lafayette Cemetery:

> There is a sense here of people seriously occupied with small tasks. We, you and I, our families, were different from the Creoles. We lived from one great event to another, tragic events, triumphant events, with years of melancholy in between. We lost Vicksburg, got slaughtered at Shiloh, fought duels, defied Huey Long, and were bored to death between times. The Creoles have the secret of living ordinary lives well. A hundred years from now I don't doubt that women like those out there will be scrubbing the tombs on All Souls' Day, a La Branche will be polishing his bar, and a dirty movie will be playing across the street.[9]

On one side, southern honor, with its grandiose codes of behavior; on the other, a contradictory but durable Creole Catholic mixture of piety, domesticity, alcohol, and pornography. Though Lance once had a "dislike of Catholics"—who appeared to him as "comical French peasants" (*L* 14)—his attitude is quite compatible with the nineteenth-century medievalist ideologies of the white South, while his contrast between Creole frivolity and Anglo-Saxon high-mindedness echoes George Washington Cable. Ironically Lance has managed to prolong a life of southern honor by becoming a "liberal," making himself exceedingly unpopular among whites, and taking up the cause of civil rights with fierce devotion. But after the political victories of the civil rights movement, Lance feels himself deprived of a raison d'être, believes himself to be living at what we might now call, following Francis Fukuyama, the "end of history," and cannot reconcile himself to the intolerable boredom that such a condition entails. Having realized that southern honor stands at the end of its tether, Lance now turns toward these Creole women wistfully. Perhaps epic deeds are no longer possible; perhaps, by the 1970s, adherence to old southern ideals appears comic when not offensive. Catholicism, however, affords more than adequate compensations: you can enjoy your po-boy and beer, delight in sex, and contemplate daily life without (as Will Barrett puts it in *The Second Coming*) "either wanting to kill somebody or swear a blood oath of allegiance with someone else."[10] Clearly it helps not to be Anglo-Saxon: the down-at-the-heels, multicultural, and complacent metropolis of New Orleans foregrounds the pleasures of difference, as it had for the *gens de couleur libres*. Lance's fantasies of apocalypse—enacted in the murder that has led to his confinement—thus prefigure his desire to escape southern ideologies, to join the ordinary Catholic world by living with Anna, his fellow survivor of catastrophe, in a little house under the levee.

If postmodernism is, in Jean-François Lyotard's famous formulation, characterized by "incredulity toward metanarratives," Catholicism in Percy's fiction proves postmodern in its incredulity toward the metanarrative called "white southern identity."[11] And just as Lyotard locates the imperative toward postmodernism in recent historical catastrophes—above all, two world wars and the unprecedented horror of the Holocaust—Percy's domestic Catholicism responds to the breakdown of the racial status quo in the South, a similarly traumatic event in the white southern imagination. His oeuvre relentlessly interrogates southernness as a determinant of personal identity. While the loss of meaning associated with this interrogation may be painful to his characters, refusal to accept this loss is regressive. Not only does the South prove inadequate as a transcendental signifier, its overcoming, however wrenching, is to be welcomed. Like Jean Baudrillard, whose theories of the simulacrum and preoccupation with apocalypse he uncannily anticipates, Percy might say, "Nothing (not even God) now disappears by coming to an end, by dying. Instead, things disappear through proliferation or contamination, by becoming saturated and transparent."[12] In a postsouthern world, the wisest accept this "transparency," this life among simulacra, rather than despairing.

There is, however, a further twist. Catholicism itself does not prove any more transcendent than white southern identity, despite Percy's intense desire that it do so. If the civil rights movement destroyed any sense that the southern racial hierarchy might be fixed in place forever, the concurrent upheaval of Vatican II destroyed any lingering belief in the church's ahistorical nature. Percy shows that the disappearance of "meaning" in the South does not necessarily spell the end of its familiar symbols, for his novels teem with recognizably southern tropes that have survived the onslaught of modernity. These tropes, however, no longer carry the heavy symbolic baggage that earlier white southerners would have discerned in them: they circulate as markers of southernness but in much the same way that souvenirs purchased at Graceland do. To invoke Walter Benjamin's terminology, they have been deprived of their aura.[13] In the same way, representations of Catholicism in Percy's novels go on, but without the portentous significance that they assume in the work of O'Connor or Gordon. Even the pleasures of Percy's Catholic characters are strangely watered down: instead of the decadent, aestheticized, sexually transgressive, and implicitly aristocratic tropes that marked many earlier representations of southern Catholicism,

Percy's Catholic representations are prosaic, quietly enduring, and almost entirely free from traces of medievalist or racialist thinking. Having deconstructed the white southern order, Percy's tropes of southern Catholic order deconstruct themselves. Transcendence, even of a daily, sacramental kind, is what non-Catholics and converts in Percy's work long for. Among "cradle" Catholics, it is rarely found.

Percy's response to his historical moment, then, involves the unwitting deconstruction of Catholicism, its transformation into a cozy domesticity that we would today call a form of "lifestyle"—that ubiquitous contemporary term that connotes both individual self-fashioning and unabashed consumption. This new departure within southern literary treatments of Catholicism would subsequently appear in such comic southern writers as John Kennedy Toole and Rebecca Wells. Though Percy's wrestling with the problem of a postmodern Catholicism first appears in *The Moviegoer,* it figures most prominently in *The Last Gentleman* (1966) and *Love in the Ruins* (1971)—the first novel written during the proceedings of Vatican II, the second incorporating Percy's response to the council itself. While *The Last Gentleman* still holds out hope for a transcendent Catholicism that will replace white southern identity as a metanarrative, *Love in the Ruins* suggests that such a hope is not viable and that henceforth Catholicism's value will be purely a matter of individual self-fashioning, something that one can take up and work variations on without reference to its truth claims.

Although in some respects, Percy's deconstructive Catholicism appears politically progressive, Toole's *A Confederacy of Dunces* (1981) and Wells's *Little Altars Everywhere* (1992) and *Divine Secrets of the Ya-Ya Sisterhood* (1996), all enormously popular novels, show how quickly and easily these progressive impulses would be co-opted by the force of a consumer economy. In Toole's novel, Catholicism would figure as the badge of a tawdry, working-class, and consumerist aesthetic on the one hand and as a parodic medievalism too complicit in this consumerism to level a coherent critique of it. In Wells's books, Catholicism is appropriated by a brand of second-wave feminism that sacrifices the political potential of Catholic inclusiveness to a boutique spiritualism that, in signifying everything, signifies nothing. These reductions of Catholicism to a trapping of lifestyle suggest not that Catholicism has lost its ambivalent connections to southern identity, but rather that both Catholicism and southern identity have become little more than fashion accessories for a protean self—a possibility simultaneously liberating and impoverishing.

In light of the different paths that their fiction would take, Percy's decision to accept Caroline Gordon's literary mentorship in the early 1950s appears ironic. Letters exchanged between them paint Percy as a militant pedagogue eager to tell readers what they need to hear and Gordon as the voice of the artist, urging him to read Henry James and to remember that novelists are not philosophers.[14] Anyone who has read both *The Moviegoer* and *The Malefactors* can only conclude that Percy listened to Gordon's advice more carefully than she herself did. In his first novel, Percy not only dispenses with any attempt to evangelize but even omits clear suggestions that his Catholic characters are more morally advanced than their non-Catholic counterparts. To the extent that Catholicism is treated positively, it is only as an antidote to southern high seriousness and pessimism. The complaint that has sometimes been lodged against Flannery O'Connor's work—that secular readers will necessarily miss her intended message—might also apply to Percy's novel were it not that even O'Connor's apocalyptic motifs are lacking in *The Moviegoer*. Whatever Percy's stated intentions, the argument that the novel insists on the necessity of Catholic belief remains tenuous and largely unconvincing.

The most obvious historical frame of reference for *The Moviegoer* is the existentialist vogue of the 1940s through the 1960s. The novel is, indeed, most "dated" in its insistence that the prosperous postwar years are, for many Americans, an age of anxiety, and Percy's admiration for Dostoevsky, Kierkegaard, and Camus, evident throughout the novel, aligns him with many other writers and thinkers of the period, including Thornton Wilder, Paul Tillich, and Ralph Ellison. Yet though Percy, as George Cotkin suggests, makes use of Kierkegaardian existentialism to promote "a philosophical retreat from politics into the larger, more enduring questions of existence and the nature of truth"—unlike, say, those student activists who found in Camus's *The Rebel* justification for their involvement in the civil rights and antiwar movements—it is important to remember that historical transformation looms largely in Percy's brand of existentialism.[15] Binx's anxiety springs in large part from a crisis of faith in southern ideology, a crisis highlighted by the changes that the civil rights movement were provoking. Percy reinforces the historical collapse of the "southern way of life" by putting its defense into the mouth of Binx's Aunt Emily, a formidable woman given to such musings on the southern Götterdämmerung as this:

> "I no longer pretend to understand the world." She is shaking her head yet still smiling her sweet menacing smile. "The world I knew has come

crashing down around my ears. The things we hold dear are reviled and spat upon." She nods toward Prytania Street. "It's an interesting age you will live in—though I can't say I'm sorry to miss it. But it should be quite a sight, the going under of the evening land. That's us all right. And I can tell you, my young friend, it is evening. It is very late."[16]

Aunt Emily's breathtakingly offhand conflation of the South she has known with the entire Western tradition ("the evening land") attests to her stoicism, as does her calm resignation before that tradition's demise. Though she clings to what she can of her paternalist tradition—for instance, by continuing to regard Mercer, her African-American butler, as a faithful retainer—she knows that her way of life is ending, as Binx recognizes: "For her too the fabric is dissolving, but for her even the dissolving makes sense" (*TMG* 54).

Aunt Emily's strength and self-possession affect Binx powerfully, even though he cannot agree with her insistence that duty, honor, and deadly earnestness constitute the good life. Early in the novel, he voices his own view of the matter: "There is much to be said for giving up such grand ambitions and living the most ordinary life imaginable, a life without the old longings" (*TMG* 9). Even so Binx lacks his aunt's certainty, remains convinced of his insubstantiality, and repeatedly gestures toward a "search" for transcendence in the world that would underwrite his existence. Yet oddly enough for a man so invested in this search, Binx ends without having arrived at a position noticeably different. Catholicism, the belief system waiting in the wings to bestow meaning on Binx's life, functions to deflate Aunt Emily's stoicism but provides no comprehensive alternative to it.

This deflation begins with Binx's Uncle Jules. If Aunt Emily represents the traditionalist, stoic South, then her marriage to the Catholic Uncle Jules might seem an allegorical affirmation of the claim that the South is covertly Catholic or at least decidedly congenial to the church. His ethnic difference, however (he plays the Creole to Aunt Emily's Anglo-Saxon), suggests that he has no anxiety about the disappearance of the South, that this catastrophe does not register on his personal radar. Like a respectable version of Cable's St.-Ange, he is "canny as a Marseilles merchant and a very good fellow" (*TMG* 49), interested in making money, enjoying Tulane football, and living pleasantly. Binx considers him "the only man I know whose victory in the world is total and unqualified" because he has wealth, friends, and social position; he is "an exemplary Catholic, but it is hard to know why he takes the trouble. For the world he lives in, the City of Man, is so pleasant that the City of God must hold little in store for him" (*TMG* 31). His ease with the world entails a complete indifference to the local: unlike Binx, whose sensitivity to place makes him uncomfortable when he travels, Jules considers it "nothing . . . to close his eyes in New Orleans and wake up in San Francisco and think the same thoughts on Telegraph Hill that he thought on Carondelet Street" (*TMG* 99). A white southerner capable of traveling to California without feeling homesickness hardly counts as a southerner at all.

This ability to live without nostalgia also manifests itself in Binx's mother and half siblings, the Smiths. Thanks to his mother, Binx is a baptized but unbelieving Catholic. Although the family prays that he will regain his faith, they do not regard his loss of it a grave matter and rarely speak of it. On the contrary, the very mention of religion "provokes in them the acutest embarrassment" (*TMG* 159), and even his mother's occasional references to God suggest "overtones neither of belief nor disbelief but rather of a general receptivity to lore" (*TMG* 142). Her actions recall Lyotard's argument that postmodernism draws on "micronarratives," language games evaluated not on the basis of their reference to some ultimate truth but of their operational efficacy. Binx's wry appraisal of his mother's faith, in fact, centers on his perception that she does not take it seriously: "It is a bargain struck at the very beginning in which she settled for a general belittlement of everything, the good and the bad" (*TMG* 142). Surely, Binx implies, one's belief about God ought to resonate with all the drama and metanarrative gravity of his aunt's stoicism; any belief that smacks of a "bargain" cannot be genuine. Poised between his aunt's belief and his family's Catholicism, Binx can do no more than acknowledge the pleasures of both: "As a Bolling in Feliciana Parish, I became accustomed to sitting on the porch in the dark and talking of the size of the universe and the treachery of men; as a Smith on the Gulf Coast I have become accustomed to eating crabs and drinking beer under a hundred and fifty watt bulb—and one is as pleasant a way as the other of passing a summer night" (*TMG* 153–54). Despite Binx's highfalutin talk about the "search"—and suggestions that the Catholic and stoic worldviews are equally "pleasant"—he cannot finally deny that crabs, beer, and the movies have certain advantages over Chopin and Marcus Aurelius.

The novel does, to be sure, provide checks against a reading that would equate the whole of Catholicism with a *laissez les bon temps rouler* ethos removed from existential anguish. Binx's friend Harold Graebner, for instance, proves just as sunk in malaise as Binx despite his Catholicism: living in stereotyped domesticity in a new suburb of Chicago, he greets Binx with barely repressed anger and suggests that the two wrestle—a proposal that, with its combination of homoeroticism and violence, evokes D. H. Lawrence's solutions to malaise in *Women in Love* and *The Plumed Serpent*. More significantly Lonnie Smith, Binx's half brother (and the only Smith to take religion seriously), derives solace from his beliefs despite the fact that he is ill and confined to a wheelchair. The conversations between Binx and Lonnie, rendered in what Binx calls the "peculiar idiom of the catechism" (*TMG* 163), have been regarded by Percy and many of his critics as crucial to the novel's outcome: Lonnie's willingness to suffer, fast, examine his conscience for the minutest traces of sin, and offer up his Eucharist for Binx's benefit foreshadow Binx's presumed conversion.

Yet there are several problems with this interpretation. Lonnie's piety and frailty, rife with what Kieran Quinlan calls "the rather pious consolations of popular Catholicism," conflict not just with his family's more casual attitude but also with the novel's constant skepticism about religious practice.[17] Binx opines that the very word *God* makes "a curtain come down in [his] head" (*TMG* 145), and Kate agrees, rejecting any obvious piety: "God is not religious" (*TMG* 197). Moreover Lonnie's own attitude suggests a death wish not unlike that of the suicidal father figures who appear in Percy's subsequent novels. He fasts, despite the fact that he weighs eighty pounds, in order "to conquer an habitual disposition" (*TMG* 163); he takes extreme unction for an illness not life-threatening; and he cryptically suggests that fasting would serve him better than the Eucharist because the latter is "a sacrament of the living" (*TMG* 164). Even his avid listening to his transistor radio—an illustration of his need for signs from beyond ordinary life—evinces an otherworldliness at odds with the larger thrust of Percy's fictional project. Unlike Binx, Lonnie focuses only on his salvation and neglects the quotidian; his death at the end seems a foregone conclusion, rather like that of Beth March in Louisa May Alcott's *Little Women*. In light of such elusive evidence, Quinlan's judgment that "for the purely secular reader, the encounter with Lonnie can hardly be seen to have the significance that a believer would, in all sincerity, attach to it" (96) is difficult to dispute.

Finally Binx's conversion to Catholicism, presumed by many readers of the novel, is unconvincing. Percy claimed in a 1971 interview with John C. Carr that Binx enacts the stages of belief outlined in Kierkegaard's philosophy, although he "jumps from the esthetic clear across the ethical to the religious [stage]s."[18] The textual clues that would support such a reading, however, are hardly decisive. The moment of truth apparently arrives when Binx, on Ash Wednesday, watches a prosperous African-American man emerge from a Catholic church. In this key passage, Percy both alludes to the tradition of integrated worship among Catholics in New Orleans (which extends back to the colonial period) and quietly affirms the equality of all human beings, which, according to the Ash Wednesday ritual, consists of our common sinful nature and our common fate, death. As Lucinda Mackethan observes, Binx "identifies his own interests with the Negro's pious act, in its mixture of ambiguity and hope," but because of the man's skin color, Binx cannot even tell whether there are ashes on his forehead—whether there has been any "pious act" at all.[19] He then asks whether the man is here "because he believes that God himself is present at the corner of Elysian Fields and Bon Enfants" or because he is merely fulfilling a social obligation and concludes: "It is impossible to say" (*TMG* 235). A year later, having married Kate and succumbed to Aunt Emily's plans for his life, Binx has achieved a kind of stability. He refuses, however, to say anything more about his "search," offering this: "I am a member of my mother's family after all and so naturally shy away from the subject of religion" (*TMG* 237). If this declaration of membership suggests an embrace of Catholicism, his reticence aligns him with his mother's brand rather than Lonnie's. Binx affirms the daily and renounces the totalizing gravity of his aunt's stoicism; as a result, "both [Kate and Aunt Emily] find [him] comical and laugh a good deal at [his] expense" (*TMG* 237). Catholicism in *The Moviegoer* may not be monolithic, but its most desirable face invites and tolerates laughter, even the mocking variety directed against it by more serious temperaments. Regardless of whether Binx has made a definite conversion, his comfort with irony and small things bespeaks a Catholicism of this world, not the next. Even his assurance that Lonnie is in heaven (expressed in a scene that recalls Alyosha's final conversation with the boys in *The Brothers Karamazov*) is, after all, addressed to children who would be taught such things as a matter of course—and does not ring with the cadence of belief.

Percy would, to be sure, express disappointment with interpretations of *The Moviegoer* that had not discerned his religious intentions. In a letter to Gordon of 6 April 1962, he resolved to leave all ambiguities aside in his next novel and engage instead in "ass-kicking for Jesus' sake."[20] Religious concerns do indeed play a more prominent role in *The Last Gentleman* and Percy's subsequent novels—and would lead many of the critics who had admired *The Moviegoer* to grow impatient with Percy's moralizing.[21] Yet if Percy's didactic impulses become more evident, his message continues to appear less orthodox than his pugnacious language would suggest. Not only would Catholicism continue to figure primarily as a set of strategies for living pleasantly, but Percy's forays into "seriousness," suggested by his penchant for apocalypse, would either be deflated (like Aunt Emily's worldview) or else have their undesirable side effects exposed. Even the upheavals of the civil rights movement and Vatican II, it would seem, cannot resuscitate the metaphysical power of Catholicism—and Percy's next two novels, which deal with these upheavals more directly, become both more strident and more despairing in their failure to record a Catholicism that remains something more than lifestyle.

≫

Few novels are as overtly theoretical about southern identity as *The Last Gentleman*. Its protagonist, Will Barrett, suffers from a loss of faith in his father's stoicism and in the white, upper-class identity that embodies it, but he pursues a solution to the problem with a rigor that far exceeds Binx Bolling's gestures toward the "search." Indeed Will's systematic approach to his problem reflects his scientific training: "I shall engineer the future of my life according to the scientific principles and the self-knowledge I have so arduously gained. . . ."[22] Hence his constant reading and receptivity to models of thought proposed by other characters: all become grist in the attempt to explain and master his postsouthern condition.

While Binx's loss of faith was presented exclusively in relation to Aunt Emily, Will's is shown as the culmination of a historical process that has been going on for several generations. The genealogy of the Barretts emphasizes the deliberate maintenance of stoic traditions, even as history's progress increasingly provokes doubt about them:

> The great grandfather knew what was what and said so and acted accordingly and did not care what anyone thought. He even wore a pistol in a holster like a Western hero and once met the Grand Wizard of the Ku Klux Klan in a barbershop and invited him then and there to shoot it out in the street. The next generation, the grandfather, seemed to know what was what but he was not really so sure. He was brave but he gave much thought to the business of being brave. He too would have shot it out with the Grand Wizard if only he could have made certain it was the right thing to do. The father was a brave man too and he said he didn't care what others thought, but he did care. More than anything else, he wished to act with honor and to be thought well of by other men. So living for him was a strain. He became ironical. . . . In the end he was killed by his own irony and sadness and by the strain of living out an ordinary day in a perfect dance of honor. (*TLG* 9–10)

Percy's genealogy forms an exact parallel to this series of stages in the meaning of representation that Jean Baudrillard would propose fifteen years later:

> Such would be the successive phases of the image:
>
> it is the reflection of a profound reality;
>
> it masks and denatures a profound reality;
>
> it masks the *absence* of a profound reality;
>
> it has no relation to any reality whatsoever: it is its own pure simulacrum.[23]

The image of the Barretts' southern identity must serve as the ground that gives meaning to their life. This violent and honor-driven southern identity is explicitly racist, classist, and paternalist: it extends "protection" to blacks (and, as the novel later reveals, to Catholics as well) because they are perceived as too weak to protect themselves. At the same time, it opposes the Ku Klux Klan not for its racism but for its lack of noblesse oblige and its vulgar violence. The great grandfather, certain of his essential self and the justice of his convictions, willingly risks death for them. The grandfather does not doubt the existence of self or convictions but cannot be sure whether his actions always correspond to them. His doubt ushers in the nonequivalence of signifier and signified and opens up the possibility that identity may be effect rather than cause of behavior. The ironic father regards his actions with reference to a deliberately constructed code that he lives by but does not believe in. Finally Will Barrett corresponds to the pure simulacrum. He "signifies" in the text as a southerner but remains acutely aware of his own lack of "profound reality," switching accents, idioms, and behaviors effortlessly as he moves from North to South to West and no longer knowing what he believes.

Will's predicament, however, serves as a microcosm, for the South of the novel has also become a simulacrum. Postwar prosperity has eroded the South's reputation as an economic problem, while the political realignments produced by the civil rights movement have wrought, astonishingly, a South for Barry Goldwater in the 1964 presidential election: "The South he came home to was different from the South he had left. It was happy, victorious, Christian, rich, patriotic, and Republican" (*TLG* 177). Yet the traces of its past persist everywhere: reenactments of Civil War battles, faithful black retainers accompanying their "masters" on hunting expeditions, and an instant, folksy sociability predicated upon extensive knowledge of one's kin. These traces, however, no longer function as embodiments of southern values. The historically inaccurate reenactment of the battle does not genuinely commemorate the lost southern cause. Its Confederates consist of "both sexes blue-jeaned and sweat-shirted and altogether disreputable. And Negroes!" (*TLG* 322). It resembles nothing so much as an excuse to party. Moreover the Delta locals, white and black alike, seem oblivious to the values of their "agrarian" culture and prefer to watch *Captain Kangaroo* on television: "How is it that uncle and servant, who were solid 3-D persons, true denizens of this misty Natchez Trace country, should be transported by these sad gags from Madison Avenue? But they were transported" (*TLG* 332). More than any of Percy's works, *The Last Gentleman* records a precise historical turning point, the last moment at which the memory of a monolithic, metaphysically defined southernness holds sway. With the suicide of Will Barrett's father, the last link connecting southern signifiers to their "profound reality" is severed. Will's periodic attacks of amnesia, which end with him wandering on old Civil War battlefields, function like a hangover: in the absence of compelling models of identity, nothing is left but the obsessive and painful revisiting of formerly sacred sites. Again Baudrillard's reflections on the contemporary world of simulacra seem apropros to Will's condition: "We live amid the interminable reproduction of ideals, phantasies, images and dreams which are now behind us, yet which we must continue to reproduce in a sort of inescapable indifference."[24] Though Will is theoretically free to do as he pleases, he finds the absence of any satisfying alternative to old codes of belief and behavior oppressive. His attempts to apply "scientific" thinking to his problem, moreover, exacerbate his pain, for they merely substitute one metanarrative for another—and both, promising transcendence, cannot deliver it in any sustained way.

The central conflict in *The Last Gentleman* is between two alternatives to Will's postsouthern anomie: the atheistic, scientific, and suicidal position of Sutter Vaught, and Catholicism, represented by Sutter's sister, Val, who has become a nun. Sutter, believing that humans require transcendence but cannot achieve it through a God who probably does not exist, argues that the only reliable escapes from immanence are the abstractions of art and science and the quasi-sacramental joys of sex. Failing these, there is always suicide, the transcendence of earthly existence altogether. Sutter is the first of Percy's non-Catholic characters who long for the destruction of meaning and abandon the accumulated memories of the South for the emptiness of the desert. His decision to live in a place haunted by memories of the atomic bomb suggests that he associates transcendence with the state of being a survivor of apocalypse. The destruction of all previous cultural forms cleanses the landscape of those simulacra that prevent any substantive break with the past, as Will recognizes when he contemplates the New Mexico desert: "This is the locus of pure possibility. . . . What a man can be the next minute bears no relation to what he is or what he was the minute before" (*TLG* 341–42). Will is tantalized and frightened by such a prospect.

As for Catholicism, Val regards her own conversion as a Kierkegaardian leap of faith, a turn of events whose absurdity guarantees its genuineness. She had been studying in the library at Columbia University, a displaced southerner forced to confront her isolation in the chaos of New York, when a nun with whom she shared a cubicle suggested that she convert. Whisked away to "a hideous red brick building in Paterson, New Jersey" (*TLG* 288) for her swift conversion and novitiate, she flunks her initiation and is sent to do missionary work among the poor, rural African-Americans of Tyree County, Alabama. In a rather heavy-handed manner, Percy presents her vocation as a triumph over the old southern ideology. Her work with black children who have linguistic disabilities scandalizes traditional southern sentiments by contributing to the still prevalent fear that Catholics wish to promote racial equality and miscegenation. Moreover Val's mission has been built on the site of the former Phillips Academy, "one of the old-style country academies" (*TLG* 283) with an emphasis in Greek and military science. This ideological apparatus of southern stoicism has given way not just to Catholicism but to a specific enterprise devoted to nurturing the voice of African-Americans.

What distinguishes Val's Catholicism from that of the Smiths in *The Moviegoer*, however, is that Val considers it a worthy opponent of Sutter's theory of transcendence, as the extended, imagined debate between Sutter and Val alluded to in the pages of his casebook indicates. Sutter and Val agree on the urgency of their respective positions, and Val acts with this urgency in mind, charging Will to see to the baptism of her cousin Jamie before his death as if Will had no choice in the matter. Val also shares with Sutter a fascination with apocalypse and has accepted her vocation in part because she fancies Tyree County a place of survivors—an ambience reflected in the mission buildings themselves, which form "a raw settlement of surplus army buildings, Quonset huts, and one geodesic dome . . . like a lunar installation" (*TLG* 284). Into this wasteland, she can awaken her fellow survivors to the wonder of language, of signs that have not yet had a chance to float free from their referents and so contain an original plenitude: "They are like Adam on the First Day. What's that? they ask me. That's a hawk, I tell them, and they believe me" (*TLG* 289). Val's seriousness seems related to her position as a southerner and as a convert, as someone, like Percy himself, tormented by the need for metaphysical certainty. Indeed the Bishop of Newark had been so alarmed by her sudden conversion and novitiate that he had required "a statement from my doctor that there was no insanity in my family," while her fellow novitiates, "mostly third-generation Irish from places like Bridgeport and Worcester, Mass.," (*TLG* 288) practice their faith more casually.

Yet despite Val's commitment, she also proves a bad Catholic, as she readily admits: "I believe the whole business . . . [but] I'm meaner than ever. . . . I still hope my enemies fry in hell" (*TLG* 289). She also stands accused of selling out, of using manipulation to garner financial support from people she despises—as when she persuades "the local Klonsul of the Klan to give us a Seven-Up machine" (*TLG* 202). Sutter's retort that she should "at least have the courage of [her] revolt" (*TLG* 296) serves as a predictable critique of her actions, but Val's own uneasiness about her methods shows that she, no less than Sutter, finds herself troubled by anything that appears to blur her distinctions between the transcendent and the immanent. If Klansmen can make donations to African-Americans and Catholics, then God must indeed work in mysterious ways, but for all Val's desire to accept such strangeness, she finally agrees with Sutter that only transcendence—not subject to doubt or qualification—can validate it.

Will is not significantly affected by his encounters with Catholicism and fails to have anything resembling a conversion. In fact his final stance implies a rejection of both Sutter and Val's competing positions. Despite being tempted by Sutter, he cannot accept what he calls "the extremity of [Sutter's] alternatives: God and not-God, getting under women's dresses and blowing your brains out," because his problem, "how to live from one ordinary minute to the next on a Wednesday afternoon" (*TLG* 340), is not served by such radically dichotomous choices. Moreover for a man whose father killed himself, suicide figures not as transcendence of postsouthernness but as yet another repetition of the stoic "final solution"—and therefore, as proof of an intolerable determinism. The novel's omniscient narrator approves of Will's turning away from Sutter, marking this moment as the point when Will becomes "normal" and ceases to experience his fugues (*TLG* 374). The threat of annihilation has had a therapeutic effect: a small dose of apocalyptic sentiment prevents him from having to experience the real thing. Yet even if Will chooses to live, it does not follow that this choice entails an adoption of Val's position. Indeed *after* he has chosen not to kill himself, he equates Val and Sutter's positions in a moment of exasperation: "To the devil with this exotic pair, Sutter and Val, the absentee experts who would deputize him, one to practice medicine, the other to practice priestcraft. Charge him indeed. Who were they to charge anybody?" (*TLG* 378). Will's reluctant acquiescence in Jamie's baptism, moreover, has no discernible effect on him: he pursues Sutter afterward, with the intention of preventing him from killing himself, but nothing in the text links this action with an advance to ethical or religious modes of life.

One could, in fact, question the efficacy of Jamie's baptism. Although Catholic doctrine does not require the consent of the baptized, Jamie is questioned by the priest to determine whether he wishes to receive the sacrament. His replies, coming in the last moments of his life, are unintelligible. The priest himself provides the only hint of the more casual Catholicism that *The Moviegoer* had validated. He asks Jamie the portentous prescribed questions as a matter of course, cutting a most unimpressive figure and appearing as if he would rather be elsewhere. His actions are consistent with what Will has condemned throughout the novel as "a species of professional unseriousness . . . almost frivolity" (*TLG* 200) and a form of "Catholic monkey business" (*TLG* 203). Will's attitude at the end suggests that his basic distaste for such lightness has not changed, that his quest for meaning still revolves, much more consistently than did Binx's, around the necessity for absolute seriousness. Impressed though he may be that "something" took place in Jamie's last moments, the reader sees no indication that he is ready to follow the priest's example.

The urgency attached to Will's search suggests that *The Last Gentleman* is a more legitimate heir to the religious program of Gordon and O'Connor than *The Moviegoer*. Even so, its relentless theorizing undermines the position that it would argue: the same theory that sees through the metanarratives of southernness and scientism renders Catholicism vulnerable to a similar critique, and the novel's faithfulness to this theoretical logic culminates in Will's failure to convert. Will's quest, continuing beyond the pages of the novel, suggests a Baudrillardian pessimism that recognizes both the desire for transcendence and, after so many historical catastrophes, the impossibility of attaining it.

❧

Love in the Ruins begins unforgettably. Percy's protagonist, Dr. Tom More, is hiding among the pine trees near an interstate exit, "waiting for the end of the world": "Either I am right and a catastrophe will occur, or it won't and I'm crazy. In either case the outlook is not so good."[25] The "catastrophe" refers to the possibility of a chemical explosion caused by the use of

More's therapeutic invention, the lapsometer, but more generally it alludes to the political and religious upheavals of the late 1960s and early 1970s, fictionalized and projected a decade and a half into the future. More presents a portrait of an America so divided between left and right that either revolution or total social disintegration seems possible: impoverished black nationalists live as fugitives in swamps and periodically attack the suburbs, while wealthy, fundamentalist Christian golf aficionados live in splendor behind electrified gates. In the face of such division, the old assumption that "America" signifies as a unified consensus rings increasingly hollow:

> Is it that God has at last removed his blessing from the U.S.A. and what we feel now is just the clank of the old historical machinery, the sudden jerking ahead of the roller-coaster cars as the chain catches hold and carries us back into history with its ordinary catastrophes, carries us out and up toward the brink from that felicitous and privileged siding where even unbelievers admitted that if it was not God who blessed the U.S.A., then at least some great good luck had befallen us, and that now the blessing or the luck is over, the machinery clanks, the chain catches hold, and the cars jerk forward? (*LR* 3–4)

Here More questions the American myth of a providential destiny but cannot rid himself of this myth's tropes. The political ferment of the time has shaken American exceptionalism to the roots, but the worn-out metaphors of this belief clank posthumously on. The same confusion and pain that attends the loss of southernness in Percy's previous novels is now revealed as part of a more general crisis. If white southerners in 1960 could still conceive of themselves as possessors of an authenticity threatened by a hostile North, by 1971 such a separation no longer makes sense. As John Egerton suggested in *The Americanization of Dixie,*

> The South and the nation are not exchanging strengths as much as they are exchanging sins; more often than not, they are sharing and spreading the worst in each other, while the best languishes. . . . The dominant trends are unmistakable: deep divisions along race and class lines, an obsession with growth and acquisition and consumption, a headlong rush to the cities and the suburbs, diminution and waste of national resources, institutional malfunctioning, abuse of political and economic power, increasing depersonalization, and a steady erosion of the sense of place, of community, of belonging.[26]

In such a climate, southern and national loss of faith are no longer opposed but rather stand exposed as different aspects of the same phenomenon.

Accordingly one can embrace or deplore the loss of meaning that threatens to engulf the United States. More reacts to this loss inconsistently, swinging from regret to ill-disguised glee. Finding the condition of the body politic intolerable, More alternates between moments of grandiosity in which he proclaims "I can save you, America!" (*LR* 58) and palpable yearnings for post-apocalyptic emptiness. In either case, he demands that meaning be real, not simulated: to be "crazy" would prove worse than the end of the world.

Even so, there is a more tangible reason More cannot suppress his exuberance before the catastrophe. His own contingency plan consists of removing to an abandoned motel with the three women he is pursuing and living out a fantasy of "love in the ruins":

> Room 202 of the motel is my room. Room 206 is stacked to the roof with canned food, mostly Vienna sausage and Campbell's soup, fifteen cases of Early Times bourbon whiskey, and the World's Great Books. In the rooms intervening, 203, 204, and 205, are to be found Ellen, Moira, and Lola respectively. . . . Even if the worst comes to worst, is there any reason why the four of us cannot live happily together, sip toddies, eat Campbell's chicken-and-rice, and spend the long summer evenings listening to Lola play the cello and reading aloud from the World's Great Books stacked right alongside the cases of Early Times, beginning with Homer's first words: "Sing, O Goddess, the anger of Achilles," and ending with Freud's last words: "—but we cannot help them and cannot change our own way of thinking on their account"? (*LR* 8)

This vision of a post-apocalyptic world combines an innocent and oddly domestic fantasy of sex, music, camaraderie, and drinking with a typically stoic veneration of lost cultural treasures. Aptly enough the Western canon that the survivors will read tells a story of decline. The opening line of the *Iliad* initiates the martial spirit and high cultural rhetoric so beloved of southern stoics; the final quotation from Freud's *Introductory Lectures on Psychoanalysis* soberly explains why psychoanalysis is a science rather than a *Weltanschauung* and writes off those unenlightened types who remain in thrall to older metanarratives. What began in a burst of enthusiasm ends in the destruction of illusion, the kind of theoretical discourse that undoes cherished belief systems and leads people to entertain suicide. The three women, presumed by More to be little more than sexual toys, will function as the antidote to the sadness of a lost world: as long as copulation remains possible, one lives in the present, aware of one's reality.

Quite aside from the sexist implications of reducing the women to objects whose sole purpose is to affirm male subjectivity (a problem that Percy himself would have probably admitted), this odd utopia presents familiar problems.[27] First, even apocalypse cannot wipe out the past altogether: the canon may be truly dead, but it remains as a trace of the past. It has become a simulacrum, no longer carrying its baggage of "greatness" and "relevance," but it has also not simply vanished to make room for the utterly new. Moreover the combination of music and sex aligns More here with two of the strategies recommended by Sutter Vaught—and thus suggests that even after the apocalypse, transcendence remains the prize to be pursued. What to do when the bourbon and chicken soup have run out, when sex has become boring, when the women rebel against their treatment, and when the charm of the canonical texts has worn off? The unspoken implication is that suicide must follow. In the absence of competing narratives, and without the renunciation of the transcending motive, apocalypse will only delay, not overcome, the malaise that comes with the "end of history."

More finds his predicament especially painful because he has lost his religion as well as his sense of national identity and purpose. He engages in no "search," professes himself a Catholic, and even attends Mass, but in crucial respects, he has lapsed: "I believe in God and the whole business but I love women best, music and science next, whiskey next, God fourth, and my fellowman [sic] hardly at all. Generally I do as I please" (*LR* 6). Percy's decision to label More a "bad Catholic" in the novel's subtitle foregrounds Catholicism as neither of his previous novels had done. But if the "badness" of More's Catholicism inheres in the discrepancy between his avowed beliefs and his actions, then there are no "good" Catholics in Percy's fiction, with the single exception of Lonnie Smith. What distinguishes More from such Catholics as Uncle Jules and Mrs. Smith is not his tendency toward contradiction but his nostalgia for a salvific metanarrative. Neither American nationalism nor science (More's lapsometer aims to heal the mind-body split but only intensifies it) can fulfill such a role, and despite his nostalgia, More doubts that Catholicism can either.

While the death of his daughter and his estrangement from his wife contribute to More's religious funk, the more immediate cause is the confusion wrought by Vatican II. Unlike *The Last Gentleman*, which was written during the years of the council itself, *Love in the Ruins* reflects and extrapolates Vatican II's full impact on the church, the whole panoply of changes that destroyed any credible belief in Catholicism's ahistorical nature. Thus the novel envisions a church whose competing tensions have led to outright schism. One group, the reactionary "American Catholic Church," "emphasizes property rights and the integrity of neighborhoods, retain[s] the Latin mass and plays *The Star-Spangled Banner* at the elevation" (*LR* 6). Another, the "Dutch schismatics" (no doubt suggested by the controversial Dutch Catechism that appeared in 1966), "believe in relevance but not God" and allow divorce (*LR* 6).[28] To their number should be added the ex-priests and nuns who retain their religious titles while pursuing nonreligious work, such as Father Kev Kevin, the chaplain of the Masters and Johnsonesque Love Clinic, who works "at his console of vaginal indicators" watching human subjects perform experimental sex (*LR* 123). Finally there is the "Roman Catholic remnant, a tiny scattered flock with no place to go" (*LR* 6).

Not surprisingly More's allegiance lies with this last group. The very word "remnant," with its echo of the survivors of Israel described in the Book of Revelation, evokes both of the alternatives to the current chaos that More would choose: the imagined post-apocalyptic condition of wondrous newness on the one hand, the reversion to an authentic and no longer credible orthodoxy on the other. This "authentic" Catholicism, however, displays its value and rightness precisely through its capacity for tolerance, its affinity with the poor, and its casual rather than transcendent attitude. More attends Masses celebrated by Father Smith, who doubles as a fire-watcher because of his lack of sufficient income. The motley congregation over which he presides contains people of different races, political sympathies, ethnicities, occupations, and income levels—and compares favorably both with the affluent, reactionary "Knotheads" of the American Catholic Church and the equally affluent, hedonistic leftists who threw in with the Dutch group. Father Smith, like the priest who performed Jamie's baptism, inspires confidence through his drabness and the rote performance of his duties. No less than in *The Moviegoer*, then, Roman Catholicism is most attractive when it eschews metanarrative claims: the American and Dutch branches stand condemned in Percy's eyes precisely because they have raised their underlying political ideologies to the status of truth and ignored the quotidian details that complicate these ideologies. Viewed in this light, More's nostalgia for a pre-schismatic church becomes paradoxical: it laments not the loss of absolute certainty that writers such as Tate had bemoaned, but a church that accepted its everydayness and inclusiveness. He misses the consolations of metanarrative but values the church's survival precisely for its micronarrative quality, for the fact that it still welcomes even such "bad"

Catholics as himself. One is left wondering why he finds the schism so disturbing.

Most readings of *Love in the Ruins* interpret it as a tale of faith lost and regained. Having seen that his lapsometers can neither defuse political tensions nor heal Cartesian dualism, More returns to the fold of the only institution that can do these things, escaping from his capture by black militants through the duct of a compressor in an abandoned Catholic chapel. In a hint that More's rediscovery of his faith parallels the nation's, the novel depicts in its epilogue a United States five years in the future, purged of its political turmoil and acting much like its familiar self. The black nationalist leader who had lived as a guerrilla fighter in the Honey Island Swamp returns to his professorship at the University of Michigan; the Knotheads move to San Diego, the leftists to Berkeley. More has married his nurse, a dour but attractive Presbyterian named Ellen Oglethorpe, who looks down on Catholicism but tolerates her husband's. The couple ends the novel in snug domesticity, preparing Christmas dinner, singing Sinatra songs, and going to bed.

This happy, domestic ending, however, obscures several persistent facts that make the novel less obviously didactic but thereby render its Catholic message ambiguous. More has not abandoned his research into the lapsometer; despite the havoc he has wrought, he remains convinced that it "can save the world—if [he] can get it right" (*LR* 382). Such stubbornness evinces a continued yearning for transcendence. More pointedly he remains a bad Catholic to the end, confessing to Father Smith his continued "drunkenness, lusts, envies, fornication, delight in the misfortunes of others, and loving [him]self better than God and other men" (*LR* 397). In short his opposing impulses are still unreconciled; his fantasies of transcendence plague him because he remains unable to achieve it.

To complicate matters further, the South makes a reappearance in the epilogue. More and Ellen have settled in the old slave quarters of a plantation, where they live what Jay Tolson calls a life "very close to the preindustrial, collard-hoeing, close-to-the-earth ideal of the Agrarians, revivified by a strong dose of Catholic sacramentalism—and by a complete reversal of the old social hierarchy, with the bottom rail now definitely on top."[29] If in one sense this existence realizes More's fantasies of simple, post-apocalyptic life—he describes himself in this setting as "Robinson Crusoe set down on the best possible island" (*LR* 383)—it also shows that southern signifiers, long submerged in the general national upheaval, have reasserted themselves. V. S. Pritchett, critiquing the novel in the *New York Review of Books*, labeled Percy a "sentimentalist" whose response to the urgent political conflicts of the day was a nostalgic turning back of the clock.[30] This charge, however, ignores the fact that the novel's Agrarian tendency, while certainly identifiable, hardly signifies as Twelve Southerners' Agrarianism had. Its tropes have repeated differently: More and Ellen embody not an embattled but beloved ethos threatened by both Yankees and African-Americans, but a single family that lives amicably surrounded by its neighbors (in this case, African-Americans, who have become 99 percent of the population of Paradise Estates). Nor does the novel endorse the kind of conflation of Catholicism and traditional southernness that Gordon and O'Connor proposed. Ellen, after all, remains a Presbyterian whose religion is more a matter of pragmatism and ethics than a system of belief: like Binx's mother, "she is embarrassed by the God business. But she does right" (*LR* 157). Her Christianity thus constitutes a micronarrative, differing only from its Catholic counterpart in its distrust of religious objects such as the sackcloth that More wears after receiving penance. For More and Ellen, religion does not become the all-encompassing, transcendent ground of meaning that Tate insisted it should be. More's status at the end, then, differs from Will Barrett's only in degree: still pursuing transcendence, he is still too bemused by the domestic comforts of his Catholicism to pursue it too far.

Nor does More and Ellen's simulated Agrarian life stand as a lone simulacrum that has floated free of old southern meanings. In a small but appropriate detail, the epilogue demonstrates that associations between a traditional southernness and Catholicism may not have disappeared but cannot retain any authentic meaning from their continued linkage. Father Smith's parish, now seeing better days, receives a gift for the chapel tower, "the original bell provided by David O. Selznik for the original Tara" (*LR* 396)—a supposed cultural treasure that the former (white) residents of Paradise Estates hide in a well to keep the black nationalists from finding it. Such meticulous trouble suggests the desire to protect and preserve a cherished southernness from attack or appropriation, but any claim that the bell expresses southern authenticity is clearly absurd. Mitchell's novel had little sympathy with the mythologization of the Old South; as for Selznik's film, its participation in this mythmaking is rendered suspect by its Hollywood pedigree, its connection to the very epicenter of image and simulacrum. The bell's final location in a Catholic chapel may be oddly fitting, given Scarlett O'Hara's own pragmatic Catholicism, but this conjunction also proves ironic in relation to any grand narrative that would equate the church with an authentic southern identity. *Love in the Ruins* demonstrates that neither southernness nor Catholicism is likely to end, that even ardently desired catastrophes will not annihilate them—but that in their increasingly transparent state, neither will they provoke existential anguish. More's life, to the extent that it has struck a happy medium between incommensurable impulses toward transcendence and everydayness, has proven successful, just like the weird annexation of Selznik's bell to the Catholic church.

In aligning Catholicism with the ordinary pleasures of a postsouthern age, Percy goes a long way toward showing that postsouthernness entails an understanding of multiple—and, increasingly, "do-it-yourself"—identities. By rejecting the equation between southern identity and stoicism that his uncle had promoted, Percy allows new combinations of identity to emerge. When Thomas McGuane, in a review of *Love in the Ruins,* complains about the proliferation of "Georgia Presbyterians, Tyler Texans, West Virginia tomboys or rounded Shenandoah Valley girls [that] rain upon the reader's eye like ciphers," he reveals his irritation with the multiplicity of formerly just plain "southern" identities that refer to all manner of specific ethnic, political, and religious categories.[31] One cannot, McGuane implies, keep up with such an assortment. At the same time, however, this multiplicity does not leave behind a traditional southernness. By using Catholicism as a variable through which to critique southernness—and then, despite his best efforts, failing to set up Catholicism as a comparably total identity—Percy's affinities with our contemporary situation come into focus. Percy shows that while "southern literature" endures, it has become saturated, a literature of micronarrative possibilities that are no longer immediately assimilable to an Agrarian metaphysic, a racist order, or a stoic code of life. While such associations cannot be expunged from the historical record—and while the contingency of existence cannot preclude their possible return—the repetition will go on, but always differently, allowing for hope. Catholicism, comfortable with difference and with the world, endures, but as lifestyle.

❦

It is fitting that Percy, who did much to introduce a domestic, deconstructive Catholicism into southern literature, should also be responsible for presenting the work of John Kennedy Toole to the public. The story of how Thelma Toole prevailed upon Percy to read her son's 1964 photocopied manuscript of *A Confederacy of Dunces* has passed into legend. Although Percy's enthusiastic response led to the novel's publication by Louisiana State University Press, no one seems to have expected its success: in addition to winning the Pulitzer Prize for fiction in 1981, *A Confederacy of Dunces* became one of the most widely read southern novels, with more than 1.5 million copies in print as of 2001.[32] Perhaps, as Percy opined, its popularity has much to do with the disjunction between the novel's riotous humor and the tragedy of Toole himself, who had committed suicide in 1969.

And yet in many respects, Toole's experience, style, and preoccupations could not be further removed from Percy's. The period when Toole was writing *A Confederacy* overlaps with Percy's writing of *The Last Gentleman,* but Toole was a generation younger and the product of a very different milieu. Though Percy was born in the prototypical New South city of Birmingham, his primary point of reference for southern identity remained the aristocratic ideal of his Uncle Will, itself the ideological outgrowth of a plantation economy. Toole's childhood in New Orleans, however, was thoroughly urban. Even his parents' economic struggles—reflected in their precarious climb from the lower middle-class Irish neighborhood of the Faubourg Marigny to genteel Uptown—suggest a trajectory like that described in early and mid-twentieth-century immigrant narratives. Moreover this urban world bears the impress of the emerging youth culture of the 1950s and 1960s, centered on popular films, increased sexual freedom, beat poetry, blues, and rock 'n' roll—all phenomena that figured prominently in Toole's cultural experience but which had little place in mainstream definitions of southern literature. Among the abiding preoccupations of southern literature as traditionally defined, only the problem of race appears in Toole's novel, and even here his novel reflects the process of change rather than the fear of it: instead of old faithful retainers or violent, predatory young black men, we see, in the figure of Burma Jones, a combative and shrewd figure who never shows reluctance to voice his grievances or to engage in forthright subversion.

Moreover the seventeen years that passed between the composition of *A Confederacy of Dunces* and its publication complicate any attempt to align Toole's work with the early work of Percy. This temporal gap raises the problem of interpretation that Jorge Luis Borges imagines in his classic fiction "Pierre Menand." Borges proposes that if someone with no knowledge of Cervantes were to write *Don Quixote* today, word for word, it would not be the same novel because of the vast differences in historical context. Although we are much closer to 1964 than to 1561, Borges's thought experiment is suggestive: is *A Confederacy of Dunces* indeed the same work that Toole wrote? Letters exchanged between Toole and Robert Gottlieb, the editor at Simon and Schuster who had considered publishing *A Confederacy* in 1964, reveal that Gottlieb's reservations about the novel stemmed from his belief that "with all its wonderfulnesses, the book . . . does not have a reason; it's a brilliant exercise in invention, but unlike CATCH [22] and MOTHER'S KISSES and V and the others, it isn't *really* about anything. . . . The book could be improved and published. But it wouldn't succeed; we could never say that it *was* anything."[33] That the book did succeed seventeen years later might suggest that Gottlieb's concern was misplaced. But I propose that what *A Confederacy* is "about" takes on a very different significance in 1981 than it would have in 1964. No less than Percy's work, Toole's novel reflects the transformations of southern and Catholic life wrought by the civil rights movement and Vatican II. But with benefit of hindsight, Toole's account of these transformations in medias res appears more prophetic. It suggests that many ordinary Catholics, as opposed to the questers who figure so largely in Percy's fiction, may have already come to view their religion more as one component of a do-it-yourself project of lifestyle, a mark of self-affirmation, than as a body of transcendent truth.

The "lifestyling" of American Catholicism that Toole evokes may owe something to the fact that during the 1940s and 1950s, Catholicism was undergoing a boom, emerging from the ethnic ghetto into the national mainstream and receiving unprecedented respect from American culture at large. Popular films such as *Going My Way* (1944) and *The Bells of St. Mary's* (1945), as well as Bishop Fulton J. Sheen's television program, *Life Is Worth Living* (1951–56), reflected a new perception of Catholicism as a source of innocent, optimistic certitude about the meaning of life. Although this perception was often naive, it offered, in Anita Gandolfo's words, a "successful fantasy that fulfilled the hopes and dreams of Americans, Catholics and non-Catholics alike, in a world troubled by war and a changing society."[34] Moreover the politics of the cold war now offered American Catholics, with their traditional opposition to Marxism, a chance to display their patriotism conspicuously. As Charles R. Morris argues, the cold war constituted "a watershed in American Catholic history: the nagging Catholic grievance that their patriotism and Americanism had never been fully appreciated was, in Catholic eyes, finally and gloriously put to rest."[35] The 1960 election of Kennedy—young, telegenic, anti-Communist, and not particularly devout—confirmed just how much Catholics had "arrived" in the United States, and Pope John XXIII's convening of the Second Vatican Council two years later went a long way toward reassuring many American Protestants that the church had embraced modernity, religious tolerance, and cultural pluralism. In these changed conditions, marked by the rise of the ecumenical movement and by the ascendancy of liberalism on the political scene, Catholicism came increasingly to be seen as an aesthetic and cultural choice, rather than as an essential matter of personal salvation.

This is not to say that Toole's characters themselves are theological or political liberals. Indeed even the ethnic ghetto is alive and well in *A Confederacy*: whereas many earlier representations of New Orleans reflected a largely Creole and self-consciously refined sensibility, Toole depicts a population composed mostly of lower middle-class Creole-, Irish-, and Italian-Americans, all talking in the harsh, Brooklynesque accent unique to white New Orleanians, moving back and forth between the insularity of their neighborhoods and the random, anonymous connections that proliferate in a metropolis. But the sense that these Catholic characters are members of an embattled and possibly subversive minority culture—as earlier generations of earlier Catholics might have been viewed—is nowhere present. They wear their McCarthyesque patriotism on their sleeves, and their political and religious affiliations are best shown in the figure of the dim-witted Claude Robichaux, who, when he is mistakenly arrested for disorderly conduct, "arrange[s] along this thigh his Social Security card, his membership card in the St. Odo of Cluny Holy Name Society, a Golden Age Club badge, and a slip of paper identifying him as a member of the American Legion."[36] Yet even Claude's reactionary politics appear not as the product of conviction but as a mere reflex. When he hears of a group of nuns providing free medical care at Charity Hospital, his first thought is that "them sisters been fooled" by "communiss [sic] and fellow travelers" (*ACD* 311). Like most of the novel's other characters, Claude inhabits his Catholicism comfortably, mixing it with a variety of political and moral stances that frequently do not correspond to stated Catholic doctrine.

What marks Toole's characters as Catholic above all is the degree to which they identify with a tawdry, working-class Catholic and even distinctly New Orleanian aesthetic, weaving it into all the corners of their lives without taking it very seriously. Their fierce provincialism and questionable taste reinforce each other but have little to do with the much-vaunted southern "sense of place" or with sacramentalism. Even as the novel's evocations of New Orleans surpass the canned exoticism of most nineteenth-century local color fiction set in that city, there are no instances in which this "authenticity" points toward a richer aesthetic or moral experience. Ignatius Reilly may believe that "outside the city limits, the heart of darkness, the true wasteland begins," and Patrolman Mancuso may consider St. Charles Avenue "the loveliest place in the world" (*ACD* 12, 42), but we know better than to trust them. Instead, we see the incorrigible nosiness of the Reillys' neighbors on Constantinople Street, the cruel gossip that occurs when a poor old woman "burning a candle for her poor departed husband" inadvertently sets her house on fire (*ACD* 313), and the casual, hypocritical bigotry that many characters display. Santa Battaglia, a minor character in the novel, sums up the milieu aptly: "If you can live down here in St. Ode of Cluny Parish, you can live anyplace. Vicious is the word, believe me" (*ACD* 205). As Andrei Codrescu has observed, many New Orleanians hate the novel precisely because it *is* authentic—because it offers up profound realism rather than caricature.[37]

This tacky aesthetic, with its often arbitrary connections to Catholic beliefs, is best shown in the real-world example of St. Expedite. Virtually unknown outside New Orleans, St. Expedite has been venerated in the city ever since a statue from Italy arrived at Our Lady of Guadalupe Church in the nineteenth century, its crate marked only with the single word "expedite."[38] Toole's novel abounds in similar examples of what Ignatius Reilly calls "religious hexerei" [*sic*] (*ACD* 91): from Mrs. Reilly's desire to buy an ailing woman a gift of rosary beads "filled with Lourdes water" (*ACD* 91) to Santa's "Our Lady of the Television" with its "suction cup base" (*ACD* 308) to the proprietor of a vending chain who "read[s] Father Keller . . . in the paper every single day" (*ACD* 185), the sacred mysteries of Catholicism are always associated—and sometimes conflated—with shabby objects of popular culture.

The only possible counterweight to this avalanche of Catholic vulgarity comes from the novel's protagonist, the outrageous and unforgettable Ignatius J. Reilly. An unemployed, overweight, highly educated, and celibate thirty-year-old man living with his mother in a decaying Uptown neighborhood, Ignatius fancies himself a cultural warrior and spends much of his time writing diatribes on the decline of Western civilization:

> With the breakdown of the Medieval system, the gods of Chaos, Lunacy, and Bad Taste gained ascendancy. . . . After a period in which the western world had enjoyed order, tranquility, unity, and oneness with its True God and Trinity, there appeared winds of change which spelled evil days ahead. . . . What had once been dedicated to the soul was now dedicated to the sale. . . . Merchants and charlatans gained control of Europe, calling their insidious gospel "The Enlightenment." (*ACD* 33)

Ignatius hates capitalism as much as any Marxist and sometimes aligns himself with the rhetoric of the civil rights and workers' movements, although his use of the jargon is laughably inept—as in, for instance, his attempt to lead underpaid black workers at the Levy Pants factory in a "Crusade for Moorish Dignity" (*ACD* 161), a cause supplemented by prayers to "St. Martin de Porres, the patron saint of mulattoes" (*ACD* 150). He even believes at one point that an alliance with the French Quarter's gay community—which he calls "Save the World Through Degeneracy" (*ACD* 315–16)—might result in world peace. More consistently, however, he invokes the conservative, medievalist strand of southern ideology that nineteenth-century thinkers such as Fitzhugh and Holmes represented, at its most parodically uncompromising. Ignatius's truest political instincts emerge when he toys with the idea of establishing a "Divine Right Party" (*ACD* 213). And his usual solutions for social ills—the extensive reading of Boethius and the promotion of "some theology and geometry, some taste and decency" (*ACD* 50)—point toward what these southern medievalists might have envisioned, were they not ultimately more southern than medieval in their thinking. When Burma Jones, the novel's single black character, suggests that he would like some of the material goods of white middle-class life—"big Buick, all that shit. . . . [a]ir condition, color TV"— Ignatius rebukes him: "In other words, you want to become totally bourgeois. You people have all been brainwashed. . . . Live contentedly in some hovel" (*ACD* 347, 349). Had George Fitzhugh ever tried to persuade his slaves of their happiness, he might have sounded something like Ignatius.

For all his intercessions to obscure Catholic saints and his praising of medieval nuns, Ignatius proves hostile to most manifestations of Catholicism that he sees around him—not just because he finds their "hexerei" tacky, but because he rejects the compromises that Catholicism has made with modernity. When "one poor white from Mississippi" tells a dean at Tulane that Ignatius is "a propagandist for the Pope," Ignatius calls this allegation "patently untrue": "I do not support the current Pope. He does not at all fit my concept of a good, authoritarian Pope. Actually, I am opposed to the relativism of modern Catholicism quite violently" (*ACD* 61). Whether the pope Ignatius has in mind is John XXIII (who died in 1962) or his successor, Paul VI, the specter of "relativism" he invokes can only be associated with Vatican II—although, to be sure, Ignatius believes that the church has been a travesty of its former self for a long time, as he shows when he opines that priests should have the power to lash penitents in the confessional (*ACD* 71).

Lest we consider Ignatius merely as a latter-day Don Quixote, however, fighting hilariously doomed but noble battles against the decay of civilization, we should remember that Ignatius also disregards Catholic teaching when it interferes with his personal pleasures, which prove just as venal as those of his fellow Catholics. Indeed we learn that Ignatius's first major conflict with the church came when a priest refused to perform a requiem Mass for his dog, Rex—a refusal perfectly in accord with church teaching but which leads Ignatius to call the priest a "heretic" (*ACD* 237) and to place a defiant Celtic cross above Rex's grave (*ACD* 43). Ignatius is also fond of masturbation (often to fantasies of Rex), of overeating, and of watching lubricious popular films in the cinema (though he seeks to conceal his enjoyment of them by denouncing the vileness on the screen as he watches). He is even, intermittently, aware that "for all his philosophy, Boethius had still been tortured and killed" (*ACD* 35) and that despite his penchant for getting himself into slapstick scrapes, he himself will never be a martyr to his convictions.

The significance of Ignatius's medievalist Catholicism is difficult to evaluate. Though it is undoubtedly true that, as Codrescu argues, Ignatius is "a merciless camera lens trained on an eternal stupidity," it is impossible to take his program for cultural reform seriously or to ignore how self-serving and willfully blind to his own venality he remains.[39] On the other hand, while the novel does promote "a strong sense of religious involvement while undercutting the very positions assumed by the adherents," as Michael Patrick Gillespie observes, it seems an overstatement to conclude that we are meant to take a more conventional Catholicism as the novel's unacknowledged norm and to use it merely "as a gauge of the central character's deviant behavior."[40] Even more so than *The Moviegoer, A Confederacy of Dunces* reveals a world in which Catholicism has ceased to function as anything but a marker of lifestyle—in this case, an urban, working-class lifestyle far removed from traditional notions of southernness. As a parody of the southern medievalist ideology of the nineteenth century, Ignatius's unorthodox faith reveals only how even stands that might have once been considered essential to the preservation of civilization have become ludicrous. Ignatius has not fully grasped the implications of his own "cafeteria-style" Catholicism— that it is merely an element of his self-fashioning rather than a thoughtful response to a crisis of civilization. His fellow denizens of New Orleans, even if they have not articulated it to themselves, know better. We may reject the cruelty and vulgarity of their own lifestyle enclave, but we cannot regard it, based on the novel itself, as metaphysically superior to the casual Catholicism of Binx's mother's family in *The Moviegoer. A Confederacy* suggests that after the civil rights movement, Vatican II, and the urbanization of the South, Catholicism is done for as the grounding of a southern metaphysic.

If *A Confederacy of Dunces* goes a long way toward aligning late twentieth-century representations of Catholicism in southern literature with a cozy, restricted, and even tawdry domestic sphere, the novels of Rebecca Wells go even further in stressing Catholicism's potential for contemporary notions of lifestyle. Both *Little Altars Everywhere* and the much more popular *Divine Secrets of the Ya-Ya Sisterhood* are, in one sense, conspicuously Catholic—set in central Louisiana, full of references to Catholic belief and practice, and even avowedly sacramental. Yet like the portrayal of Catholicism in most of Percy's novels and in Toole's masterpiece, these Catholic references lack metaphysical gravitas and moral code. They are eminently "spiritual," but this spiritualism is best seen as one component of a therapeutic ethos that sees self-esteem and self-expressive flair as the defining elements of a successful life. Wells's novels are not merely, as many readers have recognized, a product of second-wave feminism; they are, more profoundly, commodities of a culture in which Oprah Winfrey, guru of self-esteem through therapy and shopping, has become a powerful figure.

Wells's two novels focus on a group of white women, the Ya-Yas, who remain close friends from their childhood in the 1930s into their old age. Like similarly popular southern texts from the past two decades, such as Fannie Flagg's *Fried Green Tomatoes at the Whistle Stop Café* or, more recently, Jill Conner Browne's Sweet Potato Queens books, Wells's novels draw on a strand of second-wave feminism that celebrates the achievements of strong women, admires the unruly and dramatic transgression of patriarchal norms, and affirms all forms of female pleasure. The Ya-Yas' motto, "Smoke, Drink, Never Think," exemplifies all three of these impulses, and the occasional excesses of their behavior—above all, the alcoholism and violence of their most flamboyant member, Vivian Walker—are always judged against the stultifying standards of behavior for white women that once reigned unchallenged in the South and remain powerful in some quarters today. Against the force of patriarchal prohibition, self-love, self-forgiveness, desire, and the importance of making a dramatic impression are all emphasized, as are bonds between mothers and daughters. Indeed a reader of *Little Altars Everywhere,* who knows that Siddalee Walker has been beaten and molested by her mother and remains traumatized by these events well into adulthood, anticipates just what must happen in *Divine Secrets of the Ya-Ya Sisterhood*: a therapeutic journey in which Siddalee delves into her mother's past, comes to understand her and the forces that formed her, forgives her, and achieves a new conviction of wholeness as a result. As Trysh Travis points out, "[*Divine Secrets*] makes plain that no other recipe for female happiness existing today can compete with recovery's platform of acceptance, forgiveness, and gratitude that life has given us"—a conviction that ought to be regarded with suspicion, given how thoroughly corporate "recovery culture" has become since the 1980s.[41]

As Susan Douglas points out in *Where the Girls Are: Growing up Female with the Mass Media,* corporations like Revlon and Lancôme became adept during the 1980s at "appropriat[ing] feminist desires and feminist rhetoric" to sell their products, contributing to a widespread belief that women's liberation, truly understood, was little more than "female narcissism unchained," that "the ability to spend time and money on one's appearances was a sign of personal success and of breaking away from the old roles and rules that had held women down in the past."[42] Less recognized among contemporary feminists, however, is the fact that the burgeoning recovery movement, with its bevy of twelve-step programs modeled on that of Alcoholics Anonymous and its emphasis on codependency, has become a powerful industry by appropriating rhetorical moves from feminism. Ironically much recovery culture conflates narcissism with victimization: the power to heal oneself from abuse flows not from political confrontation with abusive individuals and systems but from what Debbie Epstein and Deborah Steinberg call "notions of healing [that] erase the gender politics of the patterns that need to be broken"—notions that require an acceptance of victimization and the ability to forgive.[43]

Wells's two novels offer a good illustration of this logic: in both books, psychological health is predicated on the belief that pleasure is the supreme good, that its repression always poisons human relationships, and that healing occurs when one can forgive one's victimizer unreservedly, allowing pleasure to flow again. Vivian's cruelty toward Siddalee is presented as the product of her own victimization at the hands of Buggy, her mother, who internalized both the repressive standards of conduct for southern women and the self-denying, Catholic ethos of offering up one's sufferings as a form of penance. As we learn in *Divine Secrets,* the young and naturally exuberant Vivian only wants an expression of love from her mother, but Buggy punishes her for drawing attention to herself. Buggy also stands accused of the crudest kinds of racism: not only does she listen to the anti-Semitic radio program of Father Charles Coughlin, she expresses horror when her husband brings home a brown-skinned statue of Mary from a trip to Cuba, claiming that "the Blessed Virgin is not a Negro" and that it is "just like foreigners to try to turn the Mother of God into a gaudy tart."[44] Later, as a grandmother, Buggy has become merely ridiculous, responding to any perceived attack on her by lighting novena candles, crying aloud to Our Lady of Prompt Succor, and telling her grandchildren that they will "burn in hell along with [their] Baptist father."[45] Yet even Buggy is presented as a victim in turn: had she been able to pursue her own pleasures as a young woman, without the prohibitions enjoined on her by southern ladyhood and Catholic doctrine, she might have been happy and kind, the reader is led to believe. In showing how mothers and daughters wound each other from generation to generation, both novels present an oversimplified opposition between healthy personal desire and the monolithically repressive forces of society and conventional religion. Any sense that some forms of restraint can be healthy or productive is lacking, as are any suggestions that human cruelty may be the result of something more than thwarted desire.

Predictably, institutional Catholicism functions in both novels primarily as a life-denying, sadistic dispenser of guilt and prohibition. The occasional individual priest who proves acceptable does so because he is associated with an appealing blend of cozy domesticity and sensuous aestheticism—for instance, Monsignor Messina, who reminds Siddalee of "spaghetti dinners and bright purple and gold satin robes and Blessed Virgins all smothered in jewelry and flowers" (*LAE* 218). More often, however, priests and nuns alike are demented and vicious: both the boarding school to which Buggy sends the young Vivian and the mother superior who runs it are Dickensian in their cruelty, and even Vivian's acts of violence against her children, we eventually learn, occur primarily because a repulsive priest puts her on the dangerous drug Dexamyl, in the belief that it would "get [Vivian] off alcohol and make her a better Catholic all at the same time" (*DS* 300).

For all the bitterness directed at the church, however, the women in Wells's novels do not reject it. Instead, they construct a personal, therapeutic mythology that combines elements of Catholicism with New Age beliefs that, in Travis's words, link women "to earth, to nature, to African and Native American cultures, and to the Goddess / Holy Lady / Moon Lady, a sort of Virgin Mary and Diana of the Hunt rolled into one."[46] Rather like nineteenth-century practitioners of *voudun,* the Ya-Yas brew a syncretic mixture, concocting a "Secret History of the Louisiana Ya-Yas" that describes their origins "long before the white man showed up" (*DS* 70) and in which Vivi exults: "I am Queen Dancing Creek, a mighty warrior. I am of the great and royal tribe of Ya-Yas, and no white man will ever conquer me. The Moon Lady is my mother" (*DS* 75).

The Ya-Yas become less exultant as adults, and for Vivian in particular, their syncretic, irreverent New Age Catholicism comes to resemble less a joyful system of belief than a strategy designed to keep the shocks and stresses of everyday life at bay. This is not to say that either their irreverence or its avowedly feminist impulses disappear. Although Necie, the most religiously orthodox of the Ya-Yas, occasionally chides her "sisters" for "reinvent[ing] the Catholic religion to suit yourselves," their dominant ethos remains, as Teensy suggests, associated with "eighty-six[ing] the Old Fart" [that is, God the Father] and praying instead to "Mother Most Merciful" (*DS* 12). Only Vivian seems to grasp fully the compensatory and improvised nature of this worldview: "Between Mass, sunsets, Ouija board, cocktails, and maybe a snippet of a prescription pill, I do fine. I've put together my own package" (*LAE* 199). Her gratitude at having such diverse remedies at hand points toward a deeper, seldom articulated belief that contemporary life is constructed so as to deny women any form of pleasure or community and that therefore they must take what they can get, whenever it is available.

While the Ya-Yas' lifestyle Catholicism may function as an analgesic, we should ask whether it precludes the possibility of more fundamental social changes. Indeed their do-it-yourself mythology provides a textbook example of what Slavoj Žižek has recently called "Western Buddhism," a cluster of beliefs that cultivates infinite tolerance toward the world's religious traditions, inner peace through an ironic detachment from the world's frenetic changes, and the wearing of one's own commitments lightly. Though Western Buddhism's emphasis has much in common with the domestic, casual Catholicism of Walker Percy's characters, the form it takes in Wells's novels includes not just a wider range of cultural ingredients on which to draw for aesthetic pleasure but also a thorough implication in a multimillion-dollar corporate culture of recovery. Žižek writes that even though " 'Western Buddhism' presents itself as the remedy against the stressful tension of the capitalist dynamics, allowing us to uncouple and retain inner peace and *Gelassenheit*, it actually functions as its perfect ideological supplement."[47] As such, Western Buddhism not only turns its participants away from a general critique of the social order, it also, more ominously, comes close to suggesting that any attempt to think through and understand one's situation—as opposed to merely accepting that situation, with the appropriate emotions of gratitude and forgiveness—is fatally flawed. Indeed *Divine Secrets* ends with an explicit statement of this lesson: "For Siddalee Walker, the need to understand had passed, at least for the moment. All that was left was love and wonder" (*DS* 356). The proof that Sidda has internalized "love and wonder" over understanding is her willingness to shed her doubts about marrying Connor McGill and to plunge into the domestic world that she has always held at bay. As Travis argues, the novel's emphasis on a therapeutic philosophy "allows Sidda and, by extension, all women who identify with her struggle, to 'reclaim' their 'lost treasures.' Chief among these, we should understand, is the unproblematic, heteronormative domestic world that preceded second-wave feminism." For this reason, Travis continues, the tremendous popularity of Wells's novels does not show that women necessarily "resist" a patriarchal and capitalist order through their reading: "Readers of *Divine Secrets* register dissatisfaction and desire, yes. But these are then ever-more-rapidly rerouted—by the culture around them and by their own mental predilections—into unthreatening forms."[48]

It would be unfair, of course, to characterize the many women who have enjoyed Wells's novels as mere victims of false consciousness, and a more positive interpretation of their reading is suggested by Fredric Jameson. Jameson argues that we can detect "some sense of the ineradicable drive towards collectivity" even in "the most degraded works of mass culture"; if he is correct, then the popularity of Wells's novels might function as the expression of thwarted utopian impulses.[49] For although recent southern history has been a story of success—the triumphs of the civil rights movement, the establishment of new opportunities for women, the rise in the general standard of living—many southern women seem to have also perceived a loss of community that probably has much to do with the expansion of a consumer-driven capitalism, and Wells's novels offer, in response to this loss, an image of women's community as a commodity. It is ironic that even Catholicism, with its ability to embody a universal ideal while incorporating enormous heterogeneity within it, has become susceptible to commodification in recent decades, attenuating its political potential. What was initially, for Walker Percy, a creed that affirmed human equality through its very ordinariness has become, in Wells's work, a kind of fashion accessory, with just enough aesthetic and emotional frisson to make one forget, temporarily, how empty it has become.

⚶

Today Catholicism remains a minority religion in the South, though the number of self-identified southern Catholics has grown rapidly in recent decades, from 6.5 million in 1971 to 12.3 million in 2000. This growth appears to be correlated with other significant changes in southern demographics, including increased immigration to the South, increased racial and ethnic diversity, and continued urbanization.[50] And yet the Protestant fundamentalism that achieved notoriety as a result of the Scopes trial of 1925 remains the region's most visible and vocal religious persuasion. In the Southern Baptist Convention, known for the bitter struggles between its fundamentalist and moderate wings, fundamentalists have prevailed; meanwhile smaller and fiercer denominations continue to proselytize. Protestant Christianity in the South remains public and influential to a degree rarely perceived in other regions of the country, while the identification of large segments of the Republican Party with the Christian right (and the resurgence of the Republicans in the South since 1964) suggests that traditional southern suspicion of the North now also focuses on that region's perceived godlessness. Though the numbers of Catholics in the South have grown— and though old-fashioned anti-Catholic bigotry is somewhat rarer— suspicion against Catholics remains widespread.

Though Ransom and Tate had affirmed the desirability of fundamentalism in the writings of their Agrarian period, it is unlikely that they would have enjoyed the current state of affairs much. Indeed Tate's hard-won position that Roman Catholicism constitutes the most truly southern fundamentalism seems bizarre from a contemporary vantage point. The U.S. Catholic bishops, on the center-left in most matters of social and economic policy (abortion being the most notable exception), hardly qualify as fellow travelers of the Christian Coalition. Furthermore the post-Vatican II American church is more heterogeneous than ever: it contains a large and growing number of immigrants from Latin America and Asia and continues to be riven by the theological and political conflicts that Vatican II unleashed. Recent scandals involving pedophilia among priests and cover-ups by bishops have also resuscitated associations of the church with a predatory homosexuality. In short Catholicism inspires the same reactions of fear and distrust that earlier generations of southern Protestants demonstrated, and for many of the same reasons.

The first few months of the year 2000 saw two highly publicized events that underscored Catholicism's still vexed relation to traditional white southern identities and ideologies. In January the Vatican announced that Martin Luther King Jr. was being considered by Pope John Paul II as a Christian martyr—a title that carries with it the potential for eventual sainthood. King's nomination marks a significant departure for Rome, which has traditionally given preference to Roman Catholics in its official designations of martyr and saint. The decision's ecumenical aspect, as well as the symbolic consecration of the civil rights movement that the decision would

effect, rings loud in a region where Confederate flags still fly over state capi-
tols and where prominent senators look back on Strom Thurmond's presidential campaign of 1948 with nostalgia.

Several weeks later, Republican presidential candidate George W. Bush
sparked controversy when he spoke at Bob Jones University in Greenville,
South Carolina, a fundamentalist institution known for its prohibition
against interracial dating and its claim that Roman Catholicism is a "cult."
As a result of the furor following the visit, university president Bob Jones
III rescinded the dating ban, admitting that "we can't back it up with a verse
in the Bible." First established in the 1950s when a white and an Asian student began dating, this policy remained in force after African-Americans
began to be admitted to the school in 1970. The original justification for
the rule, according to Jones, had been that interracial marriages would facili-
tate the coming of a one-world government—for fundamentalist Christians,
the harbinger of the Antichrist's rule.[51] Such logic suggests that for the many
fundamentalist Protestants, fear of miscegenation and fear of the church go
hand in hand. If on the one hand, the specter of one-world government
implies a disastrous and indiscriminate mixing of peoples and races—a "pal-
ingensia," to recall Father Rouquette's scornful term—the sinister power
invoked in references to the Catholic "cult" recalls Eugene Alldredge's
warnings about Catholic outreach to African-Americans. Since many fundamentalist readings of Revelation consider the Whore of Babylon, the beast
with the number 666, and the Antichrist to be references to Catholicism,
the effort to prevent world government also implies the effort to defeat
Catholic influence wherever possible.

If Bob Jones University's representation of the church revives Protestant
fears of priests bent on world domination, associations of Catholicism with
miscegenation and decadence continue to appear in southern literary production of the last three decades. Philip Gerard's *Cape Fear Rising* (1994),
for instance, fictionalizes the Wilmington, North Carolina, race riot of 1898
much more openly than its famous precursor, Charles W. Chesnutt's *The
Marrow of Tradition* (1901). The character who appears most clearly as the
voice of reason and justice is Father Christopher Dennen, an activist Catholic priest—whose vocal opposition to the city's racial order provides even
those who oppose him with entertainment. Father Dennen is no behind-
the-scenes advocate who limits his activism to integrating a church or dis-
pensing pointed homilies to his parishioners. His public defenses of African-
Americans and calls for justice go far beyond anything attempted by Cable's
Père Jerome, and the figure he cuts owes as much to Karl Malden's charac-

ter in Elia Kazan's film *On the Waterfront* as to the jocular priest of Lanusse's "Epigramme."

Critiques of the church's hierarchical structures also persist in recent southern novels. Alexandra Ripley's *Scarlett: The Sequel to Margaret Mitchell's Gone With the Wind* (1991) relocates Scarlett O'Hara to the Irish village from which her father hailed. There she meets her cousin, Colum O'Hara, a priest and committed Irish revolutionary. Though he can wax just as jingoistically as Father Ryan on the glories and injuries of Ireland, Colum has no truck with Lost Cause attitudes and endangers himself by raising money and acquiring weapons for Irish militants. Adopting a hard-line stance—he opposes both the Land League and the Home Rule movement of Parnell as ineffectual—he proves just as Machiavellian as Scarlett, manipulating all around him. Yet his fanaticism, compared rather heavy-handedly to that of the southern partisans who promoted secession, also appears less as genuine belief in the cause of Ireland than as a consuming will to power. Scarlett, willing to help her cousin until she discovers the fruitlessness of his plans, adheres to the New South mentality that Mitchell had sketched in *Gone with the Wind*: her Catholicism remains largely nominal and certainly nothing that will stand in the way of her business sense.

Scarlett also draws attention to Catholicism's capacities for syncretism. The Irish villagers whom Scarlett meets profess themselves to be devout Catholics, but their beliefs, like those of the Domremy villagers in Twain's *Joan of Arc*, are so intertwined with pre-Christian lore of fairies, witches, and changelings that separating the two proves impossible. Even Colum appears at times to believe in leprechauns, though he also cynically manipulates these beliefs for the good of his agenda. Inseparable from the fabric of the characters' identities, Catholicism also proves irreducible to simple political positions, to a simple and unproblematic southern identity.

Finally the increasing awareness that "the South" has never really possessed the exceptionalism claimed by its partisans—that its chattel slavery, agriculturally based economy, and underdevelopment link it historically to the West Indies, to Latin America, and to West Africa—has resulted in new, comparative understandings of southern literature.[52] The Catholicism that has figured so largely in the cultures of Latin America has left its mark on the South as well—going all the way back to the settlement of St. Augustine, Florida, in 1565—but this influence continues to grow as immigrants from Latin America move into the South, bringing their own syncretic devotions and practices with them. Such practice is on display in Sandra Cisneros's celebrated short story "Little Miracles, Kept Promises," which begins with a series of letters, in English and Spanish, from Texans and Mexicans requesting aid or giving thanks for aid received from a series of saints, each letter filled with idiosyncratic personal flourishes. The story ends with a longer, first-person narrative from the point of view of a woman who, long having associated her family's Catholicism with misogyny, now reclaims her devotion to the *Virgencita* in a gesture that puts an avowedly feminist and multicultural spin on her, conflating her with Aztec goddesses: "When I learned your real name is Coatlaxopeuh, She Who Has Dominion over Serpents, when I recognized you as Tonantzín. . . . when I could see you as Nuestra Señora de la Soledad, Nuestra Señora de los Remedios . . . Our Lady of the Rosary, Our Lady of Sorrows, I wasn't ashamed, then, to be my mother's daughter, my grandmother's granddaughter, my ancestors' child."[53] Like Wells's novels, Cisneros's story remains poised between the progressive potential of a Catholicism universal in its embrace but richly particular in its local expressions and the blandishments of a consumerist solipsism that has learned to speak the languages of feminism and multiculturalism, emptying out the radical singularity of Catholic belief.

I close with this observation on Catholic syncretism because it seems an apt illustration of the dialectical process I have sketched in this book. The variety of form and identity seen in representations of southern Catholicism has an inherently deconstructive bent; Paul Giles's account of Catholic representations in American literature applies equally well to recent southern literature: "The culture of Catholicism deconstructs the more celebrated American ideologies . . . to reveal them as provisional systems; Catholic arts and fictions in turn deconstruct the theological and philosophical bases of Catholicism . . . but the critical impulse of deconstruction in turn illuminates the fictional status of all these aesthetic creations, reconstituting them as inventions of the human imagination at particular times and places within history."[54]

At the same time, the political value of these new forms of identity, however heterogeneous, should not simply be taken for granted. In a South whose recently celebrated writers include Dorothy Allison, Randall Kenan, and Harlan Greene, the "naturalness" of traditional definitions of southern identity is less evident than ever. Similar claims of an identikit Catholicism also ring false in an American Catholic church whose cultural icons include William F. Buckley, Garry Wills, and Madonna. Yet older constructions of southernness and Catholicism have not simply disappeared; they continue to circulate in forms that are increasingly unpredictable, joining with and separating from the newer constructions. Nor is it always clear that departures always mark an advance, politically or aesthetically: if recent forms of Catholicism have suggested a new emphasis on equality, they have also been easily co-opted by the forces of consumer culture that are, more than ever, neither American nor southern but global in their reach. I end with no call for an identity politics based on southern Catholicism and with no predictions about what cultural forms these changing identities will shape. The history of representations of southern Catholicism, however, suggests that an openness to newness should be tempered by the constant effort to interrogate these forms, southern, Catholic, and American, as they come into being.

Notes

Introduction

1. William Faulkner, *Absalom, Absalom!* (New York: Modern Library, 1964), 93. Cited hereafter as *AA*.

2. See Ellis Hanson, *Decadence and Catholicism* (Cambridge, MA: Harvard University Press, 1997), 1–10, and Eve Kosofsky Sedgwick, *Epistemology of the Closet* (Berkeley: University of California Press, 1990), 140. On Bon's homoerotic and Catholic resonances, see Erin E. Campbell, " 'The nigger that's going to sleep with your sister': Charles Bon as Cultural Shibboleth in *Absalom, Absalom!*," in *Songs of the Reconstructing South: Building Literary Louisiana, 1865–1945*, ed. Suzanne Disheroon-Green and Lisa Abney (Westport, CT: Greenwood Press, 2002), 160–61.

3. Jenny Franchot, *Roads to Rome: The Antebellum Protestant Encounter with Catholicism* (Berkeley: University of California Press, 1994), xvii, xx.

4. Franchot reports that there were an estimated 350,000 conversions to Catholicism in the nineteenth-century United States, of which about 57,400 took place between 1831 and 1860 (*Roads to Rome,* 281).

5. For two traditional definitions of southern literature, see Cleanth Brooks, "Southern Literature: The Wellsprings of its Vitality" (1962), in *A Shaping Joy: Studies in the Writer's Craft* (New York: Harcourt, 1972), 215–29; and Louis D. Rubin, Jr., "From Combray to Ithaca; or, What's 'Southern' about Southern Literature," in *The Mockingbird in the Gum Tree: A Literary Gallimaufry* (Baton Rouge: Louisiana State University Press, 1990), 21–35. Important recent works of historicist southern literary criticism include Houston A. Baker Jr.'s *Turning South Again: Re-thinking Modernism / Re-reading Booker T.* (Durham: Duke University Press, 2001); Michael Kreyling's *Inventing Southern Literature* (Jackson: University Press of Mississippi, 1998); Patricia Yaeger's *Dirt and Desire: Reconstructing Southern Women's Writing, 1930–1990* (Chicago: University of Chicago Press, 2000); and *South to a New Place: Region, Literature, Culture*, ed. Suzanne W. Jones and Sharon Monteith (Baton Rouge: Louisiana State University Press, 2003).

6. Flannery O'Connor, "Some Aspects of the Grotesque in Southern Fiction" (1960), in *Mystery and Manners: Occasional Prose,* ed. Sally Fitzgerald (New York: Farrar, Straus and Giroux, 1969), 44; John Crowe Ransom, "Introduction: A Statement of Principles," in *I'll Take My Stand: The South and the Agrarian Tradition* by Twelve Southerners, ed. Louis D. Rubin Jr. (1930; repr., Baton Rouge: Louisiana State University Press, 1977), xlii.

7. Kreyling, *Inventing Southern Literature*, 28.

8. Most treatments of Catholic American writers, such as Ross Labrie's *The Catholic Imagination in American Literature* (Columbia: University of Missouri Press, 1997), tend to focus on theological intent rather than the representation of Catholicism. The most historically grounded examination of Catholic writing in American literature thus far has been Paul Giles's *American Catholic Arts and Fictions: Culture, Ideology, Aesthetics* (Cambridge: Cambridge University Press, 1992), but this work lacks any discussion of the crucial difference seen in southern representations of Catholicism.

9. Andrew White, S. J. "A Brief Relation of the Voyage to Maryland" (1633), in *The Calvert Papers, No. 3.* (Baltimore: Maryland Historical Society, 1899), 26–45; and *Voyage to Maryland* (1634), trans. and ed. Barbara Lawatsch-Boomgaarden with Josef Ijsewijn (Waucona, IL: Bolchazy-Carducci, 1995). See also Aubrey C. Land, *Colonial Maryland: A History* (Millwood, NY: KTO Press, 1981), 8–9, 49–53, 128.

10. Eugene D. Genovese, *The Southern Front: History and Politics in the Cultural War* (Columbia: University of Missouri Press, 1995), 249–50.

11. Giles, *American Catholic Arts and Fictions*, 46.

12. James J. Thompson, *The Church, the South, and the Future* (Westminster, MD: Christian Classics, 1988), 33.

13. On the anti-Catholicism of Watson, see C. Vann Woodward, *Tom Watson: Agrarian Rebel* (1938; repr., Savannah: Beehive Press, 1973), 362–68; on the Ku Klux Klan's anti-Catholicism during the 1920s, see David Mark Chalmers, *Hooded Americanism: The History of the Ku Klux Klan* (New York: New Viewpoints, 1976), 110–14; on the southern reaction to Smith, see Kenneth K. Bailey, *Southern White Protestantism in the Twentieth Century* (New York: Harper and Row, 1964), 92–110.

14. Augusta Jane Evans, *Inez: A Tale of the Alamo* (1855; repr., New York: W. I. Pooley, 1864). What little critical discussion that exists about *Inez*—for instance, in Susan Griffin's *Anti-Catholicism and Nineteenth-Century Fiction* (Cambridge: Cambridge University Press, 2004), 147–50—deals primarily with the novel's contribution to a nationalist, "American" discourse, mentioning only in passing its pro-southern convictions as well.

Chapter One

Catholic Miscegenations: The Cultural Legacy of *Les Cenelles*

1. Armand Lanusse, introduction to *Les Cenelles*, trans. Régine Latortue and Gleason R. W. Adams (Boston: G. K. Hall, 1979), xxxvii, xxxviii. Further quotations from *Les Cenelles* will be cited as *LC*. In this edition, the French text appears on even-numbered and the English translation on odd-numbered pages. For most line quotations, I cite the English translation only; for longer quotations, I include both the original French and the English translation. I am grateful to Régine Latortue for permission to quote from the editors' translations.

2. Henry Louis Gates Jr., *Loose Canons: Notes on the Culture Wars* (Oxford: Oxford University Press, 1992), 24, 25.

3. William L. Andrews, "The Literature of Slavery and Freedom, 1746–1865," in *The Norton Anthology of African American Literature*, ed. Henry Louis Gates Jr. and Nellie Y. McKay (New York: Norton, 1997), 127.

4. *The Norton Anthology of African American Literature* does contain a translation of "Le Mulâtre" ("The Mulatto"), a short story published in 1837 in Paris by Victor Séjour, who would eight years later become one of the contributors to *Les Cenelles*. This story, it would seem, merits inclusion in the anthology because of its overt political theme.

5. Preface to *Les Cenelles*, ix.

6. Though there are several definitions of the word "*creole*," in New Orleans, it generally refers to a person of any race who has French or Spanish ancestry and is a native Louisianian. Creoles are distinguished from people of English, Celtic, or unmixed African ancestry and from the "Cajuns" of southwestern Louisiana, with their French Canadian antecedents. On the origins of the word, see Gwendolyn Midlo Hall, *Africans in Colonial Louisiana: The Development of Afro-Creole Culture in the Eighteenth Century* (Baton Rouge: Louisiana State University Press, 1992), 157–59; on the contested definitions of the word between white and black Louisianians, see Alice Dunbar-Nelson, "People of Color in Louisiana, Part I," *Journal of Negro History* (January 1916): 366–68.

7. There is no evidence, however, that the *Les Cenelles* poets themselves were slave owners. On the emergence of wealth and an elite class among free people of color in Louisiana, see Joel Williamson, *New People: Mulattoes and Miscegenation in the United States* (New York: Free Press, 1980), 20–23.

8. Rodolphe Lucien Desdunes, *Our People and Our History: A Tribute to the Creole People of Color in Memory of the Great Men They Have Given Us and of the Good Works They Have Accomplished*, trans. and ed. Sister Dorothea Olga McCants (1911; repr., Baton Rouge: Louisiana State University Press, 1973), 21. See also Caryn Cossé Bell, *Revolution, Romanticism, and the Afro-Creole Protest Tradition in Louisiana, 1718–1868* (Baton Rouge: Louisiana State University Press, 1997), 134.

9. On the definition of terms of racial classifications used in the West Indies and in Louisiana, see Winthrop D. Jordan, *White over Black: American Attitudes toward the Negro, 1550–1812* (Chapel Hill: University of North Carolina Press, 1968), 174–75. On the legal establishment of a biracial order in Louisiana, see Bell, *Revolution*, 65–88; and Williamson, *New People*, 2–3, 75–82.

10. Luisah Teish's *Jambalaya: The Natural Woman's Book of Personal Charms and Practical Rituals* (San Francisco: Harper and Row, 1985) explains how practitioners of *voudun* blended Catholic devotions to Mary and the saints with the ritual of African religions (114–15).

11. Alfred J. Guillaume Jr., "Love, Death, and Faith in the New Orleans Poets of Color," *Southern Quarterly* 20 (1982): 136.

12. Bell, *Revolution*, 65, 74.

13. On the conflicts among French, Irish, German, and black Catholics in antebellum New Orleans, see Randall M. Miller, "A Church in Cultural Captivity: Some Speculations on Catholic Identity in the Old South," in *Catholics in the Old*

South: Essays on Church and Culture, ed. Randall M. Miller and Jon L. Wakelyn (Macon: Mercer University Press, 1983), 29–39.

14. Bell, *Revolution*, 11–15, 65.

15. Joseph Roach, *Cities of the Dead: Circum-Atlantic Performance* (New York: Columbia University Press, 1996), 57.

16. Floyd D. Cheung, "*Les Cenelles* and Quadroon Balls: 'Hidden Transcripts' of Resistance and Domination in New Orleans, 1803–1845," *Southern Literary Journal* 29.2 (1997): 7.

17. Latortue and Adams, introduction to *Les Cenelles*, x.

18. Edward Larocque Tinker, *Creole City: Its Past and Its People* (New York: Longmans, Green, 1953), 260.

19. Cheung, "Hidden Transcripts," 7, 8.

20. For brief but incisive readings of "A New Impression" and "A Marriage of Conscience," see Michel Fabre, "The New Orleans Press and French-Language Literature by Creoles of Color," in *Multilingual America: Transnationalism, Ethnicity, and the Languages of American Literature*, ed. Werner Sollors (New York: New York University Press, 1998), 31–32.

21. Cheung, "Hidden Transcripts," 11.

22. Blyden Jackson, *A History of Afro-American Literature*, vol. 1, *The Long Beginning, 1746–1895* (Baton Rouge: Louisiana State University Press, 1989), 229.

23. Sources disagree about the racial identity of Séjour's father. Accounts agree about his name, birthplace (Santo Domingo), and trade (dry goods merchant), but Blyden Jackson identifies him as a "wealthy white . . . dealer in paints" (*History of Afro-American Literature*, 229), while the biographical note in *The Norton Anthology of African-American Literature* calls him "a free man of color" (286) and J. John Perret names him "an octoroon" and claims that "by 1816 he was promoting quadroon balls in the notorious Washington Ballroom" ("Victor Séjour, Black French Playwright from Louisiana," *French Review* 57 [1983]: 187).

24. Cheung, "Hidden Transcripts," 12; Fabre, "The New Orleans Press," 35.

25. Cheung, "Hidden Transcripts," 13.

26. For an overview of the publications of free Creoles of color during and just after the Civil War, see Fabre, 39–44.

27. Edward Maceo Coleman, introduction to *Les Cenelles: Poems in French by Free Men of Color, First Published in 1845*, ed. Edward Maceo Coleman (Washington: Associated Publishers, 1945), xxvi–xxvii.

28. Williamson, *New People*, 62.

29. See Thompson, *The Church, the South, and the Future*, 45–46.

30. Thompson, *The Church, the South, and the Future*, 47.

31. See especially Williamson, *New People*, 26; Bell, *Revolution*, 222–82; and Desdunes, *Our People*, 124–39.

32. On Cable's religious background—and Twain's impatience with his piety—see Edmund Wilson, *Patriotic Gore: Studies in the Literature of the American Civil War* (1962; repr., New York: Norton, 1994), 551, 559–60.

33. During the late nineteenth century, white Creole writers, aware that many non-Louisianians associated the term solely with racial mixing, protested that "Creole" should be applied only to those Louisianians with pure white and French ancestry. Though Cable generally follows this usage of the term, he also occasionally suggests—particularly in *The Grandissimes*—that white Creole claims to racial purity are incredible.

34. George Washington Cable, "Posson Jone" (1875), in *Old Creole Days* (1879; repr., New York: Scribner, 1944), 149–75.

35. For such "allegorical" readings of the novel, see Louis D. Rubin Jr., *George W. Cable: The Life and Times of a Southern Heretic* (New York: Pegasus, 1969), 84; and Barbara Ladd, *Nationalism and the Color Line in George W. Cable, Mark Twain, and William Faulkner* (Baton Rouge: Louisiana State University Press, 1996), 47.

36. George Washington Cable, *The Grandissimes* (1880; repr., New York: Penguin, 1988), 26.

37. Adrien-Emmanuel Rouquette, *Critical Dialogue Between Aboo and Caboo; or, A Grandissime Ascension* (New Orleans [Mingo City]: Great Publishing House of Sam Slick Allspice, 12 Veracity Street, [1880]), 10. Cited hereafter as *CD*.

38. Dagmar Renshaw Lebreton, *Chahta-Ima: The Life of Adrien-Emmanuel Rouquette* (Baton Rouge: Louisiana State University Press, 1947), 187–93, 219–27.

39. George Washington Cable, *Madame Delphine* (1881), in *Old Creole Days* (New York: Scribner, 1944), 17. Cited hereafter as *MD*.

40. See Cable's "The Silent South," in *The Negro Question: A Selection of Writings on Civil Rights in the South*, ed. Alvin Turner (Garden City, NY: Doubleday, 1958), 130; Ladd, *Nationalism and the Color Line*, 40; and Anna Shannon Elfenbein, *Women on the Color Line: Evolving Stereotypes and the Writings of George Washington Cable, Grace King, and Kate Chopin* (Charlottesville: University Press of Virginia, 1989), 53–57.

41. Cable, *The Grandissimes*, 134, 71.

42. Franchot, *Roads to Rome*, 135–61.

43. I am indebted to Felipe Smith for bringing St. Mary's Academy to my attention. Indeed even the Sisters of the Holy Family, the order of African-American nuns who operated St. Mary's, had originally been founded in 1842 by Henriette Delille, a free woman of African, Haitian, and Cuban heritage, who had first entered the convent to avoid having to participate in *plaçage*. On Delille's history, see Sister Audrey Marie Detiege, *Henriette Delille, Free Woman of Color: Foundress of the Sisters of the Holy Family* (New Orleans: Sisters of the Holy Family, 1976). See also Bell, *Revolution*, 126–34.

44. Grace King, "The Little Convent Girl" (1893), in *Balcony Stories* (New York: Macmillan, 1925), 143. Cited hereafter as *LCG*.

45. Thadious M. Davis, *Nella Larsen, Novelist of the Harlem Renaissance: A Woman's Life Unveiled* (Baton Rouge: Louisiana State University Press, 1994), 309.

46. Anne Goodwyn Jones, *Tomorrow Is Another Day: The Woman Writer in the South, 1859–1936* (Baton Rouge: Louisiana State University Press, 1981), 123, 126, 124.

47. See, for instance, Elfenbein, *Women on the Color Line,* 111.

48. On King's identification with the Creole patrician class, see Joan Dejean, "Critical Creolization: Grace King and Writing on French in the American South," in *Southern Literature and Literary Theory,* ed. Jefferson Humphries (Athens: University of Georgia Press, 1990), 113. See also King's autobiography, *Memories of a Southern Woman of Letters* (New York: Macmillan, 1932), 60.

49. See Gloria T. Hull, *Color, Sex, and Poetry: Three Women Writers of the Harlem Renaissance* (Bloomington: Indiana University Press, 1987), 34.

50. Alice Dunbar-Nelson, "The Stones of the Village," in *The Works of Alice-Dunbar Nelson,* vol. 3, ed. Gloria T. Hull (New York: Oxford University Press, 1988), 5.

51. Alice Dunbar-Nelson, "Sister Josepha," in *The Works of Alice Dunbar-Nelson,* vol. 1, ed. Gloria T. Hull (New York: Oxford University Press, 1988), 157. Cited hereafter as *SJ.*

52. On the recurrence of the convent as a site for racial formation in twentieth-century literature, see Margaret D. Bauer, "When a Convent Seems the Only Viable Choice: Questionable Callings in Stories by Alice Dunbar-Nelson, Alice Walker, and Louise Erdrich," in *Critical Essays on Alice Walker,* ed. Ikenna Dieke (Westport, CT: Greenwood Press, 1999), 45–54.

53. On the creation of antimiscegenation laws during Reconstruction, see Saidiya V. Hartman, *Scenes of Subjection: Terror, Slavery, and Self-Making in Nineteenth-Century America* (Oxford: Oxford University Press, 1997), 183–91.

54. Walter Benn Michaels, *Our America: Nativism, Modernism, and Pluralism* (Durham: Duke University Press, 1995), 140.

55. On Watson's role in spreading anti-Catholic sentiments in the South (and for his tacit support of the "relaunching" of the Ku Klux Klan in 1915), see Woodward, *Tom Watson,* 360–68, 389.

56. Eugene P. Alldredge, *The New Challenge of Home Missions.* (Nashville: Southern Baptist Convention Sunday School Board, 1927), 73, 177, 181. I am grateful to Bill Sumners of the Southern Baptist Historical Library and Archives, Nashville, TN, for permission to quote from Alldredge's report.

Chapter Two

Medieval Yearnings: A Catholicism for Whites in Nineteenth-Century Southern Literature

1. Mark Twain, *Life on the Mississippi,* in *The Oxford Mark Twain,* ed. Shelley Fisher Fishkin (Oxford: Oxford University Press, 1996), 467–69.

2. See Georg Lukács, *The Historical Novel,* trans. Hannah and Stanley Mitchell (London: Merlin, 1962), 33–39; and Michael O'Brien, "The Lineaments of Antebellum Southern Romanticism," in *Rethinking the South: Essays in Intellectual History* (Baltimore: Johns Hopkins University Press, 1988), 53.

3. William Alexander Percy, *Lanterns on the Levee: Recollections of a Planter's Son* (1941; repr., Baton Rouge: Louisiana State University Press, 1973), 57.

4. The classic account of pastoral in southern literature is Lewis P. Simpson's *The Dispossessed Garden: Pastoral and History in Southern Literature* (Athens: University of Georgia Press, 1975).

5. I choose the word "medievalist" to emphasize the element of wish fulfillment in this ideology. Strictly speaking the antebellum South was neither feudal (in its mode of production) nor aristocratic (in its political structures) nor medieval (in its historical period). Nevertheless, defenders of the southern slaveholding order liked to argue that the South was all three, and "medievalist" best conveys both the sense that for them the South was a happy anachronism and the basic falsity of their argument.

6. Michael Kreyling, *Figures of the Hero in Southern Narrative* (Baton Rouge: Louisiana State University Press, 1987), 4.

7. Kreyling, *Figures of the Hero*, 5.

8. Quoted in Maurice R. O' Connell, *Daniel O'Connell: The Man and His Politics* (Dublin: Irish Academic Press, 1990), 130.

9. Noel Ignatiev, *How the Irish Became White* (London: Routledge, 1995), 6–31; O'Connell, *Daniel O'Connell*, 122–23.

10. Quoted in John England, *Letters of the Late Bishop England to the Honorable John Forsyth, on the Subject of Domestic Slavery* (1844; repr., New York: Negro Universities Press, 1969), 13–14. Cited hereafter as *LLB*.

11. Peter Guilday, *The Life and Times of John England, First Bishop of Charleston*, vol. 2 (New York: America Press, 1927), 151–56.

12. On the philosophical and scientific underpinnings of scientific racism in the U.S. from the Revolutionary War to 1812, see Jordan, *White over Black*, 482–511; see also Louis Menand, *The Metaphysical Club: A Story of Ideas in America* (New York: Farrar, Straus and Giroux, 2001), 101–20.

13. George Fitzhugh, *Sociology for the South, or, The Failure of Free Society* ([1854]; repr., New York: Burt Franklin, 1965), 95.

14. George Fitzhugh, *Cannibals All! or, Slaves without Masters*, ed. C. Vann Woodward ([1857]; repr., Cambridge, MA: Belknap, 1960), 243. Cited hereafter as *CA*.

15. George Fitzhugh, "Southern Thought," *De Bow's Review* 23 (1857): 344.

16. Eugene D. Genovese, *The World the Slaveholders Made: Two Essays in Interpretation* (New York: Pantheon, 1969), 192.

17. Fitzhugh, *Sociology for the South*, 206.

18. Fitzhugh, *Sociology for the South*, 113.

19. Genovese, *The World the Slaveholders Made*, 190, 191. On the continuity of Fitzhugh's thought with Tate's, see also Richard Gray, *Writing the South: Ideas of an American Region* (1986; repr., Baton Rouge: Louisiana State University Press, 1997), 150.

20. George Frederick Holmes, "Rome and the Romans," *Southern Quarterly Review* 6 (October 1844): 306, 279.

21. See Neal C. Gillespie, *The Collapse of Orthodoxy: The Intellectual Ordeal of George Frederick Holmes* (Charlottesville: University Press of Virginia, 1972), 103–4.

22. George Frederick Holmes, MS vol. 1791, November 16, 1862, in George Frederick Holmes Papers, Duke University Library, Durham, North Carolina; quoted in Gillespie, *The Collapse of Orthodoxy*, 211.

23. See Gillespie, *The Collapse of Orthodoxy*, 47–48, 211.

24. Fitzhugh, *Sociology for the South*, 15.

25. Hannis Taylor, "Abram J. Ryan," in *The Library of Southern Literature*, vol. 10 (New Orleans: Martin and Hoyt, 1907), 4625.

26. Such hagiography continues among a small circle of white southerners, both Catholic and non-Catholic. Its most recent expression is Bernadette Greenwood Oldemoppen's uncritical biography *Abram J. Ryan: Priest, Patriot, and Poet* (Mobile: Southeastern Press, 1992).

27. Oldemoppen, *Abram J. Ryan*, 2.

28. Taylor, "Abram J. Ryan," 4625.

29. Kreyling, *Figures of the Hero*, 5.

30. For an appropriately skeptical account of many of the details of Ryan legend, see Rev. Oscar H. Lipscomb, "Some Unpublished Poems of Abram J. Ryan," *Alabama Review* 25 (1972): 163–77.

31. According to Oldemoppen, "Two sources state that Jefferson Davis asked Father Ryan to go to Peoria to write editorials and assist The Knights of the Round Table, an underground organization there, working for peace on Confederate terms" (*Abram J. Ryan*, 23).

32. On Ryan's career as a priest, see especially Oldemoppen, *Abram J. Ryan*, 18–19; and Thomas Stritch, *The Catholic Church in Tennessee: The Sesquicentennial Story* (Nashville: The Catholic Center, 1987), 152–53.

33. Abram J. Ryan, *Selected Poems of Father Ryan*, ed. Gordon Weaver (Jackson: University Press of Mississippi, 1973), 5–6. Cited hereafter as *SP*.

34. Fitzhugh's judgment at the beginning of *Cannibals All!* is relevant here: "I believe that, under the banners of Socialism and, more dangerous because more delusive, Semi-Socialism, society is insensibly and often unconsciously marching to the utter abandonment of the most essential institutions—religion, family ties, property, and the restraints of justice" (6).

35. Thompson, *The Church, the South, and the Future*, 57.

36. Ladd, *Nationalism and the Color Line*, 86, 87.

37. Mark Twain, *The Innocents Abroad*, in *The Oxford Mark Twain*, ed. Shelley Fisher Fishkin (Oxford: Oxford University Press, 1996), 64. Cited hereafter as *IA*.

38. Ladd, *Nationalism and the Color Line*, 93–97.

39. Franchot, *Roads to Rome*, 16–34, 103–4.

40. Twain, *Life on the Mississippi*, 432–33.

41. Mark Twain, *A Connecticut Yankee in King Arthur's Court*, in *The Oxford Mark Twain*, ed. Shelley Fisher Fishkin (Oxford: Oxford University Press, 1996), 556. Cited hereafter as *CY*.

42. For a comparison of Twain's feminization of the church here with other female characters in *A Connecticut Yankee*, see J. D. Stahl, *Mark Twain: Culture and Gender* (Athens: University of Georgia Press, 1994), 106–9.

43. See especially Louis D. Rubin Jr., " 'The Begum of Bengal': Mark Twain and the South," in *William Elliott Shoots a Bear: Essays on the Southern Literary Imagination* (Baton Rouge: Louisiana State University Press, 1975), 47–53. Rubin reads the novel as a "fable of the New South" (50) that castigates industrial capitalism. His reading does more than adumbrate Twain's growing pessimism; it somewhat anachronistically assimilates *A Connecticut Yankee* to a white southern, even distinctly Agrarian position.

44. For further discussion of the inconsistency and love of nobility in *A Connecticut Yankee,* see Stahl, *Mark Twain: Culture and Gender,* 96.

45. The best recent discussion of Twain's deism and attitude toward religion is found in Alfred Kazin, *God and the American Writer* (New York: Knopf, 1997), 176–93.

46. On Susy's influence on *Joan of Arc,* see Laura E. Skandera-Trombley, *Mark Twain in the Company of Women* (Philadelphia: University of Pennsylvania Press, 1994), 156–62; and Justin Kaplan, introduction to *Personal Recollections of Joan of Arc,* by Mark Twain, in Fishkin, *The Oxford Mark Twain,* xxxvii–xli.

47. Stahl, *Mark Twain: Culture and Gender,* 124.

48. Benedict Anderson, *Imagined Communities: Reflections on the Origin and Spread of Nationalism,* rev. ed. (London: Verso, 1991), 5.

49. Mark Twain, *Personal Recollections of Joan of Arc,* in Fishkin, *The Oxford Mark Twain,* , 28–29. Cited hereafter as *JA.*

50. Skandera-Trombley, *Mark Twain in the Company of Women,* 160.

51. For an interesting attempt to reconcile this dichotomy, see Jason Gary Horn, *Mark Twain and William James: Crafting a Free Self* (Columbia: University of Missouri Press, 1996), 69–105.

52. Pope Leo XIII, *Quod Apostolici Muneris,* 28 December 1878, in *The Papal Encyclicals, 1878–1903,* ed. Claudia Carlen Ihn (Raleigh: Pierian Press, 1990), 13, 13–14.

Chapter Three

The Pleasures of Decadence: Catholicism in Kate Chopin, Carson McCullers, and Anne Rice

1. Emily Toth, *Kate Chopin* (New York: William Morrow, 1990), 9.

2. "Books of the Day," *Chicago Times-Herald,* 1 June 1899, 9; "Fresh Literature," *Los Angeles Sunday Times,* 25 June 1899, 2; "Books and Magazines," *Pittsburgh Leader,* 8 July 1899, 6 (signed "Sibert" [Willa Cather]).

3. Robert Sayre and Michael Löwy, "Figures of Romantic Anticapitalism," in *Spirits of Fire: English Romantic Writers and Contemporary Historical Methods,* ed. G. A. Rosso and Daniel P. Watkins (Rutherford, NJ: Fairleigh Dickinson University Press, 1990), 26–37.

4. Francis Galton, *Hereditary Genius: An Inquiry into its Laws and Consequences* (1892; repr., Gloucester, MA: Peter Smith, 1962); Cesare Lombroso, *Crime, Its Causes and Remedies,* trans. Henry P. Horton (Boston: Little and Brown, 1911); Max

Nordau, *Degeneration* (New York: Appleton, 1895); Oswald Spengler, *The Decline of the West*, trans. Charles Francis Atkinson (New York: Knopf, 1926–28). For a broader account of the historical context of decadence in the late nineteenth and early twentieth centuries, see especially Jennifer Birkett, *The Sins of the Fathers: Decadence in France, 1870–1914* (London: Quartet Books, 1986), 10–18; and R. K. R. Thornton, *The Decadent Dilemma* (London: Edward Arnold, 1983), 1–14.

5. Birkett, *The Sins of the Fathers*, 3, 4.

6. Lewis P. Simpson, *The Fable of the Southern Writer* (Baton Rouge: Louisiana State University Press, 1994), 12. See also Richard Gray's reading of Poe in *Southern Aberrations: Writers of the American South and the Problems of Regionalism* (Baton Rouge: Louisiana State University Press, 2000), 1–35.

7. Ellis Hanson, *Decadence and Catholicism* (Cambridge, MA: Harvard University Press, 1997), 2–3. Cited hereafter as *DC*.

8. "Fresh Literature," *Los Angeles Sunday Times*, 25 June 1899, 12.

9. Eve Kosofsky Sedgwick, *Epistemology of the Closet* (Berkeley: University of California Press, 1990), 140.

10. Leslie Fiedler, *Love and Death in the American Novel* (1960; repr., Normal, IL: Dalkey Archive Press, 1997), 476.

11. Mab Segrest, *My Mama's Dead Squirrel: Lesbian Essays on Southern Culture* (Ithaca, NY: Firebrand Books, 1985), 21–34; Yaeger, *Dirt and Desire*, 1–33.

12. See Toth, *Kate Chopin*, 20, 220, 232; and Thomas Bonner Jr., "Christianity and Catholicism in the Fiction of Kate Chopin." *Southern Quarterly* 20 (Winter 1982): 118–25.

13. Toth, *Kate Chopin*, 262, 272–78.

14. Charles R. Morris, *American Catholic* (New York: Times Books, 1997), vii–ix, 26–53.

15. On the nineteenth-century conflict between Irish-American Catholics and Creole-American Catholics in the South—and particularly in Louisiana—see Randall M. Miller, "A Church in Cultural Captivity: Some Speculations on Catholic Identity in the Old South," in *Catholics in the Old South: Essays on Church and Culture*, ed. Randall M. Miller and Jon L. Wakelyn (Macon: Mercer University Press, 1983), 28–37.

16. Kate Chopin, *The Awakening*, ed. Margo Culley, 2nd ed. (New York: Norton, 1994), 18.

17. Chopin, *The Awakening*, 10.

18. See especially Elizabeth LeBlanc, "The Metaphorical Lesbian: Edna Pontellier in *The Awakening*," *Tulsa Studies in Women's Literature* 15 (Fall 1996): 289–307; and Kathryn Lee Seidel, "Art is an Unnatural Act: Mademoiselle Reisz in *The Awakening*," *Mississippi Quarterly* 46 (Spring 1993); 199–214.

19. On the circumstances surrounding the cancellation of Chopin's contract, see Toth, *Kate Chopin*, 373–74. *A Vocation and a Voice* was published for the first time in 1991 by Penguin Books.

20. Joanne Glasgow, "What's a Nice Lesbian Like You Doing in the Church of Torquemada? Radclyffe Hall and Other Catholic Converts," in *Lesbian Texts and Contexts: Radical Revisions* (New York: New York University Press, 1990), 241–54.

21. *Kate Chopin's Private Papers*, ed. Emily Toth and Peter Seyersted (Blooming-ton: Indiana University Press, 1998), 181–82.

22. Kate Chopin, *A Vocation and a Voice*, ed. Emily Toth (New York: Penguin, 1991), 139–42. Cited hereafter as *VV*.

23. Fiedler, *Love and Death*, 350–51.

24. Harper Lee, *To Kill a Mockingbird* (Philadelphia: Lippincott, 1960), 45.

25. *Watson's Jeffersonian Weekly*, 25 January 1912.

26. Woodward, *Tom Watson: Agrarian Rebel*, 365.

27. Willie Morris, *North Toward Home* (1967; repr., New York: Vintage, 2000), 41–42.

28. Eve Kosofsky Sedgwick, *Tendencies* (Durham: Duke University Press, 1993), 8.

29. Lillian Smith, *Killers of the Dream* (1949; repr., New York: Norton, 1961), 116.

30. Carson McCullers, "The Flowering Dream: Notes on Writing," in *The Mortgaged Heart*, ed. Margarita G. Smith (Boston: Houghton Mifflin, 1971), 274.

31. Carson McCullers, *The Heart Is a Lonely Hunter* (Boston: Houghton Mifflin, 1940), 126.

32. Carson McCullers, *Reflections in a Golden Eye* (Boston: Houghton Mifflin, 1941), 136.

33. For representative feminist readings, see Barbara A. White, *Growing Up Female: Adolescent Girlhood in American Fiction* (Westport, CT: Greenwood Press, 1985), 89–108; and Louise Westling, *Sacred Groves and Ravaged Gardens: The Fiction of Eudora Welty, Carson McCullers, and Flannery O'Connor* (Athens: University of Georgia Press, 1985), 126–32.

34. Rachel Adams, "'A Mixture of Delicious and Freak': The Queer Fiction of Carson McCullers," *American Literature* 71 (1999): 551–84. Virginia Spencer Carr reports in *The Lonely Hunter: A Biography of Carson McCullers* (Garden City, NY: Doubleday, 1975) that McCullers understood homosexuality in terms of Havelock Ellis's theory of inversion (168) and once declared to Newton Arvin, "I was born a man" (159). In a more recent biography, *Carson McCullers: A Life* (Boston: Houghton Mifflin, 2001), however, Josayne Savigneau has challenged the naming of McCullers's sexuality as homosexual, arguing that her famous "romantic crushes" against women rarely involved physical contact and that for herself, as for many of her fictional characters, sex was largely associated with "shame, repulsion, violence" (71).

35. Judith Butler, *Gender Trouble: Feminism and the Subversion of Identity* (New York: Routledge, 1990), 140.

36. Carson McCullers, *The Member of the Wedding* (Boston: Houghton Mifflin, 1946), 118. Cited hereafter as *MW*.

37. Lori J. Kenschaft, "Homoerotics and Human Connections: Reading Carson McCullers 'As a Lesbian,'" in *Critical Essays on Carson McCullers*, ed. Lyon Beverly and Melvin J. Friedman (New York: G. K. Hall, 1996), 221.

38. Westling, *Sacred Groves and Ravaged Gardens,* 131; White, *Growing Up Female,* 107; Yaeger, *Dirt and Desire,* 181.

39. Camille Paglia, *Sexual Personae: Art and Decadence from Nefertiti to Emily Dickinson* (New York: Vintage, 1991), 159.

40. Robert S. Phillips, "The Gothic Architecture of *The Member of the Wedding,*" *Renascence* 16 (1964): 59–72.

41. See especially Sarah Gleeson-White's argument in *Strange Bodies: Gender and Identity in the Novels of Carson McCullers* (Tuscaloosa: University of Alabama Press, 2003) that Frankie's ending points "to the possibility of transformation or lines of flight that lie beyond the scope of the figure of the freak" (37).

42. On the queer implications of Rice's fiction, see especially Trevor Holmes, "Coming Out of the Coffin: Gay Males and Queer Goths in Contemporary Vampire Fiction," in *Blood Read: The Vampire as Metaphor in Contemporary Culture,* ed. Joan Gordon and Veronica Hollinger (Philadelphia: University of Pennsylvania Press, 1997), 169–88; on Rice's use of religion in the vampire novels, see Aileen Chris Shafer, "Let Us Prey: Religious Codes and Rituals in *The Vampire Lestat,*" in *The Gothic World of Anne Rice,* ed. Gary Hoppenstand and Ray B. Browne (Bowling Green, OH: Bowling Green State University Popular Press, 1996), 149–61.

43. On the use of the word *decadence* in the 1970s, see Richard Gilman, *Decadence: The Strange Life of an Epithet* (New York: Farrar, Straus and Giroux, 1979), 173–79.

44. Anne Rice, *The Feast of All Saints* (1979; repr., New York: Ballantine, 1986), 276. Cited hereafter as *FAS*.

45. Bertram Wyatt-Brown, *Hearts of Darkness: Wellsprings of a Southern Literary Tradition* (Baton Rouge: Louisiana State University Press, 2003), 181.

Chapter Four

Agrarian Catholics: The Catholic Turn in Southern Literature

1. The scholarship on O'Connor is voluminous. On the predictability of theological readings of O'Connor, see Michael Kreyling, introduction to *New Essays on Wise Blood,* ed. Michael Kreyling (Cambridge: Cambridge University Press, 1995), 17–22. For representative endorsements of O'Connor's theology, see Robert Drake, *Flannery O'Connor: A Critical Essay* (Grand Rapids, MI: Eerdmans, 1966); John F. Desmond, *Risen Sons: Flannery O'Connor's Vision of History* (Athens: University of Georgia Press, 1987); and Richard Giannone, *Flannery O'Connor, Hermit Novelist* (Urbana: University of Illinois Press, 2000). The critical tradition that accepts O'Connor's intentions at their word but believes that she fails to achieve them begins with John Hawkes's "Flannery O'Connor's Devil," *Sewanee Review* 70 (1962): 395–407. Criticism that emphasizes her southernness and her treatment of southern history ranges from the fairly traditional approach of Louis D. Rubin Jr.'s "Flannery O'Connor: A Note on Literary Fashions," *Critique* 2 (Fall 1958): 11–18, to Patricia Yaeger's "Flannery O'Connor and the Aesthetics of Torture," in *Flannery O'Connor: New Perspectives,* ed. Sura P. Rath and Mary Neff Shaw (Athens: University of Georgia Press, 1996), 183–206.

2. Flannery O'Connor, "The Catholic Novelist in the Protestant South," in *Mystery and Manners: Essays and Occasional Prose,* ed. Sally and Robert Fitzgerald (New York: Farrar, Straus and Giroux, 1969), 207–8.

3. Since the subject of this book is *representations of* Catholicism rather than expressions of Catholic thought, I will confine my reading of O'Connor's fiction to this crucial story, so as not to duplicate the many analyses that explicate Catholic doctrine in her work.

4. Flannery O'Connor, "The Displaced Person," in *The Complete Stories* (New York: Noonday Press, 1971), 202, 203. Cited hereafter as *DP.*

5. Flannery O'Connor, "A Good Man Is Hard to Find," in *The Complete Stories,* 131.

6. On Tate and Gordon's relationship to the Catholic Revival, see especially Peter A. Huff, *Allen Tate and the Catholic Revival: Trace of the Fugitive Gods* (New York: Paulist Press, 1996); for an account of the Revival more broadly, see Arnold Sparr, *To Promote, Defend, and Redeem: The Catholic Literary Revival and the Cultural Transformation of American Catholicism, 1920–1960* (Westport, CT: Greenwood Press, 1990).

7. On the relationship between Agrarianism and New Criticism, see Paul A. Bové, *Mastering Discourse: The Politics of Intellectual Culture* (Durham: Duke University Press, 1992), 128; Richard H. King, *A Southern Renaissance: The Cultural Awakening of the American South, 1930–1955* (Oxford: Oxford University Press, 1980), 63–76; Kreyling, *Inventing Southern Literature,* 4–55; and Mark Jancovich, *The Cultural Politics of the New Criticism* (Cambridge: Cambridge University Press, 1993), 141–45.

8. Robert H. Brinkmeyer Jr., *Three Catholic Writers of the Modern South* (Jackson: University Press of Mississippi, 1985), x.

9. Brinkmeyer, *Three Catholic Writers,* xvi.

10. Paul K. Conkin, *The Southern Agrarians* (Knoxville: University of Tennessee Press, 1988), 108.

11. John Crowe Ransom, "Introduction: A Statement of Principles," in *I'll Take My Stand,* xlii.

12. Allen Tate, "Remarks on the Southern Religion," in *I'll Take My Stand,* 156. Cited hereafter as *RSR.*

13. Allen Tate, letter to John Crowe Ransom, 27 July 1929, in Donald Davidson Papers, box 10, file 43, Special Collections, Heard Library, Vanderbilt University. I am grateful to Helen Tate for permission to quote from this letter.

14. John Crowe Ransom, *God without Thunder: An Unorthodox Defense of Orthodoxy* (New York: Harcourt Brace, 1930).

15. Pope Pius X, *Pascendi Dominici Gregis,* 8 September 1907, in *The Papal Encyclicals, 1903–1939,* ed. Claudia Carlen Ihm (Raleigh: Pierian Press, 1990), 82.

16. On the continuity between Tate's conception of capitalism and that of antebellum southern theorists such as John Randolph and John C. Calhoun, see Eugene D. Genovese, *The Southern Tradition: The Achievements and Limitations of an American Conservatism* (Cambridge, MA: Harvard University Press, 1994), 21–35.

17. On the relationship between slavery and capitalism, see James Oakes, *Slavery and Freedom: An Interpretation of the Old South* (New York: Vintage, 1991), 40–79.

18. On the aims and history of Distributism, and the collaboration of Distributists with Tate, see Huff, *Allen Tate and the Catholic Revival*, 52–71.

19. Conkin, *The Southern Agrarians*, 123.

20. Allen Tate, *The Fathers* (New York: G. P. Putnam, 1938), 180. Cited hereafter as *TF*.

21. Kreyling, *Inventing Southern Literature*, 34–35.

22. Allen Tate, "A View of the Whole South," review of *Culture in the South: A Symposium of Thirty-One Authors*, ed. W. T. Couch, *American Review* 2 (1934): 424.

23. Robyn Wiegman, *American Anatomies: Theorizing Race and Gender* (Durham: Duke University Press, 1995), 96. For a more comprehensive historical account of lynching as a means of political and social subjugation, see especially Terence Finnegan, "Lynching and Political Power in South Carolina and Mississippi," in *Under Sentence of Death: Lynching in the South*, ed. W. Fitzhugh Brundage (Chapel Hill: University of North Carolina Press, 1997), 189–218.

24. Allen Tate, letter to Walker Percy, 1 January 1952, in the Walker Percy Papers, series III, file 68, Southern Historical Collection, Wilson Library, University of North Carolina at Chapel Hill. I am grateful to Helen Tate for permission to quote from this letter.

25. Quoted in Adam Fairclough, *Race and Democracy: The Civil Rights Struggle in Louisiana, 1915–1972* (Athens: University of Georgia Press, 1995), 200.

26. Allen Tate, "The Man of Letters in the Modern World," in *Collected Essays* (Denver: Alan Swallow, 1959), 382. On Tate's ambitions for a revival of Catholic humanism, see especially Huff, *Allen Tate and the Catholic Revival*, 93–99.

27. Brinkmeyer, *Three Catholic Writers*, 71.

28. Lillian Smith, "One More Sigh for the Good Old South: Review of *Gone with the Wind* by Margaret Mitchell," in *From the Mountain: Selections from Pseudopodia, The North Georgia Review, and South Today*, ed. Helen White and Redding S. Sugg Jr. (Memphis: Memphis State University Press, 1972), 30; Caroline Gordon, quoted in Ann Waldron, *Close Connections: Caroline Gordon and the Southern Renaissance* (New York: Putnam, 1987), 173.

29. See especially the essays collected in *Recasting: Gone with the Wind in American Culture*, ed. Darden Asbury Pyron (Miami: University Press of Florida, 1983).

30. According to her friend Elinor Hillyer von Hoffman, Mitchell "used to talk about the Catholics the same way some people talk about New York Jews." Quoted in Darden Asbury Pyron, *Southern Daughter: The Life of Margaret Mitchell* (Oxford: Oxford University Press, 1991), 93.

31. Margaret Mitchell, quoted in *Margaret Mitchell's Gone with the Wind Letters, 1936–1949*, ed. Richard Harwell (New York: Macmillan, 1976), 24.

32. Margaret Mitchell, *Gone with the Wind* (1936; repr., New York: Macmillan, 1964), 36, 45. Cited hereafter as *GWTW*.

33. Richard H. King, "The 'Simple Story's' Ideology: *Gone with the Wind* and the New South Creed," in Pyron, *Recasting: Gone with the Wind in American Culture*, 170.

34. Caroline Gordon, letter to Sally Wood, 21 January 1930, in *The Southern Mandarins: Letters of Caroline Gordon to Sally Wood, 1924–1937*, ed. Sally Wood (Baton Rouge: Louisiana State University Press, 1984), 52.

35. Quoted in Waldron, *Close Connections*, 259.

36. Jacques Maritain, *Art and Scholasticism*, trans. J. F. Scanlan (Freeport, NY: Books for Libraries Press, 1971), 49.

37. Quoted in Thomas F. Haddox, "Contextualizing Flannery O'Connor: Allen Tate, Caroline Gordon, and the Catholic Turn in Southern Literature," *Southern Quarterly* 38 (Fall 1999): 179.

38. Giles, *American Catholic Arts and Fictions*, 194; Cleanth Brooks, "The Formalist Critic," in *Kenyon Review* 13 (1951): 72; W. K. Wimsatt, "Poetry and Christian Thinking," in *The Verbal Icon: Studies in the Meaning of Poetry* (Lexington: University of Kentucky Press, 1954), 279.

39. Anita J. Gandolfo, *Testing the Faith: The New Catholic Fiction in America* (Westport, CT: Greenwood Press, 1992), xi–xii.

40. Quoted in Haddox, "Contextualizing Flannery O'Connor," 179.

41. Maritain, *Art and Scholasticism*, 54.

42. Brinkmeyer, *Three Catholic Writers*, 79.

43. For instance, here is Donald Davidson's enthusiastic reaction to *Aleck Maury, Sportsman*: "If you will keep on writing such books, you will not only be the greatest writer of fiction yet produced in the South—you will restore the Confederacy." Quoted in Nancylee Novell Jonza, *The Underground Stream: The Life and Art of Caroline Gordon* (Athens: University of Georgia Press, 1995), 151.

44. Quoted in Haddox, "Contextualizing Flannery O'Connor," 180.

45. Caroline Gordon, *The Malefactors* (New York: Scribner's, 1956). Cited hereafter as *TM*.

46. Caroline Gordon, "The Presence," in *The Collected Stories of Caroline Gordon*, ed. Robert Penn Warren (New York: Farrar, Straus and Giroux, 1981), 120.

47. Caroline Gordon, *The Strange Children* (New York: Scribner's, 1951), 11, 25. Cited hereafter as *TSC*.

48. Flannery O'Connor would criticize Gordon's use of this Dunkard farmer in a letter of 19 May 1956 written to her friend Betty Hester ("A"): "Nothing wrong with artificial insemination as long as it's animals and bringing those Hookers or Shakers or whatever they were and their disapproval to bear just confused the moral point, if any" (*The Habit of Being: Letters*, ed. Sally Fitzgerald [New York: Farrar, Straus and Giroux, 1979], 158).

49. Brainard Cheney, "Caroline Gordon's *The Malefactors*," *Sewanee Review* 79 (1971): 364–65, 371.

50. M. E. Bradford, "The Passion of Craft," in *The History of Southern Literature*, ed. Louis D. Rubin Jr., Blyden Jackson, Lewis P. Simpson, and Thomas Daniel Young (Baton Rouge: Louisiana State University Press, 1985), 380.

51. For one version of this argument, see Katherine Hemple Prown, *Revising Flannery O'Connor: Southern Literary Culture and the Problem of Female Authorship* (Charlottesville: University Press of Virginia, 2001) ix, 2–8.

52. See Thompson, *The Church, the South, and the Future,* 79, and Gandolfo, *Testing the Faith,* 113–15.

53. Flannery O'Connor, letter to John Lynch, 19 February 1956, in *The Habit of Being,* 139.

54. O'Connor, "The Catholic Novelist in the Protestant South," 196.

55. Quoted in Huff, *Allen Tate and the Catholic Revival,* 115.

56. Jonza, *The Underground Stream,* 359.

57. Quoted in Brinkmeyer, *Three Catholic Writers,* 116.

58. Caroline Gordon, "A Walk with the Accuser," *Southern Review* 13 (1977): 597.

59. Quoted in Waldron, *Close Connections,* 361.

Chapter Five

Toward Catholicism as Lifestyle: Walker Percy, John Kennedy Toole, and Rebecca Wells

1. Huff, *Allen Tate and the Catholic Revival,* 111.

2. Giles, *American Catholic Arts and Fictions,* 375. Percy recognized this tension in his thought and sometimes foregrounded it: his essay "The Message in the Bottle," in *The Message in the Bottle: How Queer Man Is, How Queer Language Is, and What One Has to Do with the Other* (New York: Farrar, Straus and Giroux, 1975), for instance, begins with contradictory epigraphs from Aquinas ("The act of faith consists essentially in knowledge") and Kierkegaard ("Faith is not a form of knowledge"). On the rationalist strand in Percy's belief, see Kieran Quinlan, *Walker Percy: The Last Catholic Novelist* (Baton Rouge: Louisiana State University Press, 1996), 33–36.

3. Walker Percy, "Stoicism in the South," in *Signposts in a Strange Land* (New York: Farrar, Straus and Giroux, 1991), 85.

4. Percy, "Stoicism in the South," 86. See also Farrell O'Gorman, "Walker Percy, the Catholic Church, and Southern Race Relations (ca. 1947–1970)," *Mississippi Quarterly* 53 (Winter 1999/2000): 67–88.

5. Joseph H. Fichter, S.J., *Southern Parish: Dynamics of a City Church* (Chicago: University of Chicago Press, 1951), 265–66. On Twomey and Fichter's activism during the 1940s and 1950s, and the lukewarm response it generated from New Orleans's Archbishop Rummel, see Fairclough, *Race and Democracy,* 199–204.

6. Jay Tolson, *Pilgrim in the Ruins: A Life of Walker Percy* (New York: Simon and Schuster, 1992), 251.

7. For representative readings that emphasize the sacramental quality of Percy's work, see especially Gary M. Ciuba, *Walker Percy: Books of Revelations* (Athens: University of Georgia Press, 1991), 7, 8; and Allen Pridgen, *Walker Percy's Sacramental Landscapes: The Search in the Desert* (Selinsgrove, PA: Susquehanna University Press, 2000).

8. Lewis P. Simpson, "What Survivors Do," in *The Brazen Face of History: Studies in the Literary Consciousness in America* (1980; repr., Athens: University of Georgia Press, 1997), 248.

9. Walker Percy, *Lancelot* (New York: Farrar, Straus and Giroux, 1977), 23–24. Cited hereafter as *L*.

10. Walker Percy, *The Second Coming* (New York: Farrar, Straus and Giroux, 1980), 72.

11. Jean-François Lyotard, *The Postmodern Condition: A Report on Knowledge,* trans. Geoff Bennington and Brian Massumi (Minneapolis: University of Minnesota Press, 1984), xxiv.

12. Jean Baudrillard, *The Transparency of Evil: Essays on Extreme Phenomena,* trans. James Benedict (London: Verso, 1993), 4. In *The Last Catholic Novelist*, Kieran Quinlan remarks in passing that "there are occasional similarities" (197) between Percy's observations and Baudrillard's, but he does not elaborate on them.

13. On Benjamin's discussion of the aura, see his "The Work of Art in the Age of Mechanical Reproduction" in Walter Benjamin, *Illuminations: Essays and Reflections,* trans. Harry Zohn, ed. Hannah Arendt (New York: Schocken, 1968), 220–22.

14. See especially Gordon's letter of 11 December 1951 to Percy (Percy Papers, series II, file 33).

15. George Cotkin, *Existential America* (Baltimore: Johns Hopkins University Press, 2003), 87. Cotkin offers useful accounts of the influence of Kierkegaard in America during this period (35–87) and of the influence of Camus on student movements (225–51).

16. Walker Percy, *The Moviegoer* (New York: Knopf, 1961), 54. Cited hereafter as *TMG*.

17. Quinlan, *The Last Catholic Novelist,* 95.

18. Walker Percy, interview conducted by John C. Carr (1971), in *Conversations with Walker Percy* (Jackson: University Press of Mississippi, 1985), 66.

19. Lucinda H. Mackethan, "Redeeming Blackness: Urban Allegories of O'Connor, Percy, and Toole," in *Studies in the Literary Imagination* 27.2 (Fall 1994): 34.

20. Quoted in Tolson, *Pilgrim in the Ruins,* 301.

21. See, for instance, Harold Bloom's introduction to *Walker Percy: Modern Critical Views,* ed. Harold Bloom (New York: Chelsea House, 1986).

22. Walker Percy, *The Last Gentleman* (New York: Farrar, Straus and Giroux, 1966), 40. Cited hereafter as *TLG*.

23. Jean Baudrillard, "The Precession of Simulacra," in *Simulacra and Simulation,* trans. Sheila Faria Glaser (Ann Arbor: University of Michigan Press, 1994), 6.

24. Baudrillard, *The Transparency of Evil,* 4.

25. Walker Percy, *Love in the Ruins* (New York: Farrar, Straus and Giroux, 1971), 3. Cited hereafter as *LR*.

26. John Egerton, *The Americanization of Dixie: The Southernization of America* (New York: Harper's Magazine Press, 1974), xx. Percy's novel and his nonfiction of the period anticipate Egerton's reflections. His essay "Concerning *Love in the Ruins*," in *Signposts in a Strange Land* (New York: Farrar, Straus and Giroux, 1991), first delivered at the 1971 National Book Award spring press conference, is blunt: "It's not that the South has got rid of its ancient stigma and is out of trouble. It's

rather that the rest of the country is now also stigmatized and is in even deeper trouble" (250).

27. In "Laying the Ghost of Marcus Aurelius?," (in *Conversations with Walker Percy,* ed. Lewis A. Lawson and Victor A. Kramer [Jackson: University Press of Mississippi, 1985]), a 1981 interview with Percy, Jan Nordby Gretlund asked, "Are there any 'normal' women in your novels?"(211). Percy's response admitted the possibility of "anti-feminism on [his] part" (212).

28. On the Dutch Catechism and the controversy surrounding it, see Quinlan, *The Last Catholic Novelist,* 118–19.

29. Tolson, *Pilgrim in the Ruins,* 358.

30. V. S. Pritchett, "Clowns," in *Critical Essays on Walker Percy,* ed. J. Donald Crowley and Sue Mitchell Crowley (Boston: G. K. Hall, 1989), 48.

31. Quoted in Tolson, *Pilgrim in the Ruins,* 357.

32. See Walker Percy, introduction to John Kennedy Toole's *A Confederacy of Dunces* (1981; repr., New York: Wings Books, 1995), vii–ix; and René Pol Nevils and Deborah George Hardy, *Ignatius Rising: The Life of John Kennedy Toole* (Baton Rouge: Louisiana State University Press, 2001), 185–214.

33. Letter from Robert Gottlieb to John Kennedy Toole, 14 December 1964, quoted in Nevils and Hardy, *Ignatius Rising,* 131.

34. Gandolfo, *Testing the Faith,* 3.

35. Morris, *American Catholic,* 230.

36. John Kennedy Toole, *A Confederacy of Dunces* (1980; repr., New York: Wings Books, 1995), 16. Cited hereafter as *ACD.*

37. Andrei Codrescu, "*A Confederacy of Dunces,* Making the Natives Wince," in *Chronicle of Higher Education* 46.32 (14 April 2000): B7–B8.

38. W. Kenneth Holditch, "Another Kind of Confederacy: John Kennedy Toole," in *Literary New Orleans in the Modern World,* ed. Richard S. Kennedy (Baton Rouge: Louisiana State University Press, 1998), 118–19.

39. Codrescu, "Making the Natives Wince," B7.

40. Michael Patrick Gillespie, "Baroque Catholicism in Southern Fiction: Flannery O'Connor, Walker Percy, and John Kennedy Toole," in *Traditions, Voices, and Dreams: The American Novel since the 1960s,* ed. Melvin J. Friedman and Ben Siegel (Newark: University of Delaware Press, 1995), 39, 40.

41. Trysh Travis, "Divine Secrets of the Cultural Studies Sisterhood: Women Reading Rebecca Wells," in *American Literary History* 15 (Spring 2003): 146. See also my critique of Jill Conner Browne's books on similar grounds in "Making Patriarchy Work for You: Jill Conner Browne's Southern, Retrofeminist Conduct Manuals," *Southern Quarterly* 42 (Spring 2004): 113–29.

42. Susan J. Douglas, *Where the Girls Are: Growing up Female with the Mass Media* (New York: Times Books, 1995), 246.

43. Debbie Epstein and Deborah Steinberg, "Twelve Steps to Heterosexuality: Common-Sensibilities on the *Oprah Winfrey Show,*" in *Feminism and Psychology* 5.2 (1995): 278.

44. Rebecca Wells, *Divine Secrets of the Ya-Ya Sisterhood* (New York: HarperCollins, 1996), 63. Cited hereafter as *DS*. On Coughlin's notorious radio program, which ran during the 1930s, see Morris, *American Catholic*, 145–49.

45. Rebecca Wells, *Little Altars Everywhere* (New York: Harper Perennial, 1996), 69, 75, 77. Cited hereafter as *LAE*.

46. Travis, "Divine Secrets of the Cultural Studies Sisterhood," 149.

47. Slavoj Žižek, *On Belief* (London: Routledge, 2001), 12.

48. Travis, "Divine Secrets of the Cultural Studies Sisterhood," 152, 155.

49. Fredric Jameson, "Reification and Utopia in Mass Culture," in *The Jameson Reader,* ed. Michael Hardt and Kathi Weeks (Oxford: Blackwell, 2000), 147.

50. These figures are taken from Clifford Grammich, "Swift Growth and Sudden Change: The Demography of Southern Catholicism," available on-line at http://www.frinstitute.org/southern.htm. Grammich's data also show that southern Catholics are more racially and ethnically diverse than non–Catholic southerners (including, above all, a much greater number of Hispanics), more likely to live in metropolitan areas, and more likely to have been born outside the South. According to the survey *Religious Congregations and Membership in the United States, 2000,* ed. Dale Jones et. al. (Nashville: Glenmary Research Center, 2002), Catholic adherents, figured as a percentage of the total population of individual southern states, range from a low of 3.2 percent in Tennessee to a high of 30.9 percent in Louisiana. In only six southern states—Florida, Kentucky, Louisiana, Maryland, Texas, and Virginia—do Catholics constitute more than five percent of the total population.

51. For an account of the university's attitudes toward racial mixing and Catholicism, see Jones's interview with Larry King on March 3, 2000, found online at <http://www.cnn.com>.

52. See, for instance, Deborah H. Cohn, *History and Memory in the Two Souths: Recent Southern and Spanish American Fiction* (Nashville: Vanderbilt University Press, 1999); and Jon Smith and Deborah H. Cohn, eds., *Look Away!: The U.S. South in New World Studies* (Durham: Duke University Press, 2004).

53. Sandra Cisneros, "Little Miracles, Kept Promises," in *Woman Hollering Creek and Other Stories* (New York: Vintage Contemporaries, 1991), 128.

54. Giles, *American Catholic Arts and Fictions,* 531.

Works Cited

Adams, Rachel. "'A Mixture of Delicious and Freak': The Queer Fiction of Carson McCullers." *American Literature* 71 (1999): 551–84.

Alldredge, Eugene P. *The New Challenge of Home Missions.* Nashville: Southern Baptist Convention Sunday School Board, 1927. Southern Baptist Historical Library and Archives, Nashville, TN.

Anderson, Benedict. *Imagined Communities: Reflections on the Origin and Spread of Nationalism.* 1983. Revised edition. London: Verso, 1991.

Andrews, William L. "The Literature of Slavery and Freedom, 1746–1865." *The Norton Anthology of African American Literature.* Ed. Henry Louis Gates Jr. and Nellie Y. McKay. New York: Norton, 1997. 127–36.

Bailey, Kenneth K. *Southern White Protestantism in the Twentieth Century.* New York: Harper and Row, 1964.

Baker, Houston A., Jr. *Turning South Again: Re-thinking Modernism / Re-reading Booker T.* Durham: Duke University Press, 2001.

Baudrillard, Jean. "The Precession of Simulacra." *Simulacra and Simulation.* 1981. Trans. Sheila Faria Glaser. Ann Arbor: University of Michigan Press, 1994.

———. *The Transparency of Evil: Essays on Extreme Phenomena.* 1990. Trans. James Benedict. London: Verso, 1993.

Bauer, Margaret D. "When a Convent Seems the Only Viable Choice: Questionable Callings in Stories by Alice Dunbar-Nelson, Alice Walker, and Louise Erdrich." *Critical Perspectives on Alice Walker.* Ed. Ikenna Dieke. Westport, CT: Greenwood Press, 1999. 45–54.

Bell, Caryn Cossé. *Revolution, Romanticism, and the Afro-Creole Protest Tradition in Louisiana, 1718–1868.* Baton Rouge: Louisiana State University Press, 1997.

Benjamin, Walter. "The Work of Art in the Age of Mechanical Reproduction." 1936. *Illuminations.* Trans. Harry Zohn. New York: Schocken, 1968. 211–44.

Birkett, Jennifer. *The Sins of the Fathers: Decadence in France, 1870–1914.* London: Quartet Books, 1986.

Bloom, Harold. Introduction. *Walker Percy: Modern Critical Views.* Ed. Harold Bloom. New York: Chelsea House, 1986. 1–7.

Bonner, Thomas Jr. "Christianity and Catholicism in the Fiction of Kate Chopin." *Southern Quarterly* 20 (Winter 1982): 118–25.

Bové, Paul A. *Mastering Discourse: The Politics of Intellectual Culture.* Durham: Duke University Press, 1992.

Bowers. "L'orphelin des tombeaux." ["The Orphan of the Tombs."] *Les Cenelles: A Collection of Poems by Creole Writers of the Early Nineteenth Century.* 1845. Ed. Régine Latortue and Gleason R. W. Adams. Boston: G. K. Hall, 1979. 20–27.

Bradford, M. E. "The Passion of Craft." In *The History of Southern Literature.* Ed. Louis D. Rubin Jr., Blyden Jackson, Rayburn S. Moore, Lewis P. Simpson, and Thomas Daniel Young. Baton Rouge: Louisiana State University Press, 1985. 375–82.

Brinkmeyer, Robert H., Jr. *Three Catholic Writers of the Modern South.* Jackson: University Press of Mississippi, 1985.

Brooks, Cleanth. "The Formalist Critic." *Kenyon Review* 13 (1951): 72–81.

———. "Southern Literature: The Wellsprings of Its Vitality." *A Shaping Joy: Studies in the Writer's Craft.* New York: Harcourt, 1972. 215–29.

Butler, Judith. *Gender Trouble: Feminism and the Subversion of Identity.* New York: Routledge, 1990.

Cable, George Washington. *The Grandissimes.* 1880. New York: Penguin, 1988.

———. *Madame Delphine.* 1881. *Old Creole Days.* New York: Scribner, 1944. 1–81.

———. " 'Posson Jone'." 1875. *Old Creole Days.* New York: Scribner, 1944. 149–75.

———. "The Silent South." 1889. *The Negro Question: A Selection of Writings on Civil Rights in the South.* Ed. Alvin Turner. Garden City: Doubleday, 1958.

Campbell, Erin E. " 'The nigger that's going to sleep with your sister': Charles Bon as Cultural Shibboleth in *Absalom, Absalom!*" *Songs of the Reconstructing South: Building Literary Louisiana, 1864–1945.* Ed. Suzanne Disheroon-Green and Lisa Abney. Westport, CT: Greenwood Press, 2002. 159–68.

Carr, Virginia Spencer. *The Lonely Hunter: A Biography of Carson McCullers.* Garden City: Doubleday, 1975.

Chalmers, David Mark. *Hooded Americanism: The History of the Ku Klux Klan.* New York: New Viewpoints, 1976.

Cheney, Brainard. "Caroline Gordon's *The Malefactors.*" *Sewanee Review* 79 (1971): 360–72.

Cheung, Floyd D. "*Les Cenelles* and Quadroon Balls: 'Hidden Transcipts' of Resistance and Domination in New Orleans, 1803–1845." *Southern Literary Journal* 29.2 (1997): 5–16.

Chopin, Kate. *At Fault.* 1890. *The Complete Works of Kate Chopin.* Ed. Peter Seyersted. Vol. 2. Baton Rouge: Louisiana State University Press, 1969. 741–877.

———. *The Awakening.* 1899. Ed. Margo Culley. New York: Norton Critical Edition, 1994.

———. *Kate Chopin's Private Papers.* Ed. Emily Toth and Peter Seyersted. Bloomington: Indiana University Press, 1998.

———. "Lilacs." *A Vocation and a Voice.* Ed. Emily Toth. New York: Penguin, 1991. 131–46.

———. "Madame Célestin's Divorce." *Bayou Folk and A Night in Acadie.* New York: Penguin, 1999. 90–93.

———. "Two Portraits (The Wanton and the Nun)." *A Vocation and a Voice.* Ed. Emily Toth. New York: Penguin, 1991. 45–51.

———. "A Vocation and a Voice." *A Vocation and a Voice.* Ed. Emily Toth. New York: Penguin, 1991. 1–36.

Cisneros, Sandra. "Little Miracles, Kept Promises." *Woman Hollering Creek and Other Stories.* New York: Vintage Contemporaries, 1991. 116–29.

Ciuba, Gary M. *Walker Percy: Books of Revelations.* Athens: University of Georgia Press, 1991.

Codrescu, Andrei. "*A Confederacy of Dunces,* Making the Natives Wince." *Chronicle of Higher Education* 46.32 (14 April 2000): B7–B8.

Cohn, Deborah H. *History and Memory in the Two Souths: Recent Southern and Spanish American Fiction.* Nashville: Vanderbilt University Press, 1999.

Coleman, Edward Maceo. Introduction. *Les Cenelles: Poems in French by Free Men of Color, First Published in 1845.* Ed. Edward Maceo Coleman. Washington: Associated Publishers, 1845.

Conkin, Paul K. *The Southern Agrarians.* Knoxville: University of Tennessee Press, 1988.

Cotkin, George. *Existential America.* Baltimore: Johns Hopkins University Press, 2003.

Davis, Thadious M. *Nella Larsen, Novelist of the Harlem Renaissance: A Woman's Life Unveiled.* Baton Rouge: Louisiana State University Press, 1994.

Dejean, Joan. "Critical Creolization: Grace King and Writing on French in the American South." *Southern Literature and Literary Theory.* Ed. Jefferson Humphries. Athens: University of Georgia Press, 1990. 109–26.

Desdunes, Rodolphe Lucien. *Our People and Our History: A Tribute to the Creole People of Color in Memory of the Great Men They Have Given Us and of the Good Works They Have Accomplished.* 1911. Trans. and ed. Sister Dorothea Olga McCants. Baton Rouge: Louisiana State University Press, 1973.

Desmond, John F. *Risen Sons: Flannery O'Connor's Vision of History.* Athens: University of Georgia Press, 1987.

Detiege, Sister Audrey Marie. *Henriette Delille, Free Woman of Color: Foundress of the Sisters of the Holy Family.* New Orleans: Sisters of the Holy Family, 1976.

Douglas, Susan J. *Where the Girls Are: Growing up Female with the Mass Media.* New York: Times Books, 1995.

Drake, Robert. *Flannery O'Connor: A Critical Essay.* Grand Rapids: Eerdmans, 1966.

Dunbar-Nelson, Alice. "People of Color in Louisiana, Part I." *Journal of Negro History* (January 1916): 143–44.

———. "Sister Josepha." *The Works of Alice Dunbar-Nelson.* Ed. Gloria T. Hull. Vol. 1. New York: Oxford University Press, 1988. 155–72.

———. "The Stones of the Village." *The Works of Alice-Dunbar Nelson.* Ed. Gloria T. Hull. Vol. 3. New York: Oxford University Press, 1988. 3–33.

Egerton, John. *The Americanization of Dixie: The Southernization of America.* New York: Harper's Magazine Press, 1974.

Elfenbein, Anna Shannon. *Women on the Color Line: Evolving Stereotypes and the Writings of George Washington Cable, Grace King, Kate Chopin.* Charlottesville: University Press of Virginia, 1989.

England, John. *Letters of the Late Bishop England to the Honorable John Forsyth, on the Subject of Domestic Slavery.* 1844. New York: Negro Universities Press, 1969.

Epstein, Debbie and Deborah Steinberg. "Twelve Steps to Heterosexuality: Common-Sensibilities on the *Oprah Winfrey Show.*" *Feminism and Psychology* 5.2 (1995): 275–80.

Evans, Augusta Jane. *Inez: A Tale of the Alamo.* 1855. New York: W. I. Pooley, 1864.

Fabre, Michel. "The New Orleans Press and French-Language Literatures by Creoles of Color." *Multilingual America: Transnationalism, Ethnicity, and the Languages of American Literature.* Ed. Werner Sollors. New York: New York University Press, 1998. 29–49.

Fairclough, Adam. *Race and Democracy: The Civil Rights Struggle in Louisiana, 1915–1972.* Athens: University of Georgia Press, 1995.

Faulkner, William. *Absalom, Absalom!* 1936. New York: Modern Library, 1964.

Fichter, Joseph H., S. J., *Southern Parish: Dynamics of a City Church.* Chicago: University of Chicago Press, 1951.

Fiedler, Leslie A. *Love and Death in the American Novel.* 1960. Normal, IL: Dalkey Archive Press, 1997.

Finnegan, Terence. "Lynching and Political Power in South Carolina and Mississippi." *Under Sentence of Death: Lynching in the South.* Ed. W. Fitzhugh Brundage. Chapel Hill: University of North Carolina Press, 1997. 189–218.

Fitzhugh, George. *Cannibals All! or, Slaves Without Masters.* 1857. Ed. C. Vann Woodward. Cambridge, MA: Belknap, 1960.

———. *Sociology for the South, or the Failure of Free Society.* 1854. New York: Burt Franklin, 1965.

———. "Southern Thought." *De Bow's Review* 23 (October 1857): 337–49.

Franchot, Jenny. *Roads to Rome: The Antebellum Protestant Encounter with Catholicism.* Berkeley: University of California Press, 1994.

Galton, Francis. *Hereditary Genius: An Inquiry into its Laws and Consequences.* 1892. Gloucester, MA: Peter Smith, 1962.

Gandolfo, Anita. *Testing the Faith: The New Catholic Fiction in America.* Westport, CT: Greenwood Press, 1992.

Gates, Henry Louis, Jr. *Loose Canons: Notes on the Culture Wars.* Oxford: Oxford University Press, 1992.

Genovese, Eugene D. *The Southern Front: History and Politics in the Cultural War.* Columbia: University of Missouri Press, 1995.

———. *The Southern Tradition: The Achievement and Limitations of an American Conservatism.* Cambridge, MA: Harvard University Press, 1994.

———. *The World the Slaveholders Made: Two Essays in Interpretation.* New York: Pantheon Books, 1969.

Gerard, Philip. *Cape Fear Rising.* Winston-Salem: John F. Blair, 1994.

Giannone, Richard. *Flannery O'Connor, Hermit Novelist.* Urbana: University of Illinois Press, 2000.

Giles, Paul. *American Catholic Arts and Fictions: Culture, Ideology, Aesthetics.* Cambridge: Cambridge University Press, 1992.

Gillespie, Michael Patrick. "Baroque Catholicism in Southern Fiction: Flannery O'Connor, Walker Percy, and John Kennedy Toole." *Traditions, Voices, and Dreams: The American Novel since the 1960s.* Ed. Melvin J. Friedman and Ben Siegel. Newark: University of Delaware Press, 1995. 25–47.

Gillespie, Neal C. *The Collapse of Orthodoxy: The Intellectual Ordeal of George Frederick Holmes.* Charlottesville: University Press of Virginia, 1972.

Gilman, Richard. *Decadence: The Strange Life of an Epithet.* New York: Farrar, Straus and Giroux, 1979.

Glasgow, Joanne. "What's a Nice Lesbian Like You Doing in the Church of Torquemada? Radclyffe Hall and Other Catholic Converts." *Lesbian Texts and Contexts: Radical Revisions.* New York: New York University Press, 1990. 241–54.

Gleeson-White, Sarah. *Strange Bodies: Gender and Identity in the Novels of Carson McCullers.* Tuscaloosa: University of Alabama Press, 2003.

Gordon, Caroline. Letters to Walker Percy, 1952. Walker Percy Papers, Series III, File 33. Southern Historical Collection, Wilson Library, University of North Carolina at Chapel Hill.

——. *The Malefactors.* New York: Harcourt Brace, 1956.

——. "The Presence." 1948. *The Collected Stories of Caroline Gordon.* Ed. Robert Penn Warren. New York: Farrar, Straus and Giroux, 1981. 105–20.

——. *The Southern Mandarins: Letters of Caroline Gordon to Sally Wood, 1924–1937.* Ed. Sally Wood. Baton Rouge: Louisiana State University Press, 1984.

——. *The Strange Children.* New York: Scribner's, 1951.

——. "A Walk with the Accuser." *Southern Review* 13 (1977): 597–613.

Grammich, Clifford. "Swift Growth and Sudden Change: The Demography of Southern Catholicism." Available on-line at http://www.frinstitute.org/southern.htm.

Gray, Richard. *Southern Aberrations: Writers of the American South and the Problems of Regionalism.* Baton Rouge: Louisiana State University Press, 2000.

——. *Writing the South: Ideas of an American Region.* 1986. Baton Rouge: Louisiana State University Press, 1997.

Griffin, Susan. *Anti-Catholicism and Nineteenth-Century Fiction.* Cambridge: Cambridge University Press, 2004.

Guilday, Peter. *The Life and Times of John England, First Bishop of Charleston.* Vol. 2. New York: America Press, 1927.

Guillaume, Alfred J., Jr. "Love, Death, and Faith in the New Orleans Poets of Color." *Southern Quarterly* 20 (1982): 126–44.

Haddox, Thomas F. "Contextualizing Flannery O'Connor: Allen Tate, Caroline Gordon, and the Catholic Turn in Southern Literature." *Southern Quarterly* 38 (Fall 1999): 173–90.

————. "Making Patriarchy Work for You: Jill Conner Browne's Southern, Retrofeminist Conduct Manuals." *Southern Quarterly* 42 (Spring 2004): 113–29.

Hall, Gwendolyn Midlo. *Africans in Colonial Louisiana: The Development of Afro-Creole Culture in the Eighteenth Century*. Baton Rouge: Louisiana State University Press, 1992.

Hanson, Ellis. *Decadence and Catholicism*. Cambridge, MA: Harvard University Press, 1997.

Hartman, Saidiya V. *Scenes of Subjection: Terror, Slavery, and Self-Making in Nineteenth-Century America*. Oxford: Oxford University Press, 1997.

Hawkes, John. "Flannery O'Connor's Devil." *Sewanee Review* 70 (1962): 395–407.

Holditch, W. Kenneth. "Another Kind of Confederacy: John Kennedy Toole." *Literary New Orleans in the Modern World*. Ed. Richard S. Kennedy. Baton Rouge: Louisiana State University Press, 1998. 102–22.

Holmes, George Frederick. "Rome and the Romans." *Southern Quarterly Review* 6 (October 1844).

Holmes, Trevor. "Coming Out of the Coffin: Gay Males and Queer Goths in Contemporary Vampire Fiction." *Blood Read: The Vampire as Metaphor in Contemporary Culture*. Ed. Joan Gordon and Veronica Hollinger. Philadelphia: University of Pennsylvania Press, 1997, 169–88.

Horn, Jason Gary. *Mark Twain and William James: Crafting a Free Self*. Columbia: University of Missouri Press, 1996.

Huff, Peter A. *Allen Tate and the Catholic Revival: Trace of the Fugitive Gods*. New York: Paulist Press, 1996.

Hull, Gloria T. *Color, Sex, and Poetry: Three Women Writers of the Harlem Renaissance*. Bloomington: Indiana University Press, 1987.

Ignatiev, Noel. *How the Irish Became White*. London: Routledge, 1995.

Jackson, Blyden. *A History of Afro-American Literature. Volume I: The Long Beginning, 1746–1895*. Baton Rouge: Louisiana State University Press, 1989.

Jameson, Fredric. "Reification and Utopia in Mass Culture." *The Jameson Reader*. Ed. Michael Hardt and Kathi Weeks. Oxford: Blackwell, 2000. 123–48.

Jancovich, Mark. *The Cultural Politics of the New Criticism*. Cambridge: Cambridge University Press, 1993.

Jones, Anne Goodwyn. *Tomorrow Is Another Day: The Woman Writer in the South, 1859–1936*. Baton Rouge: Louisiana State University Press, 1981.

Jones, Bob III. Interview with Larry King. *Larry King Live*. CNN. 3 March 2000 <http://www.cnn.com>.

Jones, Dale, et al. *Religious Congregations and Membership in the United States, 2000*. Nashville: Glenmary Research Center, 2002.

Jones, Suzanne W., and Sharon Monteith, eds. *South to a New Place: Region, Literature, Culture*. Baton Rouge: Louisiana State University Press, 2002.

Jonza, Nancylee Novell. *The Underground Stream: The Life and Art of Caroline Gordon*. Athens: University of Georgia Press, 1995.

Jordan, Winthrop D. *White over Black: American Attitudes Toward the Negro, 1550–1812*. Chapel Hill: University of North Carolina Press, 1968.

Kaplan, Justin. Introduction. *Personal Recollections of Joan of Arc*. By Mark Twain. *The Oxford Mark Twain*. Ed. Shelley Fisher Fishkin. New York: Oxford University Press, 1996. xxxi–xlii.

Kazin, Alfred. *God and the American Writer*. New York: Knopf, 1997.

Kenschaft, Lori J. "Homoerotics and Human Connections: Reading Carson McCullers 'As a Lesbian.'" *Critical Essays on Carson McCullers*. Ed. Beverly Lyon Clark and Melvin J. Friedman. New York: G. K. Hall, 1996. 220–33.

King, Grace. "The Little Convent Girl." 1893. *Balcony Stories*. New York: Macmillan, 1925. 143–61.

———. *Memories of a Southern Woman of Letters*. New York: Macmillan, 1932.

King, Richard H. "The 'Simple Story's' Ideology: *Gone with the Wind* and the New South Creed." *Recasting: Gone with the Wind in American Culture*. Ed. Darden Asbury Pyron. Miami: University Press of Florida, 1983. 167–83.

———. *A Southern Renaissance: The Cultural Awakening of the American South, 1930–1955*. Oxford: Oxford University Press, 1980.

Kreyling, Michael. *Figures of the Hero in Southern Narrative*. Baton Rouge: Louisiana State University Press, 1987.

———. Introduction. *New Essays on Wise Blood*. Cambridge: Cambridge University Press, 1995. 1–24.

———. *Inventing Southern Literature*. Jackson: University Press of Mississippi, 1998.

Labrie, Ross. *The Catholic Imagination in American Literature*. Columbia: University of Missouri Press, 1997.

Ladd, Barbara. *Nationalism and the Color Line in George W. Cable, Mark Twain, and William Faulkner*. Baton Rouge: Louisiana State University Press, 1996.

Land, Aubrey C. *Colonial Maryland: A History*. Millwood, NY: KTO Press, 1981.

Lanusse, Armand. "Epigramme." ["Epigram."] *Les Cenelles: A Collection of Poems by Creole Writers of the Early Nineteenth Century*. 1845. Trans. and ed. Régine Latortue and Gleason R. W. Adams. Boston: G. K. Hall, 1979. 94–95.

———. Introduction. *Les Cenelles: A Collection of Poems by Creole Writers of the Early Nineteenth Century*. 1845. Trans. and ed. Régine Latortue and Gleason R. W. Adams. Boston: G. K. Hall, 1979. xxxvi–xli.

———. "Le prêtre et la jeune fille." ["The Priest and the Young Girl."] *Les Cenelles: A Collection of Poems by Creole Writers of the Early Nineteenth Century*. 1845. Trans. and ed. Régine Latortue and Gleason R. W. Adams. Boston: G. K. Hall, 1979. 114–17.

Latortue, Régine, and Gleason R. W. Adams. Preface. *Les Cenelles: A Collection of Poems by Creole Writers of the Early Nineteenth Century*. 1845. Trans. and ed. Latortue and Adams. Boston: G. K. Hall, 1979. ix–xxx.

LeBlanc, Elizabeth. "The Metaphorical Lesbian: Edna Pontellier in *The Awakening*." *Tulsa Studies in Women's Literature* 15 (Fall 1996): 289–307.

Lebreton, Dagmar Renshaw. *Chahta-Ima: The Life of Adrien-Emmanuel Rouquette*. Baton Rouge: Louisiana State University Press, 1947.

Lee, Harper. *To Kill a Mockingbird*. Philadelphia, Lippincott, 1960.

Leo XIII, Pope. *Quod Apostolici Muneris*. 28 December 1878. *The Papal Encyclicals, 1878–1903*. Ed. Claudia Carlen Ihn. Raleigh: Pierian Press, 1990. 11–16.

Liotau, Mirtil-Ferdinand. "Une impression." ["An Impression."] *Les Cenelles: A Collection of Poems by Creole Writers of the Early Nineteenth Century*. 1845. Trans. and ed. Régine Latortue and Gleason R. W. Adams. Boston: G. K. Hall, 1979. 88–91.

Lipscomb, Rev. Oscar H. "Some Unpublished Poems of Abram J. Ryan." *Alabama Review* 25 (1972): 163–77.

Lombroso, Cesare. *Crime, Its Causes and Remedies*. Trans. Henry P. Horton. Boston: Little and Brown, 1911.

Lukács, Georg. *The Historical Novel*. Trans. Hannah and Stanley Mitchell. London: Merlin, 1962.

Lyotard, Jean-François. *The Postmodern Condition: A Report on Knowledge*. Trans. Geoff Bennington and Brian Massumi. Minneapolis: University of Minnesota Press, 1984.

Mackethan, Lucinda H. "Redeeming Blackness: Urban Allegories of O'Connor, Percy, and Toole." *Studies in the Literary Imagination* 27.2 (Fall 1994): 29–39.

Maritain, Jacques. *Art and Scholasticism*. 1930. Trans. J. F. Scanlan. Freeport, NY: Books for Libraries Press, 1971.

McCullers, Carson. "The Flowering Dream: Notes on Writing." 1959. *The Mortgaged Heart*. Ed. Margarita G. Smith. Boston: Houghton Mifflin, 1971. 274–82.

———. *The Heart Is a Lonely Hunter*. Boston: Houghton Mifflin, 1940.

———. *The Member of the Wedding*. Boston: Houghton Mifflin, 1946.

———. *Reflections in a Golden Eye*. Boston: Houghton Mifflin, 1941.

Menand, Louis. *The Metaphysical Club: A Story of Ideas in America*. New York: Farrar, Straus and Giroux, 2001.

Michaels, Walter Benn. *Our America: Nativism, Modernism, and Pluralism*. Durham: Duke University Press, 1995.

Miller, Randall M. "A Church in Cultural Captivity: Some Speculations on Catholic Identity in the Old South." *Catholics in the Old South: Essays on Church and Culture*. Ed. Randall M. Miller and Jon L. Wakelyn. Macon: Mercer University Press, 1983. 11–52.

Mitchell, Margaret. *Gone with the Wind*. 1936. New York: Macmillan, 1964.

———. *Margaret Mitchell's* Gone with the Wind *Letters, 1936–1949*. Ed. Richard Harwell. New York: Macmillan, 1976.

Morris, Charles R. *American Catholic*. New York: Times Books, 1997.

Morris, Willie. *North Toward Home*. 1967. New York: Vintage, 2000.

Nevils, René Pol and Deborah George Hardy. *Ignatius Rising: The Life of John Kennedy Toole*. Baton Rouge: Louisiana State University Press, 2001.

Nordau, Max. *Degeneration*. New York: Appleton, 1895.

Oakes, James. *Slavery and Freedom: An Interpretation of the Old South*. New York: Vintage, 1991.

O'Brien, Michael. "The Lineaments of Antebellum Southern Romanticism." *Rethinking the South: Essays in Intellectual History*. Baltimore: Johns Hopkins University Press, 1988. 38–56.

O'Connell, Maurice R. *Daniel O'Connell: The Man and His Politics*. Dublin: Irish Academic Press, 1990.

O'Connor, Flannery. "The Catholic Novelist in the Protestant South." *Mystery and Manners: Essays and Occasional Prose*. Ed. Sally and Robert Fitzgerald. New York: Farrar, Straus and Giroux, 1969. 191–209.

———. "The Displaced Person." 1954. *The Complete Stories*. New York: Noonday Press, 1971. 194–235.

———. "A Good Man Is Hard to Find." 1955. *The Complete Stories*. New York: Noonday Press, 1971.

———. *The Habit of Being: Letters*. Ed. Sally Fitzgerald. New York: Farrar, Straus and Giroux, 1979.

———. "Some Aspects of the Grotesque in Southern Fiction." *Mystery and Manners: Occasional Prose*. Ed. Sally and Robert Fitzgerald. New York: Farrar, Straus and Giroux, 1969, 36–50.

O'Gorman, Farrell. "Walker Percy, the Catholic Church, and Southern Race Relations (ca. 1947–1970)." *Mississippi Quarterly* 53 (Winter 1999/2000): 67–88.

Oldemoppen, Bernadette Greenwood. *Abram J. Ryan: Priest, Patriot, Poet*. Mobile: Southeastern Press, 1992.

Paglia, Camille. *Sexual Personae: Art and Decadence from Nefertiti to Emily Dickinson*. New York: Vintage, 1991.

Percy, Walker. "Concerning *Love in the Ruins*." *Signposts in a Strange Land*. Ed. Patrick Samway. New York: Noonday Press, 1991. 247–50.

———. Interview conducted by John C. Carr. 1971. *Conversations with Walker Percy*. Jackson: University Press of Mississippi, 1985. 56–71.

———. *Lancelot*. New York: Farrar, Straus and Giroux, 1977.

———. *The Last Gentleman*. New York: Farrar, Straus and Giroux, 1966.

———. "Laying the Ghost of Marcus Aurelius?" 1981. Interview conducted by Jan Nordby Gretlund. *Conversations with Walker Percy*. Ed. Lewis A. Lawson and Victor A. Kramer. Jackson: University Press of Mississippi, 1985. 203–15.

———. *Love in the Ruins*. New York: Farrar, Straus and Giroux, 1971.

———. *The Message in the Bottle: How Queer Man Is, How Queer Language Is, and What One Has to Do with the Other*. New York: Farrar, Straus and Giroux, 1975.

———. *The Moviegoer*. New York: Knopf, 1961.

———. *The Second Coming*. New York: Farrar, Straus and Giroux, 1980.

———. "Stoicism in the South." 1957. *Signposts in a Strange Land*. Ed. Patrick Samway. New York: Farrar, Straus, and Giroux, 1991. 83–93.

Percy, William Alexander. *Lanterns on the Levee: Recollections of a Planter's Son*. 1941. Baton Rouge: Louisiana State University Press, 1973.

Perret, J. John. "Victor Séjour, Black French Playwright from Louisiana." *French Review* 57 (1983): 187–93.

Phillips, Robert S. "The Gothic Architecture of *The Member of the Wedding*." *Renascence* 16 (1964): 59–72.

Pius X, Pope. *Pascendi Dominici Gregis*. 8 September 1907. *The Papal Encyclicals, 1903–1939*. Ed. Claudia Carlen Ihm. Raleigh: Pierian Press, 1990. 71–98.

Pridgen, Allen. *Walker Percy's Sacramental Landscapes: The Search in the Desert.* Selinsgrove, PA: Susquehanna University Press, 2000.

Pritchett, V. S. "Clowns." *Critical Essays on Walker Percy.* Ed. J. Donald Crowley and Sue Mitchell Crowley. Boston: G. K. Hall, 1989. 46–48.

Prown, Katherine Hemple. *Revising Flannery O'Connor: Southern Literary Culture and the Problem of Female Authorship.* Charlottesville: University Press of Virginia, 2001.

Pyron, Darden Asbury. *Southern Daughter: The Life of Margaret Mitchell.* Oxford: Oxford University Press, 1991.

———, ed. *Recasting:* Gone with the Wind *in American Culture.* Miami: University Press of Florida, 1983.

Questy, Joanni. "Causerie." ["Chat."] *Les Cenelles: A Collection of Poems by Creole Writers of the Early Nineteenth Century.* 1845. Trans. and ed. Régine Latortue and Gleason R. W. Adams. Boston: G. K. Hall, 1979. 68–69.

———. "Vision." *Les Cenelles: A Collection of Poems by Creole Writers of the Early Nineteenth Century.* 1845. Trans. and ed. Régine Latortue and Gleason R.W. Adams. Boston: G. K. Hall, 1979. 60–65.

Quinlan, Kieran. *Walker Percy: The Last Catholic Novelist.* Baton Rouge: Louisiana State University Press, 1996.

Ransom, John Crowe. *God without Thunder: An Unorthodox Defense of Orthodoxy.* New York: Harcourt Brace, 1930.

———. "Introduction: A Statement of Principles." *I'll Take My Stand: The South and the Agrarian Tradition.* By Twelve Southerners. 1930. Ed. Louis D. Rubin Jr. Baton Rouge: Louisiana State University Press, 1977. xxxvii–xlviii.

Rice, Anne. *The Feast of All Saints.* 1979. New York: Ballantine, 1986.

Ripley, Alexandra. *Scarlett: The Sequel to Margaret Mitchell's* Gone with the Wind. New York: Warner, 1991.

Roach, Joseph. *Cities of the Dead: Circum-Atlantic Performance.* New York: Columbia University Press, 1996.

Rouquette, Adrien-Emmanuel. *Critical Dialogue Between Aboo and Caboo; or, A Grandissime Ascension.* New Orleans [Mingo City]: Great Publishing House of Sam Slick Allspice, 12 Veracity Street, [1880].

Rubin, Louis D., Jr. " 'The Begum of Bengal': Mark Twain and the South." *William Elliott Shoots a Bear: Essays on the Southern Literary Imagination.* Baton Rouge: Louisiana State University Press, 1975. 28–60.

———. "Flannery O'Connor: A Note on Literary Fashions." *Critique* 2 (Fall 1958): 11–18.

———. "From Combray to Ithaca; or, What's 'Southern' about Southern Literature." *The Mockingbird in the Gum Tree: A Literary Gallimaufry.* Baton Rouge: Louisiana State University Press, 1990. 21–35.

———. *George W. Cable: The Life and Times of a Southern Heretic.* New York: Pegasus, 1969.

Ryan, Abram J. *Selected Poems of Father Ryan.* Ed. Gordon Weaver. Jackson: University Press of Mississippi, 1973.

Savigneau, Josayne. *Carson McCullers: A Life*. Trans. Joan E. Howard. Boston: Houghton Mifflin, 2001.

Sayre, Robert, and Michael Löwy, "Figures of Romantic Anticapitalism." *Spirits of Fire: English Romantic Writers and Contemporary Historical Methods*. Ed. G. A. Rosso and Daniel P. Watkins. Rutherford, NJ: Fairleigh Dickinson University Press, 1990. 26–37.

Sedgwick, Eve Kosofsky. *Epistemology of the Closet*. Berkeley: University of California Press, 1990.

———. *Tendencies*. Durham: Duke University Press, 1993.

Segrest, Mab. *My Mama's Dead Squirrel: Lesbian Essays on Southern Culture*. Ithaca: Firebrand Books, 1985.

Seidel, Kathryn Lee. "Art Is an Unnatural Act: Mademoiselle Reisz in *The Awakening*." *Mississippi Quarterly* 46 (Spring 1993): 199–214.

Shafer, Aileen Chris. "Let Us Prey: Religious Codes and Rituals in *The Vampire Lestat*." *The Gothic World of Anne Rice*. Ed. Gary Hoppenstand and Ray B. Browne. Bowling Green, OH: Bowling Green State University Popular Press, 1996. 149–62.

Simpson, Lewis P. *The Brazen Face of History: Studies in the Literary Consciousness in America*. 1980. Athens: University of Georgia Press, 1997.

———. *The Dispossessed Garden: Pastoral and History in Southern Literature*. Athens: University of Georgia Press, 1975.

———. *The Fable of the Southern Writer*. Baton Rouge: Louisiana State University Press, 1994.

Skandera-Trombley, Laura E. *Mark Twain in the Company of Women*. Philadelphia: University of Pennsylvania Press, 1994.

Smith, Jon, and Deborah H. Cohn, eds. *Look Away!: The U.S. South in New World Studies*. Durham: Duke University Press, 2004.

Smith, Lillian. *Killers of the Dream*. 1949. New York: Norton, 1961.

———. "One More Sigh for the Good Old South." Review of *Gone With the Wind*, by Margaret Mitchell. 1936. *From the Mountain: Selections from Pseudopodia, The North Georgia Review, and South Today*. Ed. Helen White and Redding S. Sugg Jr. Memphis: Memphis State University Press, 1972. 28–30.

Sparr, Arnold. *To Promote, Defend, and Redeem: The Catholic Literary Revival and the Cultural Transformation of American Catholicism*. Westport, CT: Greenwood Press, 1990.

Spengler, Oswald. *The Decline of the West*. Trans. Charles Francis Atkinson. New York: Knopf, 1926–28.

Stahl, J. D. *Mark Twain: Culture and Gender*. Athens: University of Georgia Press, 1994.

Stritch, Thomas. *The Catholic Church in Tennessee: The Sesquicentennial Story*. Nashville: The Catholic Center, 1987.

Tate, Allen. *The Fathers*. New York: Putnam, 1938.

———. Letter to John Crowe Ransom, 27 July 1929. Donald Davidson Papers, Box 10, File 43. Special Collections, Heard Library, Vanderbilt University.

―――. Letter to Walker Percy, 1 January 1952. Walker Percy Papers, Series III, File 68. Southern Historical Collection, Wilson Library, University of North Carolina at Chapel Hill.

―――. "The Man of Letters in the Modern World." *Collected Essays*. Denver: Alan Swallow, 1959. 379–93.

―――. "Remarks on the Southern Religion." *I'll Take My Stand: The South and the Agrarian Tradition*. By Twelve Southerners. 1930. Ed. Louis D. Rubin Jr. Baton Rouge: Louisiana State University Press, 1977. 155–75.

―――. "A View of the Whole South." Review of *Culture in the South: A Symposium of Thirty-One Authors*, ed. W. T. Couch. *American Review* 2 (1934): 411–32.

Taylor, Hannis. "Abram J. Ryan." *The Library of Southern Literature*. Vol. 10. New Orleans: Martin and Hoyt, 1907. 4623–26.

Teish, Luisah. *Jambalaya: The Natural Woman's Book of Personal Charms and Practical Rituals*. San Francisco: Harper and Row, 1985.

Thompson, James J. *The Church, the South, and the Future*. Westminster, MD: Christian Classics, 1988.

Thornton, R. K. R. *The Decadent Dilemma*. London: Edward Arnold, 1983.

Tinker, Edward Larocque. *Creole City: Its Past and Its People*. New York: Longmans, Green, 1953.

Tolson, Jay. *Pilgrim in the Ruins: A Life of Walker Percy*. New York: Simon and Schuster, 1992.

Toole, John Kennedy. *A Confederacy of Dunces*. 1980. New York: Wings Books, 1995.

Toth, Emily. Introduction. *A Vocation and a Voice*. By Kate Chopin. New York: Penguin, 1991.

―――. *Kate Chopin*. New York: William Morrow, 1990.

Travis, Trysh. "Divine Secrets of the Cultural Studies Sisterhood: Women Reading Rebecca Wells." *American Literary History* 15 (Spring 2003): 134–61.

Twain, Mark. *A Connecticut Yankee in King Arthur's Court*. 1889. *The Oxford Mark Twain*. Ed. Shelley Fisher Fishkin. Oxford: Oxford University Press, 1996.

―――. *The Innocents Abroad*. 1867. *The Oxford Mark Twain*. Ed. Shelley Fisher Fishkin. Oxford: Oxford University Press, 1996.

―――. *Life on the Mississippi*. 1883. *The Oxford Mark Twain*. Ed. Shelley Fisher Fishkin. Oxford: Oxford University Press, 1996. 218–616.

―――. *Personal Recollections of Joan of Arc*. 1896. *The Oxford Mark Twain*. Ed. Shelley Fisher Fishkin. Oxford: Oxford University Press, 1996.

Waldron, Ann. *Close Connections: Caroline Gordon and the Southern Renaissance*. New York: Putnam, 1987.

Wells, Rebecca. *Divine Secrets of the Ya-Ya Sisterhood*. New York: HarperCollins, 1996.

―――. *Little Altars Everywhere*. 1992. New York: Harper Perennial, 1996.

Westling, Louise. *Sacred Groves and Ravaged Gardens: The Fiction of Eudora Welty, Carson McCullers, and Flannery O'Connor*. Athens: University of Georgia Press, 1985.

White, Andrew, S. J. "A Brief Relation of the Voyage to Maryland." 1633. *The Calvert Papers, No. 3*. Baltimore: Maryland Historical Society, 1899. 26–45.

————. *Voyage to Maryland*. 1634. Trans. and ed. Barbara Lawatsch-Boomgaarden with Josef Ijsewijn. Waucona, IL: Bolchazy-Carducci, 1995.

White, Barbara A. *Growing Up Female: Adolescent Girlhood in American Fiction*. Westport, CT: Greenwood Press, 1985.

Wiegman, Robyn. *American Anatomies: Theorizing Race and Gender*. Durham: Duke University Press, 1995.

Williamson, Joel. *New People: Mulattoes and Miscegenation in the United States*. New York: Free Press, 1980.

Wilson, Edmund. *Patriotic Gore: Studies in the Literature of the American Civil War*. 1962. New York: Norton, 1994.

Wimsatt, W. K. "Poetry and Christian Thinking." 1951. *The Verbal Icon: Studies in the Meaning of Poetry*. Lexington: University of Kentucky Press, 1954. 266–79.

Woodward, C. Vann. *Tom Watson, Agrarian Rebel*. 1938. Savannah: Beehive Press, 1973.

Wyatt-Brown, Bertram. *Hearts of Darkness: Wellsprings of a Southern Literary Tradition*. Baton Rouge: Louisiana State University Press, 2003.

Yaeger, Patricia. *Dirt and Desire: Reconstructing Southern Women's Writing, 1930–1990*. Chicago: University of Chicago Press, 2000.

————. "Flannery O'Connor and the Aesthetics of Torture." *Flannery O'Connor: New Perspectives*. Ed. Sura P. Rath and Mary Neff Shaw. Athens: University of Georgia Press, 1996.

Žižek, Slavoj. *On Belief*. London: Routledge, 2001.

Index